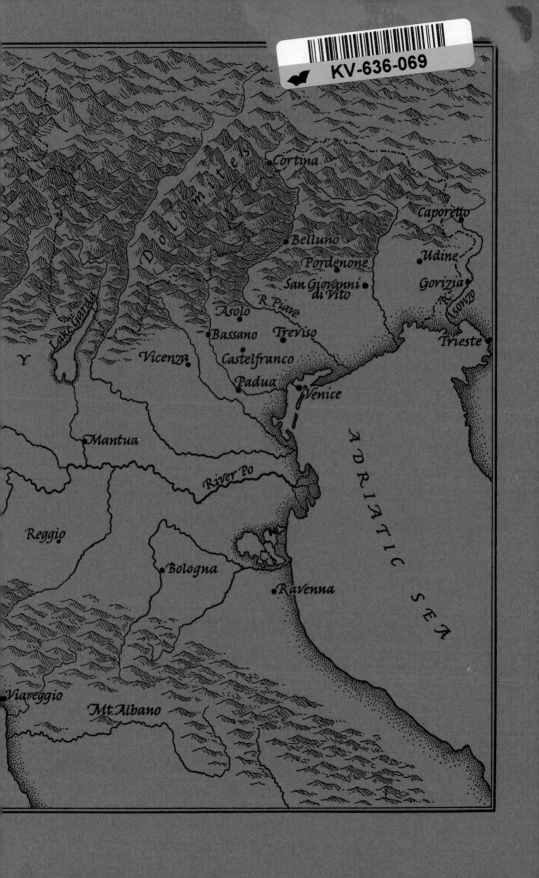

Dolomites

Cortina

Caporetto

Belluno

Udine

Pordenone

San Giovanni
di Vito

Gorizia

R. Piave

R. Isonzo

Lake Garda

Asolo

Bassano

Treviso

Trieste

Vicenza

Castelfranco

Padua

Venice

Mantua

ADRIATIC SEA

River Po

Reggio

Bologna

Ravenna

Viareggio

Mt. Albano

FREYA STARK

Letters

FREYA STARK
Letters

EDITED BY LUCY MOOREHEAD

VOLUME ONE
THE FURNACE AND THE CUP
1914-30

COMPTON RUSSELL

© Freya Stark 1974

First published in Great Britain 1974 by
Compton Russell Ltd.,
Compton Chamberlayne, Salisbury, Wiltshire,
and printed there by
The Compton Press Ltd.

Set in Linotype Granjon

ISBN 0 85955 012 5

Also by Freya Stark

published by John Murray

Foreword

Heaven from this furnace cup will drain
The fiery streams that mar its birth
And in its dinted heart maintain
The love that links with earth

Early letters, written in the furnace where the cup was moulded, show what depths were hammered out for later years. Love letters had been burnt and many dear ones lost, especially those to a most loved godfather. The remainder now included, but for some shortening and avoidance of repetition, are left as they were. The Past has poured what it has into our lap: this volume begins a collection from the twentieth century, offered in hope and gratitude to the Future.

FREYA STARK

Asolo 1974

Publisher's Note

The publication of this first volume of Freya Stark's selected letters begins a fresh account of her times and accomplishments. Though obviously complementary to her earlier books, it is intended that the letters should stand on their own as a separate and continuous commentary; and to maintain this continuity it has been possible, through the generosity of Messrs. John Murray, to include some that have already appeared in print.

For readers unfamiliar with the story of Freya Stark's early years, as she describes them in *Traveller's Prelude,* notes have been provided to set individual letters in context. In February 1914, when this volume opens, she was just twenty-one. These pages record the collision of war with youthful inexperience, the strain of continually threatened family happiness, illness, and the gradual breakthrough to the Muslim world which was to be for her the inspiration of the whole of later life.

FLORA STARK[1]

1 February 1914

My dear my own Mother,

I feel I have had so much more than I deserve, and now I am quite bewildered and overpowered. It is so good to feel that one is loved – the only real riches in the world, and I am very happy in that. I think my soul came to me quite suddenly, when I was about eleven years old, and all at once I realised how precious you were to me – since then have we not been growing nearer and nearer? When we go to the next world I hope St. Peter will not know which is which.

Here are some of my birthday flowers as a remembrance.

FREYA

FLORA STARK Dronero [Piedmont]
30 March 1915

My dearest Mother,

I arrived here quite exhausted, about 12.30 – after an hour's delay between Parma and Reggio because a *vagone* had got heated and had to be taken off. There was certainly no fear of solitude for me: we had eight people per compartment and a file down the corridors almost all the way, and most objectionable people too.

I got a pretty black hat – straw under and a silk covering, with a tiny rosebunch. It has a brim and is worn rakishly on one side. Twenty-two francs: and very ladylike and distinguished.

The Bistolfis[2] were charming to me: he was such a dear and so affectionate and good, and he wants to be our *testimonio** too! The first thing he did when I entered the studio was to embrace me and ask: 'Ebbene, quando ti sposi?' He says he will be a lot in Bologna about the monument, and that he wants to see a lot of us.

Your

FREYA

* Corresponds to best man at a wedding. F.S. was engaged to Prof. Quirino [Guido] Ruata.[3]

11 Grove End Rd., N.W.
9 August 1916

My darling Biri,

I hope you will have received the wire and not be thinking of me at the bottom of the Channel. The journey was quite good considering. At Modane I was brought into an office with three spectacled Frenchmen in a row all asking questions, so that I felt like Mr. Winkle in the witness box; their looks finally however melted to benevolence, and I was allowed to go, with many bows.

In Paris I spent the whole morning at the English *bureau de contrôle* : all the victims sat in rows with their passports in their hands and an anxious look on their faces as the lunch hour drew nearer and nearer. I was one of the very last and only got out, after twelve. Then I found a restaurant in the Avenue de l'Opéra, and then wandered about looking at the pretty shops till Cook's office opened and I could get my ticket.

I travelled to Havre with two girls from Salonika, doctors, who told me interesting things and showed me a bit of the Zeppelin which Bill [Willis] helped to get down in March. They were in uniform, and one had her hair cut and was so like a boy one couldn't possibly have told the difference if it hadn't been for her skirt. There was also a charming elderly naval officer going on leave : he told us that in the fog a day before, a German submarine got itself entangled in the Havre *reticolati* and came to the surface right in the Havre waters, and went off gaily before anyone could catch it. He said these submarines were 'great sports' and 'awfully cheeky', and spoke of them with evident affection!

There was a tremendous crowd at Havre and we were all herded together and standing for over an hour with a lot of French who always try to get on by sharpness of their elbows. The Tommies kept wonderful order : it was so nice to see the dear boys. They look so huge after the French. It was a great joy suddenly to hear one of them call out 'ladies first' and open a way for us : we went proudly past the disgusted French people!

The passport room has two long tables with a row of civilians and soldiers, and a soldier at the bottom to keep guard : and we were cross-examined by them all one after another and our life-history looked up in a file. After that we went to the customs – all looked after by women, and then on board. The charming officer had asked if he could do anything for me and I asked him to find me a berth : but for him I should have had to sleep on deck, and it was bitterly cold!

At about midnight, all the lights were put out, and we started going at a tremendous rate with quite a heavy sea, as the water was coming in at one of the upper portholes. But I slept beautifully and enjoyed it, and only woke in time to have a good breakfast before reaching Southampton.

I found dear Viva [Jeyes][4] at Waterloo, and it was lovely to be driving again through London; but also rather sad.

The Italian news is splendid, better than one could have expected even from our Alpini. It sent such a thrill of joy and pride through me when I saw it yesterday on my arrival. The taking of Gorizia really seems near; and then it's a short way to Trieste. Viva says that nurses are badly wanted, so I may think about it later on. In any case can you get at my cabinet and in the bottom drawer find all the letters relative to my work at St. Orsola [Hospital, Bologna], and send them to me?

Much love my own Biri: don't worry too much over things; one must have faith. Don't write to *anyone* about Quirino, at least not to say more than that circumstances are difficult for us both. If things come right as I hope and believe, it will do no good for all my English friends to think ill of him, and what you tell Viva is not even fair!

Here they expect the war to go till June! Who knows?

Your

FREYA

FLORA STARK
Pangbourne
14 August 1916

My own darling Biri,

Do you know that I haven't yet had a word from you? Perhaps I shall find a letter tomorrow when I return to London.

I have been having a most busy time. Had a delightful day with Prof. Ker[5] at the zoo, lunching there with Viva who then went to her office and left us to feed all the parrots and enjoy ourselves.

And now I have been here with her and George and Alice [Edwards] since Saturday in a dear little thatched cottage with the river flowing between trees and meadows just in front of the door. It has not been exactly river weather, and I got wet to the skin yesterday, but there is sun in between and the soft skies with drifting clouds suit this peaceful landscape.

There are lots of Tommies here, in bright butcher blue garments to show they have been wounded; and they have such a gorgeous time, taken out in boats with devoted and pretty ladies to flirt with and console them, and tea on the banks or in punts!

3

I wish you were here, I'm afraid I've been so horrid to you lately; it seems all I can do to keep decently civil on the outside. I don't think unhappiness is really good for one at all and the kindness of everyone almost seems to hurt me, although I am so very grateful for it.

I have a huge appetite and want to eat and sleep all day, and you will soon hear of me being too fat to stay in my dresses!

Your own
FREYA

FLORA STARK 11 Grove End Rd.,
16 August 1916

My own darling,

I came home yesterday after a very pleasant stay on the river. It is good to come back to these comfortable English houses, with the smooth lawns and roses, and bay windows, where all the troubles seem to be put aside with one's outdoor boots before entering the drawing-room!

Last night the dear Professor came with Miss Jourdain[6] to dine: I think he rather expected to be alone and would have preferred it. I wore my necklace and told him it was the first time, which pleased him: and he said the 'ensemble' was *very good*! He is such a dear man; and so kind in coming often in spite of the little time he has.

18 August 1916

The news continues good, but we lose very heavily: an average of 1,000 casualties a week for officers only.

Poor Captain McDonnell has had such a bad time: first wounded in the Cameroons very seriously; then, while convalescent, he took his flying certificate and had six months in France and was again wounded: he enjoyed that time, but he was afterwards sent with the relief force up the Tigris and had an elbow shattered and a ghastly voyage to Bombay in the heat. Now he is here trying to get well and out again, but in a very bad way I'm afraid, with nervous exhaustion. One longs for the end of all this, but it is not expected to come till the end of next year!

I am longing to get to work and hope to begin in September, either nursing if the hours are easy, or else at the Admiralty or War Office.

Your own
FREYA

FLORA STARK   The Bear Hotel, Rodborough
                                                    25 August 1916

My darling B.,

Thanks for your dear letter, sent on here. I am leaving tomorrow, after a
pleasant quiet time with dear Mr. Bale,[7] in this country of smooth rolling
hills, with the beechwoods in the valleys and winds from the Atlantic bringing clouds. The Severn shines in the distance, between a cleft in the hills, and
Wales is beyond, visible on clear days.

I have just written to Pips.* What an injudicious old B. you are in the way
of letters! He says you had asked him to come over in August to take me to
the mountains, and the poor man had to rush all the way to Ottawa (6,000
miles) for passport and was just booking a passage when he luckily heard he
wasn't wanted. I'm very glad he isn't coming, and have just been advising
him not to sell out yet at this very bad moment: after the war there will be
plenty of new settlers in quest of land.

I have had no letters from Quirino and I'm afraid he thinks it good for
me not to write. So I wait for news from you!

Herbert Russell is with us. He is a nice man, but so shy: he has a mouth so
like Quirino's that it gives me a kind of pain when I look at him.

Love to all, I wish you were here,

                                                           Your own
                                                              FREYA

* F. S.'s father, Robert Stark.[8]

FLORA STARK   Thornworthy [Dartmoor]
                                                    6 September 1916

My darling Biri,

Had such a busy week: Maurice and Dot [Waller][9] are down, and very
happy. I am pleased to see that they are even more egotistic than me! And
have neither ears nor eyes for anyone except their two happy selves.

There is a large family of girls and two boys at the cottage who are in here
a great deal, and have made quite friends. I seem to have lost my shyness:
perhaps because I don't care what people think of me any longer!

Don't trouble because [Quirino's] 'Papa' doesn't answer: it shows he feels
with you, and of course he can't tell you so, and prefers to say nothing.
What can he say, poor man? It is far better to leave things as they are and
not define them too much.

                                                           Your
                                                              FREYA

5

My darling Biri,

The plans that Clot[ilde de Bottini de Ste Agnès][10] has been making are very flattering! And really nice of her to think of me for her dear [brother] Gabriel. At present I hate the thought of anyone, and at the best of times could not marry unless I were in love really: I believe I am fundamentally English in that. I feel it would be so easy to get bored with one's husband and get to hate him: so please don't commit me irrevocably to any young man, however fascinating!

It was strange Quirino's sending the Salso papers, wasn't it? With all the account of his speech, etc.! after not writing all this time. I shall not write unless he does, and perhaps it's better to let him quite alone. Let us leave these *misères*!

Did you look in the right place for the certificate? It was in the *bottom drawer* of my Florentine cabinet in an envelope. I should be very sorry not to be able to get it, as if I do nurse, it would probably save me a time of apprenticeship and floor scrubbing!

We had a lovely ride with Maurice, over glorious gorse-covered moor. It is wonderfully beautiful now.

Must go to supper. There is so little time here: someone in every room at all hours, and always inclined for a chat!

There is good news from the two [Varwell] boys in France and Salonika.

FREYA

My darling Biri,

It has turned very cold here: one feels the autumn coming on. But the moors are lovely: the heather already it's rusty brown, and the gorse in full bloom.

Mrs. Waller is most troublesome and says she can't understand why Maurice prefers a person he has known only two years to one he has been with all his life!

He is a real good sort and the very best person Dot could have chosen: all the same there is a suspicion of pompousness now and then, quite unintentional – as if there were no edge to him. He tells stories extremely well – but keeps them all written in a note book! Think of Prof. Ker doing that! And yet I like him very much and think we get on well and shall be friends, especially as I can listen to useful bits of information without looking bored.

I heard from Quirino – just a note of his doings – but I will not write to him.

Your own
FREYA

FLORA STARK Thornworthy
23 September 1916

My darling B.,

I send you a copy of a letter from 'Papa'. You will see that he is very broken-hearted, and I don't want him to be troubled any more if he has not answered you. He has more than his share of trouble, and I would like to remain a friend to him independently of Quirino, and to see him later on. It must be worse than anything to feel that one's son has not been perfectly straight, and I believe that only my affection can comfort him for that.

I do not write to Quirino any more.

A kiss to my dearest from   FREYA

P.S. Did you ever write to Bistolfi's? I wonder whether you should tell the Bankarts that their presents will be sent as soon as the war stops: I do so hate doing it!

FLORA STARK 11 Grove End Rd.
29 September 1916

My own darling,

I found your letter here and am so much troubled about what you tell me. Please let me have news at once how you are: otherwise I shall take the next train out.

First of all are you sure that you *never* drink the canal water? After all it has made us go through we none of us have any right to touch it: * it is just a form of suicide. Please write and give me your word that you have nothing to do with it at all.

My own Biri – what nonsense you talk to me! Do you really think that I could have any happiness at all left if you get ill? I feel that it doesn't matter what one does or what happens so long as we bear it properly and do not lose our sense of proportion or throw up the sponge and be miserable just because we are one of a few millions who are going through a bad time. I am so afraid now you are alone you let yourself go to be unhappy, my dearest,

7

when there is no reason: you will see that everything will come all right in time, and then you will have wasted years in a kind of misunderstanding of the meaning of things. I do believe that our lives are in God's hands and he guides them as he wishes, and it is bad not to accept it with faith in the ultimate good, and not to take things cheerfully as far as may be: and then you will feel a tranquillity, just as anyone has found who has met sorrow and accepted it for what it is. So buck up, and don't let us be downhearted!

Did I tell you that a friend came to Thornworthy who had lost her boy in France. I have a secret thought that Win [Varwell] cared for him: and she was so splendid, and calm and gentle: it seemed as if a veil of sweetness had fallen over her.

I will now confess that Dot gave me the present of a cold on the moor, which is now quite well again. I prudently went at once to see Dr. Hunt, who told me my lungs were as good as can be and that it was nothing at all: but he ordered me brandy three times a day. As you know, the Varwells are strict teetotallers, so it was amusing.

They have all been such dears, and I feel as if I had another home there.

Send me just a card with news if you have no time for more, and tell me about the *water*.

FREYA

* F. S. nearly died of typhoid in 1915.

FLORA STARK 11 Grove End Rd.
3 October 1916

My own darling,

Did I tell you about the Zeppelin brought down yesterday night? I didn't see it unfortunately, but was wakened by the cheering: the most impressive sound in the stillness of the night darkness. I was too sleepy to have my wits, and took some time getting on a dressing gown and going down, and then it was all over: of course hardly anyone stays indoors as they should on these occasions. They are becoming very efficient in dealing with them now, and have bombs which they drop from aeroplanes and which explode inside the Zepp and burn it up, so that you see it fall through the air in flames. I hope to see one pretty soon: they are expected now the weather is foggy and there is no moon. Mr. Ruegg is a special constable and gets notice of them before-hand, so he has promised to phone us to be on the look-out: strangely enough we heard no guns last time, so that it would be very difficult to know when they are about.

Love to my own B. from

FREYA

11 Grove End Rd.
                                                    4 October 1916

Dearest,

We had a musical genius yesterday after dinner: he was supposed to be terribly shy, and Viva wanted to keep me in a woolly dress so as not to frighten him, but I wasn't going to be miserable for anyone however much a genius, and he turned out to be quite talkative and self-possessed and went on playing till midnight. He played with Dorothy – a César Franck sonata, and one of the most beautiful things I have ever heard.

I went to see Grassig* again: we discussed the plays of Sophocles, and the advantages of Republics! She is a happy woman; and so sweet always.

Quirino wrote: he says he is fixing up a place at Bologna too and came upon several things missing which he needs: will you please see that they are sent at once and be *most particular* about it. He wrote a very nice letter.

I remember quite well that the green buffet was in the bill so that it is really his, but you will see that I have asked him to send what he finds of mine. I know you will see to this with great care and at once. I enclose the letter I wrote him.

                                                            FREYA

* F. S.'s maternal grandmother, Mrs. Madeleine Stark.

11 Grove End Rd.
                                                    6 October 1916

My own darling,

Prof. Ker came to tea yesterday: we spent a happy time discussing trochaic tetrameters, and he has promised to look me out some work. He suggests the War Office.

I went to see Grassig in the morning and talked with her about the merits of Frederick II, who was a fascinating person and as attractive as any modern politician! She was rather depressing though, for what do you think she said to me, after a long and careful scrutiny? She said: 'Freya, you must now devote yourself to recovering the bloom of youth.' It is only one's relatives who say these things!

I am just longing to be at work: so sad that I can't yet nurse, but I hope to be able to in the spring. It is the only thing I really long to do now.

A loving kiss from

                                                    Your own
                                                        FREYA

11 Grove End Rd.
11 October 1916

My own darling,

It is most strange to hear of cholera at Dronero. I hope you are careful and see that the plates and things are not *washed* in canal water. At least it should be well boiled: the washing up is naturally just as important as the drinking.

Quirino sent me a card to say he had sent my things. I wonder if there is the little inlaid table: I am so fond of that and perhaps you could when you send his, ask for it, just in a brief note. But don't if you had rather not.

Hope to be at work soon. I shall not nurse till the spring, but do want that wretched old certificate: I am told I might get in anywhere with that!

I went yesterday to the office and typed quite creditably. The more I see, the more I believe common sense to be the one requisite of success. Anyway I feel quite sure of myself with any work of pedestrian kind.

News continues good. Ralph [Varwell] sends home most cheery letters, though one is anxious just now as they have been shelling Armentières. But the casualty lists are very terrible: the better part of a hundred officers killed nearly every day.

Your own
FREYA

FLORA STARK 11 Grove End Rd.
13 October 1916

My own B.,

It is so nice coming back about one o'clock up Whitehall and the Haymarket: it is all khaki down there now along those govt. offices – and the men look splendidly fit. I am just reading a history of the Retreat; most splendid, all of it! But it makes one realise how of all the Allies England was the only one prepared in any way and ready to do what she had undertaken: we couldn't have a big army of course, but all our men were fully equipped and ready at a moment's notice, and that could be said of no other country at the time. One cannot realise how those days of Mons and Le Cateau were lived through: the Germans five to one! and no interval for sleep.

I think I shall wire you for that certificate: I *must* have it, and am just getting more and more miserable with nothing to do: if you knew what it is to me!

14 October 1916

The Somme pictures were very splendid, and some most pitiful of the trenches after the fight. The men look like Cromwellians in their helmets;

they also evidently wear 'shorts' in the summer and look very trim. The pictures of the bombardment were simply terrific: one marvels anything was left alive at all. And as for the villages, one could hardly see where they used to be – not even the walls left standing.

The Gorizia pictures were good, though not up to those we saw in Turin. The best was a charge down a mountain slope of shingle, and the wounded let down by ropes over the precipices. I am glad they should be seen here, and hope ours will go abroad too. The contrast of type was very interesting: although it makes the Latin gestures look rather unfairly artificial.

I am not yet really acclimatised to Town! You would like Piccadilly in the evening: practically dark, with a chaos of buses and taxis, and people, and subdued yellow and red lamps making it into a kind of fairy landscape.

I hope this life of leisure may be done with soon. All the offices have eight hours' work and one must bind oneself to do any overtime that may be wanted and it is invariably wanted, so that means writing till 8 or 9 at night. So I think if I found a hospital to nurse just for the mornings it would be far less trying.

FREYA

FLORA STARK   11 Grove End Rd.
                                                   19 October 1916

My darling Biri,

I was so glad to receive the certificate; I thought you were keeping it from me on purpose! But I had already asked for an address at the War Office, and so shall probably be settled there: alas for the bloom of youth!

I have been typing for the last two days at the Canadian Red Cross, making out lists of 'missing'; such a sad work. I typed steadily, lists of names, and all practically belonging to September. It is very tiring, also because of shifty offices, with artificial light, and no glimpses of the hills: only a little whiff of petrol, from one's motor bus! It seems I am a most satisfactory clerk however, and I hope I shall get some work that isn't too deadly.

It is so strange mixing up with all these girls whose life is all in these rabbit burrows: they seem to talk of nothing but young men, and hats, but are very amiable and ready to be nice, and not much different from the college girl.

Viva came yesterday and took me out to lunch: we tried the Carlton Grill Room, and couldn't find a table, and only with difficulty got in at the Criterion: it is all crowded with officers on leave, and they look so nice. One feels quite 'undressed' without an officer belonging to one!

I think we may be going to St. Margaret's for the week end, and hope to see some Zepps or Taubes* over there. The searchlights are so wonderful these misty nights, like great animals shooting their heads out of the darkness, and feeling about for something to fasten on.

Your own

FREYA

* The German bomber aeroplane.

FLORA STARK

11 Grove End Rd.

28 October 1916

My own darling B.,

It is fine news to think of having a mackintosh! It's the only thing needed. Now I wonder if you can send me my best hat, the black: I am badly in need of it. The little green one makes me look so *very* old: and my funds are too low to buy one for some time to come. Also the old black velvet and fur if still decent? If I earn any money this winter I want to give it to Viva, as everyone is very poor and I had rather not be a burden.

I go on Wednesday to be interviewed at the War Office and hope to turn out favourably, although German is the only language that is really wanted.

On Wednesday we went to Mrs. Scott's for a soldiers' tea: convalescents, almost all with their heads bandaged as is usually the case this year. I wish the poor boys in Italy could be treated a little as they are here: they do have a good time! They were allowed tea by themselves (forty-six of them), and then we joined them, and they were given cigarettes, and entertainments; I don't think they cared much to be sung to, but loved to get up and do it themselves, and to join in the choruses. I don't know why it makes one want to cry always. Tipperary is no longer: we now sing 'If I were the only girl in the world, and you were the only boy!' – or 'Pack up your troubles in your old kit bag, and smile, smile, smile,' of which the moral was good, though much out of tune.

I rarely see the dear Professor, he is so busy, but he ran in for a moment some days ago, and gave me a beautiful book of Tuscan folk songs – little gems!

Did I announce to you my intention of joining Trevelyan's unit* in the spring? I hope you approve, and notice my virtue in postponing till then. Probably I shan't be able to get out there anyway, it is so much sought after.

Your own

FREYA

* Ambulance unit organised by G. M. Trevelyan.

11 Grove End Rd.
                                                                1 November 1916

My own Biri,

I went with Viva to the War Office this morning, and after waiting a long time, we were brought to a charming young lady who asked me my accomplishments. I said I knew French and Italian well, but she instantly remarked, 'That is no good at all: we want only German,' and gave me an unintelligible bit of manuscript to read. The standard must be lamentably low, because she actually passed me, and in ten days' time I will hear again from them and have to be again examined. I feel rather depressed at the thought of a whole winter spent in struggling over German.

I met a young officer just back from Gorizia, where he had been with Trevelyan, and he told me all about the nursing there and says there would be no difficulty in going out. I am so longing, longing to go: it seems the only thing I care about at all. I suppose this long winter will pass.

                                                        Your own
                                                            FREYA

11 Grove End Rd.
                                                                4 November 1916

My own B.,

A terrible looking document arrived from the War Office today asking Mr. Bale to guarantee me in all sorts of virtues: and to say that I am temperate, honest, and capable of keeping secrets of a 'highly confidential nature'. Maurice [Waller] and George [Edwards] have the same and are much disturbed at having to pledge themselves to such doubtful virtues in woman!

Two more sonnets are written, but I haven't time to copy them today. Karl [Walters] came and gave most valuable criticism: he is such a nice man and it is pleasant to discuss poetry with people who are interested in syllables, and accents, and the distribution of vowel and consonants!

                                                                        FREYA

11 Grove End Rd.
                                                                8 November 1916

My own Biri,

The week end was splendid. I really enjoyed myself. Joan [Carr]¹¹ came to meet me, and we struggled up a steep path with my dressing bag to the tiny cottage. I have never seen any country more exquisite than those Sussex downs. Amberley lies in a broad shallow amphitheatre, with a ridge of white cliff over against you : the low ground is flooded, pale, pale blue in the sunlight with a swirl and foam at the edge where the Arun River makes a current. And the downs slope away on all sides, with scarlet, copper, and flame-like beechwoods creeping towards them : wonderful woods, of old trees, with smooth shiny roots. We walked under them that afternoon, and it was like long aisles of a temple, with the gold leaves falling silently about one.

The party consisted of us two and a sister, called Ursula, a fascinating girl with straw gold hair and eyes that slant a little upwards at the corners. The Sunday came with the most terrific gale I have ever seen : one thatch roof lay mostly strewn about the lawn, and when we put our heads out of doors the rain was like hail on our faces. Ursula said what a splendid thing to sail on the river. I backed her, Joan was torn between the excitement and the fear of the danger. The wind was roaring like big guns : we had to run past the trees, as big branches were being hurled off. Unfortunately the boat was beached under some elms, so we had to haul it out in fear of our lives : Ursula and I did the work while Joan looked doubtful : we pulled the boat, a long narrow thing for sculling, to the edge of the flood and I was left to hold her while they went for the sail : and it was all I could do to keep her inshore against the wind. I really think it is the maddest thing I have ever done! Just as we started we saw a train on the opposite shore going at full speed, and the wind was so strong that the smoke was blown along in front of the engine! We had a glorious time. I held the mainsheet, and learnt the mysteries of *gybing,* and *close haul.* It was very cold : the burberries were no good against that downpour, and we sat in soaking garments, thinking with joy of the horror of our absent families if they could have seen! And the pleasure was enhanced by the knowledge that we must certainly have drowned if we upset.

We came home wet through and famished, and found tea and a young man waiting : he was a nice young man, whom we astonished with the history of the day.

Do you know to what lengths the U.S. navy has gone? Two of their men of war were between an English merchantman and a German U boat, and the Germans asked them to get out of the way to let them torpedo the Englishmen, and *they did it*! I should like to see our navy doing that!

FREYA

FLORA STARK   11 Grove End Rd.
                                                10 November 1916
My own Biri,

Thanks for the two cards. It is sad to hear you did not get my letter from St. Margaret's: I carefully avoided putting in all the most interesting things, but they are evidently very strict in all that district. Perhaps it's still reposing at the Censor's and you will get it in due time.

I have just heard from Joan that her Fred is in town wounded, getting on all right. She herself was laid up with a temperature after our soaking in the boat, but I am as well as possible and all the better for it, which shows I can do what I like!

A kiss to my dearest from her

FREYA

FLORA STARK   11 Grove End Rd.
                                                16 November 1916
My own darling Biri,

We had your letters yesterday. I am glad Miss Smith told you of the event,* and Viva is writing for my picture: the other presents I hope he will keep. I am sending his rings back of course.

We both feel that this explains a great deal; if there was an earlier tie he may have had a difficult choice to make, or perhaps he came again under her influence while I was away: these things happen, and I believe the more one knows the less is one inclined to blame. Certainly I feel it puts him in a better light, and explains much that was dark to me.

I am very glad for his sake that he should have married: I believe she is a very nice woman and clever, and quite young. I should like to know more about her if you happen to hear. Of course I feel he should have been more straightforward and told me the real reason, which I would have understood and accepted: but even there, it is possible that there were very good reasons why he could not tell.

Anyway that is done with, and I would not worry any more about it if I were you, Biri. I do believe that a sense of proportion is the most important thing one needs, and sometimes I feel that yours is rather wobbly: please don't become intense, or get a religious craze, or chronic melancholia. Dorothy told me yesterday that you were the sort of person to head a 'Movement', and I have been alarmed ever since.

I do hope you are all most careful about the water!

Your

FREYA

* Quirino's marriage.

11 Grove End Rd.

20 November 1916

FLORA STARK

My own dearest,

I am working for a fortnight at the British Museum, copying at 30/- a week, what one may call sweated labour! The hours are good, 9.30 to 4, and the lady I do it for is very pleasant: I wish it were to go on, instead of the wretched German. The War Office is anxious to have me and so I feel I must go: if I simply can't stand the hard work I must give a week's notice.

Don't send any hats! They will only be ruined by the journey, and they cannot be worn now when no one dresses and I am not going anywhere. Do you think they would look suitable among a lot of clerks? – or that I have energy to go to tea parties after eight hours' writing?! I have all I need in that way, and also heaps of shoes, blouses, combies.

I had such a nice letter from Prof. Ker the other day about my poem, which he liked. He may perhaps come soon again.

It is so late. I must go to bed, but had to write now as there is no time in the morning.

FREYA

11 Grove End Rd.

26 November 1916

FLORA STARK

My own dear Biri,

I am afraid there is going to be a diminution in my letters! After writing all day, my hand is so tired in the evening that I put if off till Sunday, and just do nothing at all after dinner. You mustn't think I have been run over by a bus or blown up by Zepps if you do not hear from me for seven days.

I am getting on quite well at the British Museum; my employer (doesn't that sound grand?) is most kind and spends her time begging me not to

16

work so hard – to leave early, etc. . . . just as if it was the greatest kindness to earn £3 from her. The last days also I had less drudgery, and some amusing copying of old legends on herbs, really interesting work. There is a dear little lunching place close to the Museum; you get three courses for a shilling and a sight of all the Intelligent Women gratis. And they are the most disinterested restaurant people I have ever come across – yesterday I happened to order something I did not like, and they begged me to have something else instead, and when I had no time for that, deducted part of the shilling! And there are bright majolicas on the walls, and picture papers on the tables to amuse one.

It was nice to get your letter, my dearest. Don't make too many plans for a distant future: it seems to me we have lost so many years of happiness by keeping our eyes fixed on the distance, and the reality is never good enough for that: so often, when the wished for thing comes, we find the taste and savour has gone, and that we have grown beyond it or caring for it. And there is always so much that is good round about us! I shall try before leaving England to prepare myself some work that I can do in Dronero; I thought a history of those valleys might be good, and I should enjoy it, and be able to go to Turin to find the necessary books. Then we can have little jaunts together when we have saved up, and sometimes run across to England! I feel that I should like to be like other girls, with friends of my own age, and *young men*! and that is not done by knocking about the world, but by a home and the friendships that grow with custom, don't you think? I am sure you could get that in Dronero, and make your circle, and that we could live happily enough there; and everyone will help you, and understand; I believe they have all only been surprised at our living in solitude so long. I have really debated with myself whether I ought to set to and earn some money, or stay at home with my own very dear mother, and I think that is the right and happier thing. So let us make it a Home, my Biri, and look calmly enough at things to make the present beautiful and trust to God for the future.

I am reading about Italian folk-poetry in my spare moments, a most rich and interesting subject; that is another debt of gratitude to my dear Professor. I think I had better stick to Italian subjects, as I will be able to get the books in Italy.

Viva sends love and says it's ridiculous to write such long letters (and she doesn't approve of going to Serbia!).

Your own

FREYA

17

11 Grove End Rd.
                                            [?] November 1916
Dearest Biri,

Ralph [Varwell] says those muddy Somme trenches are too awful, water one day and ice the next! But he is glad to say that his horses are in better quarters than himself. I thought that so nice and English.

I should be so glad if you could make Vera[12] return my wedding presents to the various people, as that is high time. At least return to the Bankarts – the salver and jug: to Aunt Sarah – teaspoons: and to the Varwells – the fish knives. Dot doesn't want hers – and I don't know if Aunt Mary [Androuztos][13] would want hers sent back. All those things are much on my mind.

Are you going to have an Xmas tree this year? We shall be all by ourselves at home – and hope to notice the day as little as possible. Who knows that it may not be the last War Xmas!

No more, except most loving wishes to all and a long kiss from Your
                                                        FREYA

11 Grove End Rd.
                                            [?] December 1916
Dear B.,

Quirino has just written to me asking if it is with my approval that legal proceedings are being taken against him.

I need not – should not need to say – what I feel about this news. I wait to reply till I hear from you; but please tell Grillo to stop at once.

Please tell me the details; what sum of money you wanted from him and on what grounds.

Please *write at once*.

I shan't say more: you seem unable to understand what it means to have the memory of the happy days smirched over. Nothing, nothing could have hurt me like this.

Please wire if possible as I must know before writing an answer. Please send an exact history of what you have done in this matter.

                                                    Your
                                                        FREYA

                                            [Next day]
P.S. I have thought it over and asked Viva and Mr. Bale – and have written the enclosed to Quirino. But I am very sorry to have had to write again, which I did not intend doing.

[Translated from original Italian.]

Dear Ruata,

I did not know what Avvocato Grillo had done. I am not sure what it's about: probably it is a question of the transport and expenses of some boxes which at your request were sent to Bologna, and the charges for their return have been debited to my mother. I have written asking that the proceedings should be stopped. If you wish you can pay the bill, as a debt of honour, but the decision is entirely yours.

Would you please send the things that you wish to return to me to Maria in Sicily, if she will be kind enough to keep them for me until I return to Italy. The only object to which I am much attached is the portrait (painted) which you did not return with the letters. Since this has no value, would you be kind enough to send it *to me here*.

Believe me, with sincere good wishes,   FREYA STARK

FLORA STARK   11 Grove End Rd.
                                                   [?] December 1916

Dear B.,

I saw Viva and she told me of your letter. I have also heard from Ruata, and he sent a copy of Grillo's letter where I see that in spite of your promise by telegram he *still* asks for money – even the payment of my trousseau.

I don't think I can bear much more of this. If you could know the misery this action of yours is causing me, you would care more for my happiness than for your point of pride.

I sent you my letter to Ruata: you see that I promised 'he should not be asked for anything' and that I only wanted my portrait – and I thought you would respect my word to him.

Dear B, I am just heartbroken. I can't force you, but if this does not stop I shall come over at once and do what I can.

You had no right to begin it: there are things too personal and sacred for anyone to tamper with, and you had no right to spring this misery on me without my knowledge.

I wish Grillo to ask for *nothing but the portrait*. No fines, apologies, or anything. He can say that he does this by my express desire (renouncing the other claims I mean). On this condition I shall not answer the letter.

Will you wire me what you do: first what you intend to do and then when the thing is finally settled and done with. Viva will write you, too, to the same effect.

                                                   Your

                                                   FREYA

11 Grove End Rd.
23 December 1916

Dearest Biri,

Your wire has just come, and I am much relieved to hear it is all stopped. I hope this is the last of the whole business.

I am trying to get off my Xmas letters, but have little energy, and one cannot wish anyone Happy Xmas this year. One good thing about this peace note shows the Germans don't feel like holding out very much more.

I hear the most awful descriptions of the mud on the Somme. Some men were so stuck in it they couldn't get out for three days, and had to remain out in the open under fire, having food passed to them when possible.

Your

FREYA

FLORA STARK   11 Grove End Rd.
5 January 1917

My darling Biri,

Your letter came this morning, and was such a joy to me. I am so glad of what you write about the gossip *à propos de moi*. I don't think Quirino 'wants to pay: at least so he explains in a letter to me which is quite nice in tone. So I should let the matter drop, if we have the portrait. I cannot help thinking, B., that if I have forgiven what he has done to me, you can 'forgive what he has or hasn't done to you. If he speaks well of me, that is all that matters, as that is all that concerns our good name. But please let me know about the portrait and when and how the correspondence with Grillo is closed; as it is worst of all to feel that things are happening without my knowledge.

Your

FREYA

FLORA STARK   11 Grove End Rd.
14 January 1917

My own dearest,

I can only write Sundays, as I really do feel very tired all the week, and usually sit and look at the fire in my spare time. But I seem to get on at the work, and do it as quickly as anyone at my table; my chief gets more and more benevolent, so that is all satisfactory: only of course I don't mean to stay very long at it.

The Professor came to see us the other day and was so kind and dear as always. I told him of my affairs, and he was really sympathetic and wonderfully helpful in his silent way. I think very often silence is more helpful than speech.

I give Viva 20/- of my 30/- and the other 10/- for luncheons, so just scrape along. That wretch of a doctor has just sent a bill for £5. Isn't it a waste!

FREYA

FLORA STARK   111 Clifton Hill, N.W.
                               20 January 1917

My dearest Biri,

I am staying with Mrs. Webb till Thursday I think, and she pretends to be very pleased to have me, and is very kind, even to getting up early for my impossible breakfast.

Did I tell you about Mr. Rowntree, who tried for so long to come and see me? He achieved it at last, and turned out very nice indeed, with the greatest appetite I have ever seen. I think I shall let him invite me out to lunch occasionally: Mrs. Webb says he is a real good sort, the kind that gives small parties at his flat and has many mild flirtations of blameless description. He is a Quaker too, but not a shirker.

What wild notion are you going to write me next?! I never heard such a project as to send a six months baby travelling under present conditions: I don't suppose you expect the Germans to overrun the whole of Italy! Florence, or Rome, are out of reach even of the 'heavies'! We hear a good deal here, and I am certain that you are much safer where you are than risking pneumonia in the French trains and U boats in the Channel; these are really going to be a serious danger. Some people left Marseilles three weeks ago and were continuously torpedoed and fired at for three hours before shaking off the horrid little insect.

I am sorry as to what you write about Grillo.

You want me to send you the letters: I can naturally not do so without your telling me why: if I give them to anyone it should be to Quirino.

I want you to understand this, that the sooner this wretched business is *definitely closed*, the sooner I shall be able to begin to try and forget. You are wrong to think that I do this for Quirino: I do it for myself. You do not seem able to understand that the hurt all this is to me is far greater than any satisfaction . . .

You see you are in his hands: a brave person can face facts bravely and not try to get round them.

If you ask for the portrait, and I do not get it, it is all that you can do with dignity, and please, if it is not too late, let the matter rest there. You will have the additional comfort of thinking that it saves me much unnecessary pain.

Will you please write and let me know all that is being done, and when it is all *finished with,* and I may try and think of happier things?

Dear Biri, I don't want to be brutal, but I put it gently to you and you instantly did what I most disliked.

I cannot help being sorry, Biri, to find you on the side of bitterness and anger so that I must fight against your influence to keep the sweetness of my sad experience and let it turn to good instead of evil: I should have preferred so much to have done this with your help.

When I told Prof. Ker of Ruata's marriage, he said 'It is so bad, that it is easier to bear.' And I told him that I would far rather suffer more and have him clear of blame – and my dearest Professor said 'You are right, and I am wrong.'

I hope you will let me write more cheerful letters soon, but till it is finished, please keep me 'au courant' and tell me what Q. has answered; as I think of it all the time anyway and only am anxious when I hear nothing.

FREYA

FLORA STARK11 Grove End Rd.
4 February 1917

My dearest Biri,

I have just had two days' holiday (they give one weekend every six weeks) and I am so annoyed because I had to spend most of it in bed, stifling a cold. The W.O. insists on all windows being open, and as there has been fog, snow, and all sorts of weather lately, it wasn't at all pleasant and probably the regulation was made in August!

I seem to be getting on quite well at my place, and have got to know quite a number of nice women, with whom I lunch and tea: but it is very strenuous, and I am so worried at not hearing from you about the end of that wretched business that any off hours are no rest. Do let me know at once: I hoped you would wire – because until I *know* it is done and finished with I shall not be able to get back any peace and serenity of mind. So please let me know.

Things really do look bad for Germany now. Evidently the conditions are even worse than was known. One hopes the blow may be dealt before the next harvest; and save us another winter.

We are all scraping pennies for the War Loan: all offices collect every week, even sixpences, and factories too – and huge sums are the result. You have a card and put on sixpenny stamps, and when they amount to 15/6, you get a War Savings Certificate.

Much love my own dearest. Do set my mind at rest –

Your own

FREYA

FLORA STARK

11 Grove End Rd.
15 February 1917

My darling Biri,

The portrait has just come – and such a joy to me! Nothing could have pleased me more or been dearer. It is very like, except that it looks so very anxious and overstrained; not the *serenity* I should like to see! You really seem to be the only person who can paint yourself.

I'm nearly dead with sleep, am so tired in the evenings: it is so vexing not to be able to do more. I think a real strong physique would be the greatest blessing of all.

Tomorrow however is a half day, and I'm hoping Prof. Ker may come to tea.

Last holiday I went with Viva to the National, and saw the Buccleuchs' Rembrandt, such a wonderful, beautiful old woman reading: so calm, with beautiful lines, and the marvellous warm, golden background – she was like a queen in her dignified old age.

I lunched with Mr. Rowntree, and then came home to find a girl whom Bill admires, and whom I thought like a doll, but am no judge in these matters.

Always your own

FREYA

FLORA STARK

11 Grove End Rd.
23 February 1917

My own Biri,

I have finally settled to start my nursing again – owing to a very good offer to get English training for six weeks at a little hospital (civilian) in Hornsey.

I shall live there, free of charge, and only get one afternoon a week off and Sunday either the morning or aft.: so I look on it as a kind of *retraite*! The hours are very heavy; 7.30 a.m. to 8.30 p.m. with two hours' rest in the middle: but if I can stand it I shall feel sure of being fit to volunteer for abroad, and shall be altogether in a much better position than with my Italian certificate only.

I'm so glad to start nursing again: it is the one thing that gives a tangible result and makes me feel of any use at all in this old world. I hope you will approve of it.

The Prof. came some days ago and brought me the most *wonderful* photos of the Cogne hills, Grivola, Tersiva, the whole chain: he is too good to me – he always comes, whenever we ask him, and tells us his stories: really there is no one to come up to him; he is the best of friends, and one feels so sure of him, that he would never change: that is the rarest and best thing in friendship.

Yesterday I actually went to a dinner party, at Mrs. Webb's. I sat between two charming officers, who talked about Salonika, and France, and were most interesting; and after dinner we played bridge – which I don't do brilliantly, but it didn't matter.

Your own

FREYA

FLORA STARK

11 Grove End Rd.
28 February 1917

My own dearest,

I have given up my work, and all the tired feelings seem coming out in my bones! But I was flattered, having had such good conditions offered me if I could stay – and my head said I had done some 'particularly good work'. It was very interesting and if the hours had been just a trifle less strenuous, I think I should have stayed till the end of the war.

FREYA

FLORA STARK

11 Grove End Rd.
5 March 1917

My own Biri,

It was good to see a letter from you on my return from Southampton. My weekend there was very pleasant; though a little spoilt by the fact that Mrs. Carr came just those days and of course wanted to see her daughter as much as possible, so that I had to try and 'not be in the way', which is never

particularly amusing. She is a very energetic woman, I should think has never spent a real lazy day in her life – does arts and crafts, and wears her hair in a 'natural' way, a loose knot low down, which isn't becoming. She looks very young, and is rather like an elder sister to the three girls – one feels she is really much younger than Joan. I like her, but she is very fatiguing, not only because she is so energetic, but because she belongs to a rather 'super-cultured' set and hasn't got a broad enough humanity to get beyond it. You will like Joan very much; she is going to bring Fred to Dronero on her first long holiday, and we are going to set to work seriously and write! I do so long to get some real work; I must find something that I can do there without needing too many unprocurable books – and you must discover some people who are interested in such things and we will gradually get a pleasant little circle: then who knows but I might do something worthwhile!

A lovely stiff wind sprang up, and we got hold of a good sailor and went scudding up a broad sheet of Southampton Water with the breeze on our 'quarter' and our boat on a fine slant with the water swishing right up to the edge. A glorious run; the river opened up before us in a long series of grey folds and bends; occasionally the trees screened us, then we would right ourselves, the sail would flap for a minute, then fill again, and bend nearly to the water, driving us along with a feeling of incomparable freedom.

Travelling is not very safe even in the Channel. When I was down there a hospital ship was sunk just outside the port – but luckily everyone was got off, even the bad stretcher cases. A troopship with a huge number of Canadians was also sunk, and all saved. Neither of these have appeared in the papers, and I daresay there are a good many more.

I am to go to Hornsey next Monday. It is to the north of London, on a hill, with open spaces round, a nice garden, and a beautiful view towards Hampstead, and on my free Sunday afternoon I want to walk to the heath by Highgate, where it all looks like open country; so you see it will be rather nice.

I feel very pleased with myself, as, besides paying Viva, my earned money has allowed me to go on without touching the Italian things. I should like to go on earning something at Dronero: I wonder if I could write for some English paper?

My rooms sounds very nice, my dear dearest old B. I do really want to come soon you know. It is such a waste not to be together while we can. Will you try to arrange our lives so that there may be a little *leisure* to be together 'after the war'? Is my little sitting-room to be arranged too?

Joan says when I'm back she will keep me posted in the new books we ought to read; and I thought I would dedicate the money I economise now to buying them, so we may keep in touch with what goes on. Don't you think that a good plan?

Your own

FREYA

FLORA STARK

Hornsey Cottage Hospital

16 March 1917

My own Biri,

I have only two hours of free time in the day, and have wasted three quarters of the precious time by not having energy to fetch my paper to write. But my poor legs. They feel so tired. I am only just realising what a wonderful experience St. Orsola was, where I had all the interesting things to do and none of the drudgery. Here it takes a lifetime to reach that stage, and all my brilliancy in bandaging, giving anaesthetics, etc. . . . is of no use. I'll tell you the timetable – one is called at 6.30 – breakfast 7.15 – then cleaning the wards, sweeping, dusting, brushing their hairs, etc. till 9 – then one gets the luncheons – then one clears them, then the doctors come and there is a scurry till 12.30 – then the real lunch – then a short respite while we eat – more sweeping (the wards are swept four times a day), washing of various things, then teas to be prepared, and then they have to be got ready for bed. It is usually but not always all done by 8.30 – and by that time I go about like an automaton.

The etiquette is very strict, and the Matron is a small goddess whose smile and frown settles everything for us in this world and the next. Luckily she is very pleasant and kindly with a twinkle in her eye. After the Matron comes Sister, amiable but uncertain, with not a very good accent, and a nose with an inquiring and rather complaining look down which the spectacles seem constantly on the point of sliding. They have all been very nice to me, though evidently not thinking much of my muscles – but I do hope to be able to manage the work. Tomorrow I have the afternoon off, and am longing to see Viva again, and be in a place where everything is done for one, no fetching and carrying, and one pours tea out of a silver tea pot and feels like a lady.

I am hoping this training may get me out to Italy and near you, my own mother: – that is what I long and long for.

Being in hospital brings back so much to me, and the first day I could hardly bear it; this is so different, with none of the glamour of my wonderful time in Bologna.* In spite of all I am so thankful to have had that, which nothing can ever take away.

You hardly ever write to me, Biri. I have sent at least four since your last.

FREYA

* F.S. was trained and met Quirino there.

FLORA STARK   Highgate
                                                          19 March 1917

My very own Biri,

I had the whole afternoon off yesterday, and it was so lovely to get back to Grove End Rd. and wallow in comfort. My appetite is really something tremendous now, and I am beginning to get fat again, but my limbs still ache all over.

I sleep with a nice Irish girl, who has shown me the work and been very friendly; and she has the Irish gift of putting thoughts into words; it is wonderful how it is in the race, and how the English lack it. The nurses are all a pleasant cheerful lot, except for their silence at meal times. But they none of them expect me to be able to do the work, so I just must buckle to and 'learn them', as the Professor says.

One is quite out of London here; something between a country town and a suburb, and there is a hill opposite with a fringe of poplars on the top which I look at from the windows during my many journeys up and down the length of the corridors. I think I am too shy really to be ever much of a success with people, though everyone is very nice to me; but I am always treated a little differently to the others, as something of a freak. It's so trying, and I work so hard to be just like everybody else.

This week I have the men's ward all to myself to look after. Shall tell you about them tomorrow.

Your own

FREYA

VERA DI ROASCIO   Hornsey Cottage Hospital
                                                          20 March 1917

Dearest Vera,

Thanks for the photos of the little angel: she looks just like a small St. John carved in wood.

I have been here over two weeks now, one third of my time, and am getting fairly accustomed to the hard work – even the getting up at 6.30. It's all quite useful to know; and I shall be able to polish and scrub with real art when I get back. They let me do a little real nursing now and then; I went to the operating theatre last Wednesday when Dr. Edmunds was there and held up a woman's arm while he operated, and came off quite creditably without fainting or getting tired as I believe they all expected me to do. But most of it is just housework, and washing and feeding people.

It's easy to ask about my plans, but how can I make any with all the regulations that crop up every week. I hope to get to Italy anyway, but it will have to be as a nurse unless one of you gets really dangerously ill. There are so many difficulties now with the submarines that this rule has no exceptions – especially since Miss Hobhouse made use of an Italian passport to get to Germany and write pro-German articles in the papers here. I don't think it'll be for much longer now; wouldn't it be good if we got the summer together after all, and could enjoy it in peace. Everyone seems to think it will be over before autumn.

I look after two men, two small boys of four, and a *baby*! and it's the worry of my life, and starts yowling at all the wrong moments. I wash its clothes out in all my spare moments, only to find a new relay waiting, and when nothing else is doing I stuff its fat little tum with bread and butter to keep it good and smiling. But I come to the conclusion that I should not like to be the mother of a dozen.

This work is much better for me than the office, though I sometimes feel far away from everyone and everything: I'm afraid we shall never feel exactly at home with other people; I always have the feeling of a kind of strangeness between us, and that I am looked on as a new sort of animal – quite agreeable but incomprehensible.

Viva is making a cookery book of recipes without flour. Can you send me some from yours – anything with maize in it for instance.

Love to you all.

FREYA

FLORA STARK   Hornsey Cottage Hospital
                                                          30 March 1917

Dearest Biri,

This morning the Turkish rout is good news, especially for England. I expect we shall make a good thing out of the eastern victories, and everyone will be able to recognise the English selfishness again.

Aunt Marie wrote asking to come and visit me. She has been so good to me, and so wise too in many ways. It's a pity that she only likes people who are unlucky or unhappy, but it's an amiable weakness after all.

I believe I get on fairly well here – though I haven't the same amount of work to get through as some of the others. I begin to feel the real nurses' point of view, of not caring how the patient feels so long as his outward appearance is presentable. But I'm careful not to sacrifice them too much to a smooth sheet and creaseless bedcover, remembering my own sufferings in this respect.

Joan is in town and I hope to see her Sunday: her husband is back at the front, so the anxious days begin again – and there will be some terrible fighting now.

FREYA

FLORA STARK   Hornsey Cottage Hospital
4 April 1917

My own Mother,

I shall be half way through my term here by the end of next week, and seem to be doing satisfactorily. They are all very pleasant to me; and bring things for my sore hands and look after me. I find that now I can get through my work nearly as fast as the others and feel much more confident in myself.

I think that I must send you my dearest and best wishes today, to be in time for your birthday. The next we shall spend together and I hope they are all going to be very happy, my own darling. We ought to have done with troubles now, after all the time we have had.

It must be so lovely now with spring creeping up from the plain. Here it has been snowing almost daily and I bless my fur coat every night when I come back in it. But there is a lovely moon, and the buds are growing fat on the boughs. I think with great longing of a gallop, and a rest in the heather.

Do you know the feeling of coming to life again? It is what I have now, and it is a great blessedness to feel the joy of life coming back. I seem to be filled with a great hunger for happiness, and all the good and interesting things of life – and not for myself only, but for you too my dearest. In a way, sorrow is a wonderful and helpful thing – because it gives a sense of right proportions, and places life in perspective, so that one is far less at the mercy of circumstances than before. I feel as if now I should be able to get much more out of things, and enjoy the good in whatever circumstances bring to me – don't you think that is so? One is much more *serene* after a great sorrow, and that gives a happiness which nothing external can really affect.

FREYA

Hornsey Cottage Hospital
                                                              9 April 1917

My own darling,

I have just a few minutes left for you after writing to poor neglected Pips.
You wouldn't think that two hours was a short time for two letters, but one
does things slowly when sitting in the sun, and I stop to look at the fields
and curve of woods and houses, all made gentle and lovely by the mistiness
of the spring coming over them.

Here is a letter from Pips, just come which I thought you might like to see.

He seems to be thinking of settling down in some new place. But I don't
think we shall want to change, shall we? We must manage to arrange things
so that we get a few months off every year to be frivolous and come to London or go exploring somewhere, and we shall make ourselves a happy little
corner – even my Biri's neutral-tinted mind will become normal again.

Twelve o'clock! Goodbye – a hug to my own mother from her

                                                              FREYA

Hornsey Cottage Hospital
                                                              12 April 1917

My dearest,

Tomorrow I shall have a whole day off, and am going to Viva's this evening for a good sleep, and then to a theatre with Dot and Pud. So it's to be a
gay time. Fancy, the first morning for over four weeks that I shall get up
later than 6.30.

I am now doing a full probationer's share of work and seem to get through
as well as some of the others.

Did I tell you that sometimes I am allowed to do a dressing all by myself?
It's a great thing, when you think how Dorothy was a whole year in hospital
and never went into the operating theatre at all. This is run in a very simple
and homely way, with far less formality than most places, and everyone is
on good terms more or less. People are judged by the work they do; if one is
slow, or does things badly, somebody else has to come and help, and so there
is a feeling of good comradeship which is very pleasant, and also the responsibility of getting everything in good order lest someone else has to do extra
work. It's all very good training, not so much for what one learns to do as
for the attitude and point of view, and one realises that things are not so
difficult after all if one sets about them in the right way. I'm collecting many
ideas for housekeeping in Dronero later on after the war.

The people here are rather bourgeois, rather *too* refined for us. They seem
to live in a little world of settled conventions; there isn't much tolerance for

anything outside. I never realised what an enormous importance their church has to them; it seems the one note of colour in a very grey and formal atmosphere. And they are all so anxious to assert their position, and make sure it is as good as anyone else's. This is specially among the patients; I have my two old men who are the most insufferable snobs, one who wishes to be thought a gay old spark, talks of pheasants and champagne and drops an occasional *h*, and the other a sanctimonious old prig who finds all the longest words in the English language and places them without any connecting link in his sentences. The sort who go to polytechnic lectures, and make one think of democratic education as an abomination.

I can hardly believe that I shall only be here another fortnight. The time has gone so quickly. Perhaps in another two months I shall be with you, my dearest, if only for a little. It would be fine to work out on the Isonzo, under Trevelyan, wouldn't it? The war will not be over till the winter anyway. If I get to Gorizia I shall be within reach and able to see you occasionally, and still be doing my bit; so I mean to try for that with all my might.

Is Vera going to stay at Dronero now? How is she getting on? Is she still very discontented. Do you know, Biri, I have come to see so many things more clearly now, I think I could make matters a little easier with her, and I shall have a try when I get back.

I wanted to buy a cheap lingerie dress, but Viva says I must make my serge do. But I wonder if you could rout me out one or two pretty lace collars to put over the velvet collar and lighten it up a little?

No spring here; but a new sort of blizzard every day, and oh! such icy mornings. We have summer time too, which makes the mornings still more unattractive. But it's pleasant to jump out of bed into a boiling bath.

Always your own

FREYA

FLORA STARK Hornsey Cottage Hospital
14 April 1917

My darling,

I shall go to the moor as soon as my time here is up, and be back by May 15th. After that I shall hear about Gorizia, and if that isn't possible I shall see if I can get back to Italy in the ordinary way. If I can't do the nursing I shall bring some work that I can start, and see if I can't make something by writing. I have one or two ideas that might turn out. I ought to start some real work, and I must find something that can be done out there and for which the Italian libraries are sufficient: because I don't want any work that means being away from you. If ever I want it, I feel confident of being able to get a post of £100 or £200 a year in England, as I am quite clever at that sort of work that is wanted in offices, etc . . . I know that by the way my work was appreciated at the War Office. So I feel that is all right, and while we are in Dronero I shall try and start some literary work which may bring in nothing but will perhaps give me a position and lead on to something useful. Do you think I am able to write? I am always so discontented with my own efforts, and that keeps me from getting on.

It was so hard to come back to work and get up again at 6.30, although I was welcomed back most cordially. It will be quite sad to come to the end of my stay; I have been very happy here – and I have a feeling of coming to life again, and being well and able to take an interest in things. I do hope to have done with illness now for many years.

Viva lives now surrounded by cookery books. We had maize-bread for breakfast, cornflour rissoles instead of potatoes, and barley cakes for tea.

Your own

FREYA

FLORA STARK Hornsey Cottage Hospital
19 April 1917

My darling Biri,

Yesterday I was again allowed in to an operation – also a serious one – and I thought it was never going to end. The intense heat, and the smell of ether, and the standing still with nothing to do, make me feel intensely sleepy, so that there always comes a stage when I ask myself 'Is it sleepiness, or am I going to faint?' It goes off after a time, and never bothers me while I have anything to do. I was left on guard by the patient while she woke up, and she started kicking about so violently I thought she would fall off the bed. You can't think how useful a few extra inches would be to me here.

I feel limp sometimes – but have lost the wretched feeling of inertia that hung over me so long. So long as one doesn't feel tired right into one's bones it doesn't matter. Oh, won't it be lovely when we get a real holiday, with no war in the background.

Your own

FREYA

FLORA STARK Hornsey Cottage Hospital
24 April 1917

My darling,

Your dearest letter came just before I left Viva's. I think you are quite right about Pips; what he mostly wants is independence, and no worries, and he will be happy with Dronero as a 'base' from which to travel.

I saw Prof. Ker yesterday and he, like the dear man he is, is writing to Mrs. Trevelyan, who will let me know if she can help about Gorizia. Isn't that fine. So I shall hear next week. I shall then go to the moor, only for a week, and another week divided between Constance, Torquay and Exeter. I have no money! But shall borrow from the bank £20 to pay my expenses and outfit when I leave, and pay back in July.

I have been having a gay old time; six men in the ward, four of whom quite helpless, and have to be washed, and fed with feeding cups : besides which one is very very ill of pnuemonia, and delirious most of the time, and another has delirium tremens and I find him half out of bed, with nothing on. I have been there nearly all the time, never coming for my supper till nine o'clock, and I think I have got through that heavy work quite well, but I shall be glad of a rest, and sometimes when six o'clock comes along, and the men are not half washed, and all the beds to make, and my old drunkard has just made his clean bed all horrid again – I feel like the cook who had so much to do she thought she might as well go to bed!

Viva had a fine time at St. Margaret's; she saw the scrap in the Channel, all the flashes, and rockets lighting the scene, and the ships from Dover scooting out to join the fight, their lights passing at incredible speed over the dark water – and next morning saw our own disabled destroyer limping home, escorted by a flotilla of light craft, and lying very low.

Must stop now – with all my love. I think your idea of the medieval saints is very attractive; perhaps it has been done. I must ask Mr. Allen.[14] It merges into the story of the Universities – of course Monte Cassino alone would be a fascinating story to write; I believe the Salernian school belongs there, and all the Moorish learning came into Europe by that route. But it is a huge subject – and one must be able to read the script of the old Mss. It would be nice to go for a few months to Monte Cassino, you to sketch, and I to spend my time in the old library. The Professor wants me to return as soon as possible to 'the higher life'.

A loving kiss to my dearest from her

FREYA

FLORA STARK   11 Grove End Rd.
                                                         11 May 1917
My darling Biri,

I can't realise how it is that I have let a week go by without writing; but suddenly, when I just seemed to have arrived at Thornworthy, I found I had to come back to town post haste, and six days had already gone by. It was so beautiful down there – hot sunny days, with a little sudden wind that came round corners and seemed to spring up out of the earth. We were out all day: I had one ride all alone when Dot and Pud were in Exeter, and went exploring up over Assacombe, and a good gallop home by Fernworthy.

I also looked at the plantation and arranged for the sale of a little timber which is rotting there at present: Mr. Varwell is going to manage it for me, and if there is anything from it I'll put it in War Loan for Pips. I didn't manage to go over my little plot, but looked at it with great satisfaction across the stream: there is a mysterious pleasure in owning a scrap of earth, far greater than that of any other possession. I wonder why.

I was called back from the moor by a note from Mrs. Trevelyan, who wished to see me, so I went down in fear and trembling yesterday. Mrs. Trevelyan is an attractive little woman; enthusiastic, but not intense – not a society woman, and I should think very practical. She thought it would be possible to arrange for me to go out some time in June; then I would have to wait, perhaps a fortnight, perhaps two or three months; but I would have to join up when called upon. As far as the work goes, of course I couldn't do anything better or more useful, and I should be glad personally too to be within easier reach of you. So I would go on with it unless you have any reasons against it.

The hospital isn't near the fighting line (worse luck!) and there are twenty nurses under the charge of a Sister and Matron, so one is well looked after. I thought that if the fact of me nursing would shock people [in Dronero], you might say that I am to do housework, that the nursing is done by older and more experienced women. I'm afraid that is more or less true, as the Sister does all the interesting jobs.

But if you would prefer me not to go, I shall try and get out of it. But I do so want to come out and see you again, my dearest.

I had only one hurried day in Torquay; I looked over Rozel* and was shown it by a very supercilious sort of maid-manager. I impressed on her the value of the pictures, which she seemed not to realise; one of the oils had a little bit peeled off, and I noticed that our nice old bureaux were beginning to have their toes wormeaten. So as the inventory is being revised, I got Mr. Green to make a note on it and these things will be specially carefully looked at by the valuer. The only things we might want are the dinner service and a blue china garden seat (modern).

Don't make me keep away from Italy without good reason. I think I ought to volunteer for nursing: there is such a shortage now, and it really seems to suit me.

Your own

FREYA

* House belonging to F.S.'s father.

11 Grove End Rd.
22 May 1917

My darling Mims,

I have been putting off my letter, expecting every day to tell you something definite about my plans – but the delays and difficulties are endless: I still hope to manage it some time next month. Viva got Mrs. Cantlie interested in me, with the result that I became a V.A.D. without having to pass any of the exams: that's not bad, is it? Your telegram came yesterday, and rejoiced me very much. I'm afraid it won't be as exciting as you think: I'd rather be in tanks, like Bill!

I had such a cheeky letter from Ralph yesterday, written in his dugout: they are splendid, these boys. He says the country is good for galloping, only one must keep a look-out for barbed wire. He is near Bullecourt, all in the thickest fighting, and the other day when the Boche counter-attacked in the early dawn and broke through our front line, he had to rout out his men in their shirts to race the enemy for the guns, which were between the first and second lines. His people got their first and were able to mow the enemy in fine style (at quite close range of course) – all in their night shirts!

The dear Professor dined here on Friday, and was so charming. I don't think he likes the idea of my going nursing: I am sorry to think of being far away from him again, but one hopes this isn't going on very long now and we may manage to come to London together quite soon for a visit.

Tomorrow I go with Joan to her allotment. I have been working all to-day in the Brit. Museum, reading about the old Burgundians, who were the ancestors of the Droneresi as far as one can make out.

I dined with Mr. Allen on Saturday, and beat him at Chinese chess, a weird and wonderful game. He was very charming, spoke most encouragingly of my historical researches, and advised me to hunt in all the municipal archives. I think a history of the Marquisate of Saluzzo might be quite interesting.

Ever so much love, my darling.

Your

FREYA

11 Grove End Rd.
25 May 1917

My darling Biri,

This afternoon Viva took me to the American embassy, where Their Excellencies were entertaining the nurses of the first American unit for France. I enjoyed myself immensely: the nurses were very jolly, and liked being talked to. They had spent three days and nights without undressing, with their lifebelts on all the time: and one day they received six S.O.S. signals and were warned by wireless to change their course. All expect to go off on Tuesday, and to get quite near the front: they looked very capable, and had the frankness and openness which is so nice in Americans. They have a very good uniform, neither too showy nor dowdy, but extremely hot for summer.

FREYA

FLORA STARK 11 Grove End Rd.
5 June 1917

My darling Biri,

I am working nearly every morning at the British Museum. I struggle with the bad Latin of an 11th century chronicle written close to the Mont Cenis – Monte delle Ceneri – and very fascinating. There is a great deal of material, all picturesque and not very reliable, but the difficulty is to reach a point when one has read enough and can begin to write. Yesterday as I was 'ferreting about in one of the catalogues, a very very old gentleman came up to me, and said pathetically: 'I wish I were young.'

The dear Professor is always dear, but he has too many goddaughters. A new one every time, and he produces them without the rudiments of tact. He asked us to tea Friday previous to a Carducci lecture, and of course I thought we were to be the two and only as it were: but there was another anaemic-looking girl (she was pretty really, but I didn't like her) and it spoilt it all. I believe she thought me just as much in the way.

Ever so much love. I do hope to see you soon.

Your
FREYA

FLORA STARK 11 Grove End Rd.
8 June 1917

My own darling,

Boris Godunov was very interesting: not difficult music: very decorative and picturesque, with no 'art shades' in it, and some wonderfully fine marches. Beecham is doing it, at Drury Lane, and in English – which we thought rather a pity. We were amused by the audience in the intervals; the boxes were very well filled – the Duchess of Marlborough, who looks snake-like and pre-Raphaelite; and Lady Randolph Churchill, who was behaving very badly and seized on the hat on the girl next her and clapped it on the unruffled brilliantine of the poor young man at her side.

Arnold Ward* has got together a good many people in Parliament to propose an amendment to the Woman Suffrage clauses, suggesting that the bill should be passed but not made effective till six months after the war, when a referendum is to be taken from the women to ascertain their wishes, and then a men's referendum whose decision would be final. I feel sure that if the referendum were to include all classes of women it would be anti-suffrage by a great majority: but it is to include only those who would vote under the provisions of the bill: and that result is more doubtful.

Yesterday morning I met Arnold Ward, who is a huge, heavy man with rather sleepy observant eyes and a brusque manner. He thinks of what is being said to him and not of the person saying it, and is therefore not very popular in the House; but I liked him very much. His sister Mrs. Trevelyan has rather the same sort of manner. He has managed this business very well indeed.

In the afternoon there was a meeting of all the influential people in a Committee room of the House of Commons, and Viva gave me a ticket. I felt most awe-inspired going along the dark corridors, with the members standing about in little groups, and a great air of business and antiquity about it all. Viva introduced me to Mrs. Humphry Ward, who received us rather with the manner of an empress: a little too much so I thought: but she does give one rather the impression of one of England's monuments.

Mrs. Trevelyan has just written that they are over-staffed at Gorizia for the moment; it is too vexing. But she is going to try and let me have a letter saying that they will give me the first vacancy. Meanwhile it's very trying to be hanging at the end of a string with nothing doing. I did get an offer for Salonika, but I suppose you would have a fit at the mere mention?

I heard from Pips yesterday, and was electrified to find a cheque of £5 inside for my Torquay trip. Wasn't he a dear to think of it? It was most opportune too, now that I am living on borrowed money!

Your own

FREYA

* Son of Mrs. Humphry Ward, and Member of Parliament.

FLORA STARK   11 Grove End Rd.
                                                   17 June 1917
My own dearest,
    I am much overjoyed, as I went to see Mrs. Trevelyan again, and they have given me a letter definitely promising the first vacancy. I showed this to George, and he thinks it will get me out.

I expect you heard all about the raids. I was in luck this time, as on Wednesday I just happened to be going to see Grassig and a bomb fell quite near there. I didn't see that, but I saw the four Taubes very clearly against the perfect blue sky; – one could hear the throb of the machines, and see them gleaming like lighted windows when they turned and the sun caught them. They couldn't be mistaken for our own, as the shape is so different. They seemed to be making straight for *me,* that was the feeling it gave, coming slowly up over the street where my tram was till they were right overhead: all round and below them, beautiful little white clouds, like cigarette rings, were curling and scattering the shrapnel from our guns, but it looked as if it fell far short. Our own aeroplanes were not up, I suppose so as not to get in the way of the guns. Everybody took it quite calmly, although they nearly all got out of the tram and took shelter; but I didn't as I was afraid of missing the view, and I hoped to see one come down.

FREYA

FLORA STARK   11 Grove End Rd.
                                                                                4 July 1917
My own dearest,

It was very nice to get a letter at last, but why you should have got Mario to address it and give me the most awful shock thinking something had happened to you I don't know. That and Vera's black envelope are on a par.

Prof. Ker came here this afternoon, and we had a good long talk about this great work of mine and he saw my notes and gave me excellent advice. I shall want books very badly, and if you are in Turin I wish you would find out if there is any library whence I could take a few vols. to Dronero. Perhaps Bistolfi would know. I shall want things like the *Biblioteca Storica Subalpina* and the *Monumenta Historiae Patriae* and other ponderous collections of the kind. I think the book should be quite good – if only I can write, which yet remains to be seen. It is a matter of drudgery and collecting for the present.

How lovely to see you soon.

                                                                         Always your
                                                                              FREYA

FLORA STARK

                                                                          [?] July 1917
Dearest B.,

Don't you think the Allies' notes have been splendid? What a blessing we changed our government in time!

38

All the news from France is most hopeful; everyone one sees looks forward with confidence to next year.

Poor Bill can't get into the Tanks after all; the Navy won't spare him. His mother will be glad, but rotten luck for him. I can just feel how disappointing it would be. They are all dying to get into them: the first battalion is just being organised. I wish I could send you a picture of the brutes: – they look like nothing on earth.

Love to all.

FREYA

FLORA STARK 11 Grove End Rd.
12 July 1917

My own darling,

I am just out of bed after inoculation, and am now off to the dentist; and all this for the service of one's country. Who would not rather go to the front straightaway?

We had a thrilling time on Saturday with the big raid. Viva first noticed the exceptionally loud banging of the guns; we went out by the front door, and there were about twenty Taubes coming straight for us from Highgate way, clearly defined in black against a grey cloudy sky. By the time they were nearly over us, our own aircraft were up, their formation was broken, and a number of separate duels were going on, with a great noise all round as if the ground were bubbling up in a series of spasms. The shrapnel was falling all round Selfridges, so that they were quite near; and looked more so being monster machines of a special type. Altogether we counted any number bewteen thirty and fifty by the end, and they drove away like a flock of starlings. We retreated to the kitchen when they appeared to be right overhead, but then went up to the drawing room to see; and got a splendid view.

A loving kiss from

FREYA

P.S. I read your suffrage article in the *Corriere* with deep disgust! Anyway the bill isn't through the Lords yet, so don't crow too soon.

FLORA STARK 11 Grove End Rd.
17 July 1917

My own darling,

It was nice to hear from you again after so long. Will you come to Turin some time the first week in August? I won't know anything more definite myself till the last moment, but will then wire you; so keep ready to start.

Yesterday was a great day: twenty wounded soldiers to tea; arrived in a storm of rain, and we had to squeeze them in to play cards, and look at picture books. They were a nice lot, and did so enjoy themselves, and the quantity of cigarettes they smoked is beyond words.

18 July 1917

Last night we went to Hampton Court with Col. Segrave and wandered about the beautiful gardens in the most pleasant peaceful way; then had dinner at the Mitre and came home about eleven. The Colonel was in very good form, only so easily put out by minor details such as the cooking of the peas and the exact situation of our table. He gave us champagne, the first I have tasted since the war!

Must stop now and go on with my work. I think I shall be inoculated today again. Dear love to all.

Your

FREYA

FLORA STARK
11 Grove End Rd.

24 July 1917

My darling Biri,

I shall leave either the 1st or 2nd and there are some ladies with whom I shall travel. I'll come straight on to Dronero, as there is the chance of my staying only such a short time – and as the journey sounds so abominable I think you had better not come to meet me. One could almost walk it in eight hours!

I have the infant's things – but how to take my luggage is the most awful problem. Tea, being a foodstuff, I cannot bring.

Tomorrow Prof. Ker will dine here. It makes me sad to leave him, and Viva.

Your own

FREYA

ROBERT STARK
Rome

1 September 1917

Dear Pips,

Here for a day en route to the hospital. When are you coming? Do you mean to be in time to march into Trieste?

Love from

FREYA

Rome
2 September 1917

My own darling,

I am leaving tonight; I've had a lovely sleep, and a drive round Rome yesterday, and now live on the fat of the land in this most gorgeous hotel.

The R.T.O. into whose hands Captain Harvey delivered me was most polite; he gave me his corner seat, his eau de cologne to wash with in the morning, saw to my breakfast, and luggage, but oh! he was such a dull old boy – had lived here twenty-three years and seemed neither to know or care anything about it.

It was lovely running into Rome in the early morning. We saw the sea-planes dipping to the lake near Orbetello looking like beautiful birds in the clear light. The sea was a band of sapphire colour behind the low land and scrub.

I went to St. Agostino after tea, by tram, and walked through Piazza Navona watching all the children and sellers of strange sweets and things, and then inquired my way through narrow streets till I reached the church. I found Clot's Madonna; there was a crowd of votaries who went up to kiss her shoe, and the candles lit up all her jewels; it might have been Aphrodite or Demeter. One has the feeling here of a pagan city; the Rome of Popes and cardinals, and not of the Saints and Martyrs; one thinks of Boccaccio's saying, that one must come to Rome to lose one's religion.

Your
FREYA

Villa Trento [near Udine]
4 September 1917

My darling Mother,

I am here quite safely and happily, after a long night's sleep and no work till tomorrow, so I am just looking about today and putting away my things. It is the most lovely place, one of the old Venetian villas with the two statues at the entrance and hill and *vigna* behind; just a few cypresses on the brow of the hill to show the old aristocratic country – and the beautiful opal distances of the Veneto.

The sound of the guns comes through the sunlight and seems to beat on one's heart with the thought of all those men. I went out with two of the nurses yesterday and watched it all in the sunset time, beautiful rolling country, rising gradually to the barrier of the rocks; – well worth fighting for – 'Evviva l'Italia!'

By the time one gets to Venice one notices the difference in the type of officers; because all those *embusqués* of Turin are gone, and you find the people who are doing the real work. One of the first impressions was really sad. Between Udine and here my carriage filled up with a party of young lieutenants rejoining their various regiments after leave and they started talking about things in general and life in the towns they had left; of the carelessness and heartlessness about the war – and the attitude of the women! One can only hope that they chanced on the very worst entourage, but really the bitterness and their absolute *scoraggiamento* about it all hurt one to listen to – so much so that I had to look out of window as I found myself almost crying. I hope no Englishman can talk like that of our women. When one thinks of their life out here, and that all the sweetness it has comes from the people they have left at home, one sickens to think how these wretched people can spoil it and take away the one thing that can give them courage and hope.

It was so nice to arrive at last, and everyone has been kind to me. There are quite a number of people altogether; we have supper out of doors, in front of the house, with the road and its constant stream of lorries just beyond. Nearly all the wounded [censored] . . . I am told there is not very much theatre work as only the essential operations are done here – the rest sent back to the rear.

Mind you let me hear often.

Your own

FREYA

FLORA STARK

Villa Trento

8 September 1917

Darling B.,

Your letter just came, bringing me much joy. I hope you will write often. As for me, seeing that the weather here seems to be the one and only possible topic – what am I to write about except that I love you? I am feeling very tired these first days, as my feet had forgotten what the long standing was like, but that will pass and it is such a pleasure to see the people getting better. I wish you could be here too. Will try and write tomorrow, but always a loving kiss from

Your

FREYA

FLORA STARK

Villa Trento

9 September 1917

Darling B.,

I can't tell you about things here, except that I like the work and hope to get on all right with it. One loses touch with the outside world and I haven't

42

seen a paper all these days; the last was the fall of Riga and one just hates the news and is glad to plod on at something that holds all one's thoughts and gives a tangible result of good. I have been sad these days because Viva tells me Prof. Ker's godson was killed; what poor wrecks we shall all be by the end of it all.

There are a lovely lot of books here, if one has the energy to read. At present I am really happy with Theocritus; the beautiful hot landscape is all round one as one reads and is all so far-away and peaceful; one wonders why anybody ever wishes for anything except to lie in the sun and watch a few sheep, and have the gift of *singing*. It is also interesting to find the origin of so many later things, like Lycidas and Spenser and Ronsard – only this was actual life and rings quite true and genuine; - it might be the life of the shepherds at La Gardetta if our climate were different.

Am writing this in bed. I have a lovely painted room, shared with four other V.A.D.s. You would love this house and to be let loose to furnish it properly; – it is the regular Venetian villa on a small scale, and would make the most ideal place, only Count Trento – to whom it belongs – doesn't seem to have troubled much about it. I expect all he cares about is the *vigna*. We have to be very careful in my ward; if the disinfectant falls through the very slight board and plaster arrangement of the floor to the wine vats below, a whole barrel of this year's *vendemmia* may be done for!

Your

FREYA

FLORA STARK

Villa Trento

13 September 1917

My own darling,

Gabriel sounds most attractive; of course if he is a mountaineer, he must be and it will be fine to discover new routes up the Rocca Provenzale. I must say that the dangerous moments are the real ones to live for and one wouldn't be nearly so happy without the knowledge of the precipice below.

It's very pleasant to find how splendid the Piedmontese are. Some of the very best patients here, who have borne everything without a murmur, turn out to come from Piedmont. I have one nice boy now from Mondovi. Their character really does vary in the most extraordinary way according to the district they come from.

Do write often, as often as you can dearest; one can't help feeling homesick in between whiles.

Your

FREYA

Villa Trento
15 September 1917

Dear old Vera,

I hear that the small prodigy is more wonderful every day and beginning to walk. Do you think she will remember me? Do you find my Kodak all right for taking her with? I'm getting a fine collection of snapshots ready for you and yesterday I went up the hill at the back of the house and started a panoramic view of all the exciting places one can watch from here.

All these hills are lovely in shape, and last night the sunset turned them to a red gold like old mellow wine – a most gorgeous sight. It's quite different from Dronero, and much warmer in tone; the distances all seem to glow and quiver with a light of their own – and in the evening there are trailing mists that seem caught in the rows of maize. The maize is enormously tall here – far above one's head, – and it is altogether a fat and smiling land, with big oxen, and lots of children playing about.

The work goes on quite steadily and I am not showing the slightest sign of your prophesied breakdown. We get some hours, at least, off every day, and when I have the energy I go out to try and get rid of the smell of disinfectants.

I wish you could get me some white embroidery work to do – a table centre or something. Will you make me a good design, and send it along as soon as ever you can with cotton and all, so that I need only start? if you find some poetry to put in I should be still more pleased, as I didn't bring any at all. There is a little brown leather book of George Herbert's in my shelf near the window.

I hear you already talk of fires, and it is fairly cold over here also, especially when one gets out of bed and only cold water to wash in.

I wish you were here.

FREYA

FLORA STARK   Villa Trento
16 September 1917

Dearest Biri,

It is nice to get your cards; I take an interval in the morning's dressings to look into the post box and it is pleasant to find something waiting there. Yesterday I heard from Viva after staying in a castle at Dartmouth where Mr. Biron has houseparties: she says the men were charming and the ladies wore lovely clothes. All that seems in another world altogether just now, and it gets quite hard to realise that people really have all their legs and arms and are not needing someone to prop up their pillows all the time.

I had such a delightful ride yesterday, along one of the roads towards the front, and got a few snapshots which I hope may turn out all right. As soon as there is a really sunny day I will take one of my ward, and ask if I can send it you so that you may see some of my poor boys. We are having such an awful time in there just now as there is a hysterical Romagnolo – a man who just lets himself go and behaves like a madman; he lies and yells for hours at a time.

If still in time, and there is room, a white blouse, the one with filet lace, would be acceptable (why was I so foolish as to get stiff collars here!).

FREYA

FLORA STARK   Villa Trento
                                                      25 September 1917
My very dearest

I am really not fragile, morally or otherwise, and to be so constantly with the sorrow of other people is the only way of forgetting one's own; one gets back a sense of proportion. But I shall be so hungry for happiness after the war; at present one hasn't got the heart to ask life for such an out-of-the-way commodity.

Do you know that we actually get music here? There are two very good players who come from one of the outstations, and brought a small Austrian organ last Sunday – just for that evening. Such a pleasure and rest: I thought of your dear playing and all beautiful things. There is also a V.A.D. who sings; but I won't say anything about that.

It is rather pathetic to see how the men who come here wounded try to read about what they have done in the papers, and don't manage to recognise it. The war is so much more personal here, and therefore far sadder; sometimes I just hate the sound of the guns – it seems like a horrible Juggernaut eating up these poor lives.

Your
FREYA

FLORA STARK   Villa Trento
                                                      27 September 1917
Dearest,

I had a whole holiday yesterday, and went to Udine to shop. Do you know it? There is a charming piazza, with the old loggia very well restored, and the columns of St. Mark. An aristocratic little town, with the most wonderful amphitheatre of hills.

I had a fine walk yesterday, back into the foothills, and it is quite like

45

Asolo country, looking north; most attractive to tramp over in peace time. We should start somewhere here, and then cut across Istria, and right down the Adriatic, and then find some little fishing smack to ferry us across to Brindisi or Taranto; I believe hardly anyone does this trip overland, and one must come across wonderful places, Diocletian's palace, and all the old Venetian towns, and fascinating creeks and islands. Even here one can already notice the mixture of Slav and Italian; some of the church towers look quite Russian except for the colouring. But it is still the *Veneto biondo*, without much red in it; all maize and vines, and a wealth of fruit trees that must turn it to a garden in the spring time.

I am waiting for Vera to send me some work to do, that I can take out and sit in the sun with. There are delightful warm banks in the *vigna* where one could laze away most happy afternoons. Our free times vary a great deal, but at present I get three or four hours every day, so that I can really enjoy myself. All my people seem to be getting on well too, so that one feels quite happy about them.

Your own

FREYA

FLORA STARK

Villa Trento

29 September 1917

Darling B.,

Two letters running is luxury! I get time to read little bits of them through the day, so that they remain in my mind rather like a patchwork quilt, till the evening when I can enjoy them in peace. I am just now under a pine tree, with the most gorgeous sunset round me, and have been listening to R.L.S. on 'walking tours' and contemplative pleasures in general. I think I am getting old; they seem the only ones I want – watching other people do things and to look down on the world from some pleasant hill top. The sky is full of aeroplanes; it will be strange not to hear the noise any longer, it is so familiar now.

I think there would be no *embusqués* left if they could come near the front and hear what is said of them by these poor wounded; one loathes the whole tribe. I was listening today: one man who has lost an arm and leg and another very badly wounded (from Mondovi too) talking about some rich people who have got a snug post near Milan. It makes one quite sick to think that the feeling of so much injustice must add so greatly to the burden of those who do the fighting.

They were also talking about the Turinese, and it was refreshing to hear what the Piedmontese out here think of them. Yes, I find my Italian very useful; I don't always think it advisable to translate to Sister, especially in the matter of strong language – our words are so much less picturesque!

Your own

FREYA

FLORA STARK   Villa Trento
8 October 1917

Darling B.,

I'm afraid my last letter was some days ago – but now I shall make up by sending you some *real* news of myself, as the letters as a rule are censored here by a member of the unit, so that one always feels as if someone were reading over one's shoulder and I can't tell you any of the fascinating gossip. Now two of the V.A.D.s are going on leave and offer to post for me.

It is the funniest place here; every sort of person all jumbled up together, from the mechanics, who are paid, and not 'gentlemen', to the drivers, and Mr. Trevelyan's set. The girls are all very nice, except two rather common ones who spoil things by flirting all the time. What the Italians think of us I don't know. We have the utmost liberty till 10.30 at night, when we are supposed to be in our rooms. In the summer nights one is invited out on the hills by whichever of the men one happens to know, and it is quite embarrassing not to stumble over all those *têtes à tête* dotted over the hillside. As a matter of fact it is very pleasant just because they are very nice girls and we are all much annoyed with the two who are not so. The only real trial was the one I worked with, now on holiday, a journalist and artist of uncertain age, kittenish manner, dyed hair, *fearful* snob and says clever and peculiarly illnatured things.

Before the Inspecting Lady came here to reorganise, the V.A.D.s and men used to sleep out of doors dotted about promiscuously round the house; is was perfectly all right, but think of the feelings of the Italians! Now the V.A.D.s sleep on one side of the moat, more or less hidden by tents, and the men on the other. We also eat more or less at separate tables, though we invite whom we like to our table, and all sit together when dining out of doors.

I haven't any young men friends. The only one who asks me for the regulation moonlight walk is away now; there is no danger anyway, as Mr. Trevelyan is the only really fascinating person besides Geoffrey Young, whom I have not spoken to. But I know quite a lot just sufficiently to pass the time of day, and have already been presented with one Australian and one Italian helmet as trophies.

47

I am not to give you any military news. When you see reports of artillery action on the Faiti, Ternovo, or Bainsizza, you know we can look on at them and see the huge black clouds of the shells. The English have a record here; they go nearer the front than any Italian car of the Red Cross, and Trevvy is anxious this should be kept up; that explains our heavy casualties lately. The dangerous piece is up the S. Gabriele, where the road is hidden from the enemy behind a precipice of rock; they can't see who goes along, but have the range and shell the place constantly. (When the road is open, they usually don't fire on the Red Cross). I am told it is the most exciting feeling to rush along an open road, where nothing else dare show itself, flying a huge red cross and trusting the enemy will not fire. There is one station where one can see the road from a balcony and watch the cars racing by and count those that are hit, and the men do this and see how many are smashed, and then have to go and race along there themselves. A trying thing at first too are the Austrian searchlights that suddenly illuminate and make one conspicuous when all round is black as night – and you may be jammed in a row of lorries and unable to move. The searchlights are extraordinarily powerful; I was sitting on the hill when the one from behind the Carso (Austrian) fell upon me in a belt of light about three or four yards wide – a most uncomfortable feeling.

Your

FREYA

FLORA STARK

Villa Trento
12 October 1917

My darling,

Have been especially busy today, as fifteen patients left this morning and we took the opportunity to have a grand spring clean and scrubbing and are now as spick and span as can be, but feeling melancholy with a half empty ward.

It is bitterly cold already. The hills just beyond where the fighting is are all already powdered with snow. On the clear crisp days one can look across to the Dolomites and see new wonderful ranges stretching away westward, quite white already.

I had a letter from Margaret Jourdain about the air-raids, and descriptions of East End aliens encamped with their families in the tube stations. Viva had a bit of shrapnel through the greenhouse, too; so you see one can die an early death just as easily in London as anywhere else, and much more easily than at Villa Trento.

Margaret sent me a lovely quotation à propos of my Montaigne:

Fifteen, Horace,	And when I look back,
Sixteen, Tom Paine,	To say the truth,
Seventeen, Plato,	I stand aghast
Nineteen, Montaigne.	At the age of youth.

Always your own

FREYA

FLORA STARK   Villa Trento
                                            16 October 1917

My very dearest,

We had a great time some days ago, [a fellow nurse] Ruth Trant and I, going to call on a Major she knows who looks after the observation balloons in this sector. The Major telephoned to one of the balloons to get itself ready to be visited, and we were soon running along one of the lovely smooth roads towards the front, with trench on one side and barbed wire the other, all rusted and looking singularly evil in that peaceful country.

The balloon lives in a quite out-of-the-way valley about forty minutes' drive from the actual front, and when we arrived it was sailing just above our heads, like a great galleon in full sail, held down by about forty men in their shell helmets. All the officers were introduced, and explained the monster to us; they opened out the parachute – a huge umbrella of fine white silk, parked in a small case and hooked always on to the officer. There is room for one or two men in the little basket and they stay up about three or four hours. We were very hospitably treated at the mess, and given a most gorgeous lunch with the luxury of tablecloth and napkins. I felt most uncomfortably nervous at first, after being introduced to what seemed an unending number of beautifully brushed officers in dazzling blue and white collars, all making the same bow, and looking exactly alike. But they were so much relieved on discovering that we could speak Italian and French, that our conversation instantly became animated.

I had a letter from a patient – four pages and one full stop – saying that, when leaving, his heart was overcome with tenderness at the thought of being in a hospital where I was not! and would I send my photograph, and write to him often, and let him know if ever I went to the Abruzzi and he would come to see me. He was a dear little boy – we used to call him 'the bambino', and I looked after him a lot: so it was very pleasant to receive so much gratitude, but I think I shall tell him that it is not permitted for nurses to send their photographs.

There has been one air raid, with guns and machine guns firing round about – a very short sharp sound, like something snapping in frosty air. The men all knew the enemy planes at a glance; but I could see no difference; they did not seem to be curved like the Taubes. Nobody bothered to take cover; I suppose one is more fatalistic in the war zone than in London.

I hope you are not worrying yourself over things: most things are little things after all – 'ce n'est pas la peine!' Talk of a restful time out here. I have spent the last three days with a delirious carabinier, who calls us the most appalling names, and has been having a pulse of 118. It isn't so wearing now, because he is better, and will pull through finely I hope.

Your own

FREYA

FLORA STARK   Villa Trento
                                                 19 October 1917
My darling,

Just a line to say goodnight, in a slack moment in the ward. I am so tired today, having been called the most objectionable names all the time by our huge carabinier, who thinks we are illtreating him because we refuse to bring drinks. Talk of smoothing the sick men's pillows. I think really nursing is one of the most prosaic jobs: the last three days seem to have been spent entirely in avoiding his huge fist, which has come down bang on my chest once, like a sledge hammer. But he does get better. He is a Bolognese too!

It has settled to a muggy wet winter; soft gleams of sun in between, very lovely. I had a ramble all by myself this afternoon in and out of the little hills, a fascinating country for children, full of little ponds, with frogs jumping in and out, and lost pathways, and tiny trickling streams hidden in the thorny acacias.

With all my love always,

Your

FREYA

FLORA STARK   Villa Trento
                                                 23 October 1917
My own darling,

It was lovely to get a letter from you, after so long. It seems to me that you live in a whirl of gaieties, I hear nothing but parties: I expect to find you a wreck by the time I come home. I wish I had been there to see the beautiful A[chille de Bottini]; does he talk as much as his sister [Clot]?

And what do they both look like? Do tell me what I am to expect as a future fate. I think Gabriel sounds much less alarming.

We were inspected the other day by the Lt. Colonel of our army corps, such a pleasant energetic-looking man: Dr. Brock told him I lived in Piedmont when they came to our ward, and he spoke Piedmontese and I answered . . . very badly, but he seemed much pleased; and he was most flattering to Sister about the ward. It is really very pretty now; all the men have red winter bed-jackets and look nice against the whitewashed walls and rafters: it is also comparatively peaceful, as our carabinier has stopped using such awful language.

One of the men here, just come from an out-station, plays Chopin and Schumann and all the things I love, and it is such a treat and luxury: I had the lounge all to myself yesterday while the evening was coming on, and just lay on a sofa and listened in the half dark, and outside the cypresses grew deeper and deeper against a clear wonderful sky, just flushed with the hidden sun. The work of the wards itself is so drab – depressing in one way – that one has a real hunger for everything beautiful; just a sight of the blue sky or the line of the hills gives one a feeling of such deep gratitude. I can't tell you how intense it is; one could kneel down and worship the loveliness of the earth, it is like a great comforting presence, an immense serenity, and the far line of shells and smoke is just a horrible gash that spoils the surface, but cannot reach the inner loveliness, or spoil it. Sometimes, especially in the evening when I am alone in the ward, and the lights are out, and only the dim sleeping figures around me, all the business of life seems so unreal, a kind of cinematograph of shadows; but the beautiful things, the shapes and music, and the sound of verses, are always a reality. I shall never be afraid of death, not even for the people I love – one thinks of it so often out here.

Your own

FREYA

[On 27 October 1917 F.S. left the Villa Trento. See *Traveller's Prelude* for the diary of the Caporetto retreat.]

[After the Armistice F.S.'s father, who had been over from Canada, bought her 2½ acres near Ventimiglia, on the Italian Riviera. The old name of the land was L'Arma – a name F.S. liked and kept.]

ROBERT STARK   Grimaldi
                                                        29 November 1918
Dearest Pips,
   Here we are, Mama and I: it is lovely and warm. We have been over
the estate, and it is just as nice as when we saw it first: and there are seven
rooms of quite good size which we shall have done up now. I will write and
tell you all about the arrangements we make: thinking of letting the *vigna*
for two years, till you come to start it properly.
   The Armistice hasn't yet sent down prices over here, so I think it's best
to do as little as possible to the place till things settle.
   Lots of love to you from   Your
                                                             FREYA

ROBERT STARK   Paris
                                                             8 May 1919
Dearest Pips,
   You see I managed it this time, and am en route to stay about six weeks
in England and will write to you there. There seems nothing special on in
Paris though it looks very gay. L'Arma finally getting on when I left
yesterday morning.
                                                     Your
                                                             FREYA

ROBERT STARK   Monte Rosa
                                                          14 August 1919
Dearest Pips,
   As soon as we get home I shall write you a description of these beautiful
places. B. and I have been tramping about with Professor Ker – from
Courmayeur (we climbed to the Col des Géants) here to Valtournanche.
Now we go down across the valley – ridges to Macugnaga and back to Lago
Maggiore.
                                                     Your
                                                             FREYA

FLORA STARK   L'Arma
                                                         8 January 1920
My darling B.,
   We had threats of rain and nothing in particular to subsist on for some
days, but today and yesterday were gorgeous again and soon I hope the
excavation will be begun, and hope to have it ended by the end of the month.

The carpenter is steady, but incredibly slow, so I think we must give him the staircase to do on piece-work. Will you find out how much we ought to give?

I have asked Vera if she could give you two fowls to bring down; we could keep them quite easily and do need eggs so badly.

Granny is well; she felt the bad days rather and I kept her in bed, but had a walk today in the sunshine and is now busy teaching me Spanish. I conjugate verbs while sewing in the evening.

My love to you dearest B. Don't be too long.

Your loving

FREYA

ROBERT STARK L'Arma

2 November 1920

Dearest Pips,

I believe I haven't written to you for ages, since the *vendemmia* last month; it has all been a rush ever since. I wish I had been with you for the camping. I should love to be out with you looking for bears and climbing.

I sold the grapes for 2,500 francs clear and have about a thousand worth of wine now fermenting in the *cantina*: there is white and red – the pale pink you like, and a few bottles of raisin wine, specially good, which will be kept for when you come. I am writing your name on the bottle. It is great fun making it, and deciding how long it is to ferment.

Altogether I am quite pleased with the first year of this little place. It has given four percent on what it has cost altogether, land, building and all. Don't you think that is quite good? The grapes were the best in the neighbourhood, huge yellow bunches, a joy to behold, looking as if the sun lived inside them. Now I have a small bit of strawberries and a lot of peas and some artichokes to attend to, and am planting lots of potatoes to sell about Easter time. And I have a *man*! He is quite young, just married, and wants to settle in life. I have taken him for one year as a labourer, with the promise of giving him an extra share of whatever profits there may be: and by the end of that time one will know how things develop over here. I will not have to slave away like last year I hope, but will do some of the work also so as not to be in any danger of dispossession by Bolshevists.

They have been pretty bad here and in the big towns things are more or less at a standstill: in Turin the workers (so called) took hold of the factories, filled them with machine guns, and there were killed and wounded every day. And prices are getting higher and higher: I sometimes don't know what to do for housekeeping: it is a blessing to have vegetables and

53

milk of one's own. We are all going back more and more to old patriarchal ways of living and it is not a bad way either.

The building is not yet done: there seems to be no end, and the various saints whose feasts have to be kept are endless. We have had over a month of rain, torrents and hurricane, with huge waves over the promontory, and mud to wade in whenever one goes out. Professor Ker came in September, and now Viva and Mr. Bale, and it is very disgusting to give them this sort of weather. But they like the place and the house very much and we got a few good walks – a fine one round Cap Martin in a wood of old pines and olives, and one or two good scrambles in the hills.

The *Literary Times* come at intervals and are very welcome; they are the only way I keep a little in touch with what goes on in literature. I have been reading Borrow – *Romany* and *Lavengro* – and enjoying every word; that is the way to talk of travels! That and Jane Austen have been my two authors lately.

Have you got enough warm things to get through the winter? I hope you will keep a sharp look-out for that pneumonia and not let it come again; do be careful dear old Pips. I should like to know you take all precautions.

Lots and lots of love from

Your
FREYA

FLORA STARK L'Arma
26 February 1921

Dearest B.,

Thanks for letter and the money. I waited and waited and at last had to sell out stocks, having borrowed all I could from Benbows and worried *no end*.

Lucia has been in tears – her mother wanting her back. How detestable these old peasant women are – no more sense of a promise than a Boche. Now will you interview her before the old sinner's obstinacy has time to congeal? It is no fun for me to keep this house as a winter resort for people who don't stay: explain this in forcible language, the horrid old pig.

Your
FREYA

L'Arma
15 April 1921

Dearest Pips,

I have also been indulging in colds and have been laid up, and so putting off writing this week in answer to your letter of March 10th. I have been thinking it over and trying to see all sides of the question, although it is difficult when wanting you so much to be back here again.

I quite see that giving up Canada is a loss: but on the other hand I believe we have *quite enough* to live on if you sell it for £6,000, and I would *much* more happily do without a larger income and have you these few years sooner. I would not say this if it meant real poverty for us all, but we shall really have enough to get along happily with your and Mama's and my incomes put together and this place to develop.

I wouldn't mind selling therefore, dear old Pips. If I were strong enough to come out and really help you it would be different, but as it is I'm afraid I'm no good for real hard labour. I have been knocked about these last seven or eight years and seem only to be good for an ordinary kind of life. I feel you are hesitating because of me, as Vera is well off and settled in life, and I do want you to feel how *very* little – nothing at all – it matters to me to have more than just enough to be quiet on. That we should certainly have, and anything beyond that isn't worth comparing a minute with the joy of having you again.

Your

FREYA

ROBERT STARK L'Arma
24 May 1921

Dearest Pips,

The hot days have come all of a sudden, and all the little grapes are bursting into flower faster than I can pick off the leaves that choke the air off them. Do you know or remember the scent of them? It is as sweet as mignonette, almost to send one asleep while working out among them. It is delicious here now: bathing in full swing with a lovely freshness still in the sea and one has discarded stockings. I do so wish you were enjoying it all too.

The elections are over at last and not very satisfactory as the Socialists have kept practically all their seats and it was expected they would get a squashing defeat. The Government has no majority unless the Clericals vote for it, so that they are practically dictators at present. France seems to be the only country that can manage her affairs at all well.

I had one gorgeous walk the other day with some Bordighera people up into wild country between Bordighera and Pigna, up a valley off Dolceaqua. One can go for hours without meeting a soul: much more lovely really than the Alps.

I do long to hear of your being able to sell, and to come here and let us enjoy you at last.   Your loving

FREYA

ROBERT STARK   L'Arma
                                                      12 July 1921

Dearest Pips,

I just got a p.c. of yours and a lovely fat bundle of *Literary Supplements* enough to last me for weeks and make me feel that I still belong to the living and thinking world.

You ask about Yardworthy,* but I wrote ages ago to say I would rather keep it if possible. When I go I will see if it isn't possible to get someone to rent it for ten or twelve years and put a little shanty there. I would be so sorry to give it up altogether.

Vera and the infants are here, all getting to look like little niggers. Paolo is a small barrel: I went up to him the other day when he was murmuring in his sleep to hear what it was all about and he was saying 'pasta asciutta' to himself in the most tender voice imaginable. It is nice to have them here playing about in the water.

It isn't tactful to ask if you have any spare cash hanging about, poor Pips, but if you happen to be able to send me anything for my bank debt it would be a very great help. It still stands at £250, as my own resources are only barely (very barely) enough to keep up with the living expenses with these high prices. It is an awful worry to me because there is absolutely nothing more left on which I can save. We will pull through however, and have done better so far than I could have believed possible a year or two ago. So don't trouble if you *can't*, but if you *can* I shall be so thankful.

                                                          Your

FREYA

* Robert Stark's remaining farm on Dartmoor.

FLORA STARK   Thornworthy
                                                 17 September 1921

My dearest B.,

I will take an hour before tea for writing to tell you of the journey. Until I actually woke up in London I felt this was all some kind of dream. Even

56

the sight of that beautiful Kentish land of rolling meadow and trees could not make me realise that this was England; but it is sinking into me, and coming back hour by hour, and I am so happy to be in the dear country again and to hear English spoken in the lanes and streets.

We had a most agreeable journey – mostly eating and drinking – with a little sleep thrown in. From Marseilles to Avignon was sunset over the mouths of the Rhone, a clear gold sky on a sheet of cold and luminous water, with dark low hills and flaming lagoons in the foreground and then the moonlight and a white road by the waterside: it was among the most beautiful things one can remember. We had breakfast on the boulevard at Paris; then lunch on the train, already surrounded by travelling English. The crossing was sunny with a breeze on the sea, enough to make me sedentary, but not sick. At Dover the Prof. got me into a gorgeous saloon with brown velvet armchairs and a Jewish family. I believe it was a Pullman, and I was much thrilled at the solemnity of the rich and their surroundings. And we went through Kent and a beautiful sunset till the lamps were lit and shone along the Thames, and we slid into London. Viva was there. It was such a joy to get into that house again: I might never have left it.

Viva and I went to see caricatures of the Rossetti coterie by Max Beerbohm – great fun – and then for tea and ices at the Piccadilly. Maurice came to see me next morning before I went off, and who should turn up at Paddington but the Professor himself, with a book – isn't he a good friend?

I travelled up easily and my vis-à-vis at lunch came from Palestine and was most interesting; and the West Country was in sunlight. Pud met me at Chagford and we walked on heather in the evening: it is like a dream to see it all again. Tomorrow I shall ride.

With lots of love,

Your

FREYA

FLORA STARK   Thornworthy
                                        21 September 1921

My dearest B.,

I have been riding twice, the second time it felt more natural and the saddle and I begin to have the same impulses; it is unbelievable joy to be out on the heather and surely no place *more* beautiful than the open moor.

I do nothing here but sleep and eat. My clothes are all right, and Pud has lent me shoes. The habit was much too long, they are worn just below the knee, and the breeches *hang in folds* round my calves, so what I must have been in the way of fatness once is astonishing to think of.

Your

FREYA

FLORA STARK   11 Grove End Rd.
                                                                      14 October 1921

My darling B.,

I had two exciting episodes learning to jump. Mouse is an excellent pony at it, and William got me higher and higher till he put up a hurdle of five bars and Mouse took it sideways and went right over the hurdle and the higher spike above it: it was a lovely jump altogether, scarcely showing day-light. Soon after however, I really came off.

I left on Tuesday, driving to Exeter with the whole family and then on to Woking where I found Mrs. Whibley in a pretty little French car. The Whibleys[15] were most agreeable and pleasant. It is a delightful modern house in a little wood of its own and a garden in the making: so comfortable – bath, hot water waiting on the washstand, early tea, comfy chairs, and the most delicious coffee Mrs. W. makes herself in a brass pot.

Your

FREYA

FLORA STARK   11 Grove End Rd.
                                                                      18 October 1921

My darling B.,

I meant to bring you a beautiful surprise as a Christmas present, but now that Pips is going on ahead, I thought better send sooner. I have got you a brown fur coat; it is pony skin, and looks a little leathery and stiff, but I have hunted half over London – even the ugliest imitation sealskin are £15 or so. I thought a real skin, even if not fine and silky, was better than these imitations and would look more refined, especially as we come into places from the country. I dare not tell Viva, partly because I have got it at a 'dress agency' – I had the old lining left in as it might cause trouble at the douane, and you can line it with a pink or mauve silk petticoat you have.

In the morning I went with Dot and Maurice to the Home Office and we looked out on the Cenotaph in Whitehall and saw General Pershing deposit a wreath there, and he did it with great dignity and composure – and has a kind human face, not machine-made as if he couldn't turn his neck around like so many of the Americans.

Among others we saw Winston going by: he is just like the caricatures only tremendously powerful and not a bit ridiculous to look at. When it was over, our hosts let us out by a side door into Downing Street, where we sprinted hard and managed to come up with the troops as they went down Victoria Street, the U.S.A. ahead in steel helmets, then our Grenadiers with their band, the Welsh and the Scots behind them looking as if the earth was too low to be trodden on. Not being a pacifist, I wept so that I couldn't even cheer them. The U.S. were fine men, but ours had the style, every swing of the arm was the same right down the line – it was a great sight.

In haste – with dearest love.

Your

FREYA

FLORA STARK   11 Grove End Rd.
                                               21 October 1921

My darling B.,

I went to Finsbury Square this morning with Viva to see Sir Denison Ross, who was most amiable, tripping about with his round tummy and bulgy eyes and lively manner, in a room hung with Chinese inscriptions and Arabic MSS. on the tables. He was in a great hurry, but seemed well impressed by my grammar, which I took with me. I told him I could stay only till Xmas and wanted coaching, and he went out and came back in two twinks saying 'You will have four hours a week here, two with a young Englishman, and two with an Arab from Mesopotamia!' Imagine my joyous feelings – so joyous that I forgot to ask the fee. I begin on Nov. 1st so as to have a free week first for Pips. I think I should get on fast.

Lots of love dearest B., from

Your

FREYA

FLORA STARK   11 Grove End Rd.
                                               27 October 1921

My dearest B.,

I have got such a pretty toque – jade green taffeta, very close fitting with frills of the same round it: looks nice with the black coat and only 30/-; and another for 10/- because it was a little knocked about, made of coppery-brown little ribbons shot with gold.

Pips arrived on Saturday last, looking very well, and has been busy ever since getting his apples in to the Crystal Palace exhibition. If he gets a prize I will make him buy a new suit: otherwise no hope! He has got a new burberry and a cap, and that is all – having only £15 balance at the bank. It is hard on me, as I feel we *must* ask Viva and ought to ask Dot and Maurice to a theatre, and I will have to pay the tickets and that means about £2. I do so dislike being poor. When you see Pips do let him understand – without rubbing it in however – what a hard struggle it has all been.

We went for lunch to A. Marie and felt much chilled by the earnest atmosphere of the settlement: – I strongly feel if I lived in the East End that I should prefer to be one of the *undeserving* poor. All my time seemed taken up in avoiding (1) a sewing class; (2) to start arts and crafts; (3) to join their dramatic society; (4) to study Rabindranath Tagore in a class; etc . . . But it is well known that persecution and philanthropy go together.

Your loving

FREYA

FLORA STARK   11 Grove End Rd.

6 November 1921

My darling B.,

I am so rushed for time with Pips here and seven lectures a week of Arabic that I shan't manage a proper letter.

We saw *Chauve-Souris*, a Russian variety show full of the most delightful things. Pips enjoyed it ever so much, even after paying £3 for the tickets, which is what amusements cost in this degraded age.

Tonight we dine, Viva and I, at the Carlton with Prof. and Olivia [Horner][16] – and the night before last I went to my first real dinner since the war, with some of Pips' grand friends, and had two glasses of champagne and felt very cheery and vivacious in consequence. So I hope the rest of the week will be quiet to let me catch up with my work.

The Arabic is great fun. I am the most intelligent of my class – the others all seem rather stupid as a matter of fact – but I have a good deal to catch up being put in with people who started a while ago. The Arab from Mesopotamia was a sad disillusion – a fat young man in a swallow-tail coat with purplish lips and a fat smile.

I have got myself good boots for country or skiing; also a cheap mac – and that is all I can do in the way of clothes.

It is lovely to think you may get over next year. I do believe the worst of our times are over. I think Pips is going to help too: he quite sees how hard it is to live nowadays on £200 a year.

Lots of love, dearest Biri,

Your

FREYA

ROBERT STARK   L'Arma

27 March 1922

Dearest Pips,

I think this ought to reach Creston about the same time as you – and I hope it will find you not too much knocked about by the Atlantic nor shrivelled up with all the cold that the burberry didn't manage to keep out. If your waves were bigger than ours, they must have tossed you a good deal: the whole front of Mentone was more or less under water and Dorothy had the joy of seeing a fat Monte Carlo lady, all dressed in satins, washed from head to foot as she was sitting in the open tram!

Herbert [Olivier][17] left on Friday. We ended up with a frantic struggle to make him pay his numerous workmen instead of picking roses. Masses of priceless furniture arrived the day before he left, beautiful inlaid bureaux and ebony chairs, and he had a lovely time dotting them about all over the house: then we upset him very much by remarking that unless he collected them into one room again the whitewashing of the rooms would spoil them all! There is a curious feeling of peacefulness now he is gone.

We had a lovely day going to explore for more furniture for him in Alassio. It was a good thing you didn't come, you could never have paid your fare out to Creston, there were such lovely things – inlaid chests of drawers for 500 lire.

Your

FREYA

ROBERT STARK   L'Arma

22 May 1922

Dearest Pips,

You would like our climate now. I am sleeping up in the loggia, with the old moon looking in about two in the morning and the sunrise between Ventimiglia and Castel d'Appio, very comfortable to look at from bed. That charming doctor of mine recommends great laziness in the morning: so I can have the luxury of being late and also feeling virtuous!

When I have time I go into the *vigna* to pick off the extra leaves that are now covering up the bunches and preventing their flowering. There ought to be such a *vendemmia* this year; Nicola calls me every morning to admire a new prodigy of a vine and says it is all his pruning; while I say it is my manure at last showing results. The days are so still: Ventimiglia and the hillside are reflected in the water, and the evening brings out the lovely pastel tints, and the fireflies.

Herbert's masons are all over the place, putting up and pulling down staircases, etc . . . I do hope he will not end in the bankruptcy court: we have given up any attempt at slowing him down. I reserved quarter of the water of the big cistern, and the use of Herbert's pipes: also a mutual right of way and refusal of the property in case of sale: and also the right to quarter of the water of any cistern to be built in the future. I though I should go mad at the notary's what with Italian legal language and Herbert fussing over it. Then some imp of mischief prompted me to tease him by saying that of course we might still evict him unless he got the transfer of his property made out, and he spent nearly a day considering how he could prove in a court of law that the villas were really his!

Viva and the Edwards have asked Mama to go and stay for a while with them, and I think she may go and I shall remain here quietly and then go to meet Prof. Ker who has invited me to the hills: I am not to climb, but it will be nice to look at the snow even.

I am reading the *Aeneid* in the afternoon on the loggia. There is such a fine boat-race in the Vth book, one feels as if it were going on just beyond the point.

Arabic goes on, very slowly, too; it seems to get more and more difficult: and it is hard to concentrate on unpronounceable verbs when the sun is so hot.

Lots and lots of love

FREYA

FLORA STARK   Dronero
                                                                14 August 1922
Darling B.,

Vera, Mario and I went to Col Maurin for three days. It was glorious for me, but there was not a very serene domestic atmosphere otherwise; Vera found she could not walk at all on anything with an edge, and poor M. stayed with her at the bottom of the mountain all day – and the next day – and never got a good word for it – which I really thought rather hard. I went up with Menico and Provenzale, and we climbed crumbling rock for three hours overhanging the glacier – and not roped! It was an exciting climb –

we took one and a quarter hours for the last seventy metres, testing every stone to hold on by.

Yesterday, coming down to Chiappera, we went by the Rocca Provenzale and I went up with Provenzale alone. He was so pleased to do it – after twenty years! He is a most charming man, with the eyes of a boy and all his enthusiasms intact. He couldn't go up alone now because there is one bad place at the top and he feels too stiff for it – so I went ahead, squirming on my tummy on a little ledge, with the valley down below and my legs really trembling because I was quite frightened. I had to wait there for ages (not looking down) for a lull in the wind which was blowing; then however I got round the corner, and found decent hold for my hands and feet, and hauled up the rope and Provenzale joined me, and we nibbled bread beside the cross. The coming down is quite easy, down the crest overhanging Chiappera. I am feeling very stiff today. Provenzale told me that only two 'alpinisti' have done that pass – two boys from Dronero – possibly Carlo Savio? – and also the other climb I believe I am the first woman to have done.

When you come will you bring my yellow slip and black sequin tunic in case I need it.

Lots of love dearest B.,

Your own
FREYA

ROBERT STARK

Dronero
August 1922

Dearest Pips,

It is a lovely view looking out towards Savoie isn't it from Col Maurin? And lovely going up over those pastures with the soft turf. It was good to feel able to do these things again. I wish you had been with me, sitting over our lunch with all the valleys spread round us and tracking out our old walks: do you remember the Col Traversières and going down on to Belluno in the mist?

Your own
FREYA

ROBERT STARK

Dronero
29 August 1922

Dearest Pips,

I am going to L'Arma in a week or so: have been waiting for cooler weather, as I seem not to be very brilliant in the heat and it has been beyond anything this year. Even high up at Madonna delle Grazie the grass is burnt and dry, and here there are no wells left. The reports from Nicola are quite good considering, and the carnations are pulling through. But I am longing to be down there and to see them for myself.

George [Edwards] is going to see Mario next month, and we will see if he cannot get your £2,000 back before they go down again in value. If we do not get it I don't quite know what we can do; I must think of some way to make a little money and help the housekeeping along – *sufficient for the day is the evil* however.

Your

FREYA

ROBERT STARK

Torquay

9 November 1922

Dearest Pips,

Here am I – have spent a busy pleasant sunny morning walking round with Fred hearing about things. The sale [of Rozel] is to be on the 29th and they suggest a reserve price of £6,000.

I don't know if you wanted any of the pictures to be sold? I thought of sending them all up to London and showing them to a friend who collects for Americans and rich Jews and who would get us as good prices as anyone could, and meanwhile you can let me know what you think about it. It is rather sad to part with good pictures, isn't it?

I will write from the moor and tell you what the bracken looks like: I am counting the hours to be out there and on a horse. It is the most gorgeous autumn, all red and gold and today has been perfect – with the sea as blue as the Mediterranean only a softer horizon. I went up along the downs and looked at the little beaches down below, and remembered strawberries and cream at Babbacombe.

Goodbye. Do write.

Your own

FREYA

ROBERT STARK

Thornworthy

22 November 1922

Dearest Pips,

I waited a few days to write because there was a meet of the S. Devon at Chagford yesterday, and they were coming to draw Frenchbeer Cleeve. I went out on Mouse who had been doing no work and eating lots of corn for days, so that I did hope to be able to give you a fine account of gallops. But we had the most wretched luck; only after three o'clock did the hounds find a trail and then the wretched fox only went out to the edge of Batworthy Mire and turned back to cover. Isn't this heart-breaking for the only day out after a year? It was gorgeous being out again, and I found myself fairly safe in the saddle by the end of the day. I had almost forgotten what November is like down here, and it is lovely to come and have good still weather, and wander up over the old places.

Many kisses dear old Pips. Do not get pneumonia again. I am always wishing the winter over when I think of you out there.

Your

FREYA

ROBERT STARK   Torquay
                                               1 December 1922

Dearest Pips,

I am posting you a poetry book which I hope you will like: I found it the next best thing to a real run with hounds and spent one wakeful night unable to put it down till it was finished – Masefield: *Reynard the Fox*.

As to Rozel – there was no decent bid at the sale: nothing above £3,000: Mr. Green agrees that the first offer that comes over £5,000 had better be taken.

It was sad to leave the moor. It was perfect out there and I had one gorgeous ride out across Assacombe to the Warren Inn and then down to Tin Mines (keeping to the road after one dangerous excursion among pits and holes). It all looked deserted and desolate. There was a hawk whistling and hovering over my head in the sunlight, quite low down and not a bit shy, and another one perched on a wall not 200 yds. off: and rabbits in and out of their holes everywhere. It was a sharp frosty morning and all the low bunches of heather looked as if they were covered with white blossom. I followed the road over the hill by the stone avenue thinking of all those distant ancestors who dug for the Phoenicians, and so up till I reached the good ground and had one glorious gallop to Lakelands. I find that I liked going by myself over the moor almost better than anything else; there is no sound of lorries, so all the beasts and birds go on doing their jobs without paying attention to you, and it is like a voyage of discovery.

I spent my last evening calling on the young Endacotts – then came back over Kestor and thought I should like to try and climb the wrong side of it, the one looking towards the Long Stone. I got half way and then found that the granite was heaved up in the wrong sort of layer and also that the wind just caught me turning the corner. I thought I would go down again: but turning back, that looked so remarkably unprepossessing that I settled myself firmly to think, and found that, quite independently of any sensations of my own, my legs felt shaky and not at all safe. I thought I must do something quickly or I should get demoralised, and just flung myself up at the granite holding on by the wrinkles of it with my finger tips and trusting to my balance, and sure enough I got up quite easily and feeling much relieved though flustered.

Goodbye dearest Pips. I wish it were not to be another Xmas away from you.

Lots of love from

Your

FREYA

FLORA STARK

17 Carlton Hill, NW8

10 December 1922

My dearest B.,

Olivia [Horner], the Professor and I spent a joyful day at the zoo, giving chocolates to the badgers and small monkeys and talking to the baby seal. In the evening I went with Viva to see the Mt. Everest film: that was marvellous – the mountain itself and the three attempts to get to the top. It looks an easy climb – the only difficulties come from the height. The man who explained the film was one of those who made the first and last attempt. They lost seven porters in an avalanche and this, the young man said, 'distressed us *almost* as much as not reaching the summit.'

Your

FREYA

FLORA STARK

17 Carlton Hill

21 December 1922

Darling B.,

Such glorious news. The Prof. has booked a sleeper for me on Friday week for New Year at Loch Lomond. Isn't that wonderful?

Mr. Bale nearly had a fit when I told him about H. and the securities – and he said that if I had given them it would have been more than he could bear – so I am glad, though I have been feeling pretty awful about it. It is so much easier really to say yes than no.

Your own

FREYA

ROBERT STARK   17 Carlton Hill
                                                          24 December 1922

Dearest Pips,

I am afraid you will have to squeeze £20 or £25 out of somewhere. I
don't know how it goes, but money in London seems to be like snow in the
spring and I have had to borrow more from my long-suffering bank, and
promised to pay back *very soon*. I am so sorry, Pips, as I know how hard it is
for you to come by. I am beginning to think that I ought to marry a rich
man so as to relieve my parents of anxiety.

                                                          Your
                                                          FREYA

FLORA STARK   The Tarbet Hotel, Loch Lomond
                                                          31 December 1922

Darling B.,

This is the last of the year – and I am writing to you from one of the
loveliest places in the world – looking across the Loch to Ben Lomond, a
white mountain, with the sides still red with bracken. We got here early
yesterday morning – at 7.30, but still night and Venus shining low in the
sky. We travelled in luxury, and I enjoyed my first experience of a sleeper,
only I was far too fascinated with my little room and bed to be able to sleep
at all.

Today we went down the Loch, and lunch on a rock at the edge. And we
have had fine sunlight and now a shining moon. It is a wonderful time altogether.

                                                          Your own
                                                          FREYA

FLORA STARK   Loch Lomond
                                                          7 January 1923

Darling B.,

I have had such a wonderful time here, it seems almost impossible to tear
oneself away. We have been out every day and almost all day, eating sandwiches on a rock, occasionally in rain, sometimes with most beautiful mild
sunshine and pale winter skies. The colour, the shapes of the hills, the birch
and oak woods and glens are all too beautiful for words.

It is a most hospitable, friendly people and it has been a joyful time for me.
I now leave tomorrow and hope to start on 13th for Turin. I shall see about
Arabic on my way through.

Olivia is very nice and vivid: sometimes I should like to see the dear Prof. myself without her – but that is too much to expect. She is fine for walking with.

Lots of love dear B.

Your

FREYA

ROBERT STARK   L'Arma

13 February 1923

ROBERT STARK

Dearest Pips,

I suppose this letter had better begin from my return to Italy – and an exciting week spent with Clot in Turin. She was ill and at first it was agreed as more correct and proper that I should lodge in a convent so as not to live in the dangerous proximity of two young men [her brothers]. As the time drew near however, Clot decided that my reputation could bear it and I had a lovely time and acquired much knowledge of the real life in cavalry regiments besides a large repertoire of the most improper songs; but I expect you have quite a good idea of it all.

It was a rush down into summer here. I got to Ventimiglia at 2 a.m. on a moonlight night and thought it a pity to waste the time in a hotel so walked out without meeting a soul, with the sea shining and great waves of mimosa and stock-scent coming to me round every bend of the road.

Our carnations are really beautiful: the blooms are among the very best on Ventimiglia market and there is no want of buyers. The heartbreaking part of it is that just about a month ago when they had reached a good price and we were really feeling confident, this Franco-German trouble sent down the exchange and all trade stopped with a bang. I am feeling thoroughly depressed over it and not knowing whether to keep Nicola or not. I do wish you were here to advise; I do sometimes feel like Atlas with a world squashing him down. However it is something to feel that now this is a property that everyone admires; very different from three years ago!

Lots of love to you dearest. I do so long to have you here; it is very lonesome pulling along by oneself.

Your own

FREYA

L'Arma
17 March 1923

Dearest Pips,

Your letter asking for news has just arrived. I hope however that by this time you have had my budgets. I think I would have sent more just lately only that Providence remembered that sunstrokes were among the few accidents that have not yet happened to me, and so it decided to try it on in a mild way. It was not really bad, only bothering especially just now that I am so behind-hand in the *vigna*, but now it is quite right again and I am out all day, pruning in a way that would make your hair stop curling and stand straight on end.

It is lovely being out in the *vigna* now with everything rushing out. There has been lots of rain so I hope for a better summer too. When you come you will see great improvements in the garden part round the house; I am looking after that myself and have got in lots of roses, lilies of valley and iris and am sticking in the wild narcissus and anemone that I find about. Meanwhile I have started a violet bed, and have also learnt to graft vines and hope soon to see the pergola creeping up.

Mama will have told you all about George. He has been such a brick. He and Mario will meet to settle things in London, but it seems that they will get settled. I feel that *anything* definite is better than the former state of things.

I am so awfully relieved to think of Rozel sold at last (at least I suppose that is where the money comes from?).

I shall be very busy indeed with Arabic for the next month as I have a real *Persian* lecturer from Cambridge coming to coach me through the Easter vac. It will be very exciting and I hope to speak it really well by the end of the time. But what we shall do with him when not studying Arabic I don't know.

FREYA

L'Arma
14 April 1923

Dearest Pips,

I am working very hard with Arabic and getting on slowly. The Persian has left; he told me he would make a lot of money out of his holiday by writing a book in Persian on Monte Carlo, so who knows but we may not be responsible for the demoralising of a nice uncontaminated nation! I think he rather liked Monte Carlo; he used to go off in the afternoon and be seen no more till late at night. He had no visa on his passport and I had great difficulty in persuading the Carabinieri as a personal favour to let him through, and then the wretched little creature was so conscientious that he insisted on showing his papers at twelve at night and woke the poor customs inspector out of his bed to come and look at a passport without a visa which they had illegally promised not to notice.

Tanti baci from

FREYA

PROFESSOR KER

L'Arma
7 May 1923

Dearest Professor,

Is it really true? I have just had the Dover letter and it is as exciting as journeys of my own – to think of you all truly in Italy. I think I shall really be walking with you along Lung 'Arno – or looking over the Fiesole landscape, hills and valley. Lucky family. I am bathing here, just trying what it is like to tell you when you come; the Mediterranean is still cold, although the sun is upon it; it washes away all my domestic troubles, which are many just now, Rosa and Domenica having developed a vendetta feud.

Arabic goes on. The exam is early July, but I don't know yet if I can do the work. I don't think anything much of exams: but they impress Mama and make her do the housekeeping and so procure me Time! That is the whole secret.

I do think there is a difference in the look of things since you are across the border. I am so happy about it, dearest. Come soon.

Your loving

FREYA

ROBERT STARK

L'Arma
7 May 1923

Dearest Pips,

My money I have invested in Italian War Loan, and I only hope it may all be all right. I talked it over with George before – but the best and dearest business adviser ever has gone; dear Mr. Bale died the other day. London will be very different without him when I go.

I heard from Mama that she wrote to you about my difficulties and am vexed that you should have been worried about that. Prof. Ker lent me the amount to cover my deficit last winter and he does not want it back in a hurry, and I shall save up gradually for it; I think I shall be able to do so now – especially as I have discovered a new and most exciting way of making money . . . smuggling Old Masters across the border! I really have done this: a Sienese primitive 5 ft. x 3, a most lovely Madonna on wood. My picture dealer friend came to spend two days here and spoke of his difficulty; I said airily (not knowing the size of the wretched thing) that I could easily get it through for him; and he said 'If you do I will give you £100 commission.' So the thing was brought here one evening and I spent a sleepless night wondering how to manage. I thought of a boat and using it as flooring with the face down. Then however some Scotch very respectable neighbours were leaving, with innocence and virtue written large all over them. So we got a cart which happened to fit the Madonna exactly; I bribed the nice girl by all her feelings of friendship and the prospect of a new leather bag – and we put the picture face down without even a piece of paper round it; we piled the luggage on top; and draped our scarves over the bits of gold frame that *would* show; then she and I ascended the cart; the parents walked behind. We stopped at the douane; the little *guardia* strolled out, shook hands, we offered to show him our luggage, but he was all amiability and hoped we should have a good voyage and return. We passed the French douane at a trot, and I have just received my commission now. Isn't that a thrilling story from real life? I do think however that I earned my commission, because it was a most awful moment and the night after I kept waking up in a panic.

It is so late, I must go to sleep. I am working rather hard between Arabic and garden.

Lots of love dear Pips.

FREYA

ROBERT STARK

L'Arma
30 May 1923

Dearest Pips,

It is beautiful weather now, warm and gorgeous and lovely to bathe, only I don't seem to be up to it and so shall wait till August. We are going to get away to the mountains at Macugnaga for a month and that will be fine. Mama has not been at all well, with *gout* of all things! but she is better now. I am doing Arabic hard for my first exam, do not get enough time at it to hope for much success. Some day you will hear of me in the deserts of Arabia discovering buried cities.

Goodbye till next letter dearest Pips. I wish you were here sitting under the olive tree.

Your loving
FREYA

London
                                                              27 June 1923
Dearest B.,
    Did I tell you that my exam people want me to know an extra 300 years
of history all at the last? I shall have two days after to do all my jobs.
                                                              Love from
                                                              FREYA

Rome
                                                              5 July 1923
Dearest B.,
    Exam has been most successful and I am through very well. I heard the
result at once as a special kindness before going on holidays.
    Will you bring my little blue coat after all as I may look at League of
Nations for a few days.
                                                              Love from
                                                              FREYA

Macugnaga
                                                              8 July 1923
Dearest B.,
    I found your letter and to my great dismay am fixed here clotheless;
I do not know what I can do till you come, but please do not delay longer
than necessary. As you know I have *nothing* not even a woolly or pair of
thick stockings, and my only choice is to sit in the hotel or spoil my only
tailor-made.
    Now as to all you write. *Kitchen out of question this year*. The seat etc.
has been quite enough and I see no means of affording any more for a long
time.
    Money – I send you Lire 420, which ought to carry you out here. Send a
wire to say when you can come. I can't understand all these change of plans
with no apparent reason, and thought it was arranged that you would come
as soon as possible. I am really on the verge of exasperation!
    It is lovely here. I only hope for a little climbing – shall get into training
and hope for one or two real excitements when all are gone.
                                                              Love from
                                                              FREYA

72

Macugnaga
                                           Mid-July 1923

Dearest Pips,

We are just here for three weeks, and I am having a thorough good rest. I had three weeks in London working very hard and got through an Arabic exam at London University: I did it on the chance, having had only five months (and interrupted) instead of a year to work at it, but my lecturer informs me that I have a talent for grammar, and was so pleased that he is going to let me take a diploma without going to attend the courses in London. This is very pleasing and makes things easy for me. The result of my exam was the offer of a teaching job in Egypt, but I did not think it worth while to accept unless something really too good to miss comes along. I have been reading up Mohammedan history and finding it very interesting; quite a new world opening out – and I am so glad to have brain-work that can be done away by myself in the country.

Here are Prof. Ker and his two goddaughters, Olivia and Poldores [MacCunn],[18] and Viva is over the hills at Zermatt. I am thinking of crossing over the glacier to see her and, if I feel fit, of doing something amusing like the Matterhorn before restoring myself to my family.

We had great luck to arrive before they cut the hay, so the place is covered with flowers, red and yellow lilies, fields of campanula and wild pink, and the rhododendron still out near the glacier. But it is very hot and stuffy and thunderstorms breaking themselves against M. Rosa, and the Prof. does not care for much climbing any longer so that we feel rather like horses on a curb. We had one good walk up to 3,000 metres and looked over to the Jungfrau and the Dom and Eichhorn. Monte Rosa itself is one of the most beautiful shaped mountains there could be, with all her crests and glaciers pouring down.

                                                Your
                                              FREYA

L'Arma
                                             3 August 1923

My darling old Pips,

Your letter reached me in Zermatt, and cheered me up no end talking about mountains and huts – and those good things. We are back now, only arrived this morning at 2 a.m. in the moonlight, and the plain of Lombardy was like a steam-cauldron to come into. It is wonderful what the hills do: I feel renovated as soon as I get up over 1,000 metres – and even with all the sadness of this time* we are both feeling remarkably fit.

We went to Zermatt with Viva for a week after arranging everything at Macugnaga. Mama went by train and I up over the pass and it was glorious to get to the top of the wall and look over on all the giants, Mont Blanc with sun on him high above all the rest, and all the beautiful white shapes rising out of that immense field of ice and snow.

It was wonderful blue clear weather and as I had the guide I could not bear to part with him immediately so we rested that night, and got a good Swiss *porteur* and next morning started for Matterhorn. I wanted to go over the top and down the Italian side, which is more difficult, and it appears that the guides in Zermatt discussed the matter in relation to my fragile appearance and betted against it. However we got to the Swiss hut, which is about 10,000 feet up at the bottom of the actual crest of rock, and there had a pleasant evening looking out on the wonderful ring of hills, Monte Rosa and all her group in snow and moonlight. There were four other caravans going up, but we had first start because of our difficult descent, and I lay awake in my comfortable little room watching the moonlight and listening to the stones now and then rolling down the *couloir*, or the wind moaning round that gigantic corner. We started at one o'clock – with no lantern – a most mysterious feeling climbing up gullies and faces of rock in that uncertain light. One is much too busy to look down, but when we reached a little ledge about 4 a.m. and the daylight began to float in upon us and we sat down to drink tea, I saw that the whole side was one unbroken sheer slope, incredibly steep, and no place for giddy people. I was not in very good training of course and got breathless when hurried, so let the others go on ahead – but we caught them up when it came to the real rock-work. There is a terrific steep bit at the top with a rope to help you and just *wrinkles* of rock to hold you and a wind blowing like ice to get you off the top – and then when you do arrive there is a long ridge – about fifteen minutes – with nothing at all on either hand: here you have an irresistible wish to crawl on all fours, but the guide informed me that I must 'andare franca' so I just walked along and thought it very like life, with the abyss and the unknown on either hand – and there we left our companions and started going down the other most tremendous slope, I feeling rather like someone in the acrobatic kind of cinema. The other side has lots of ropes, and one overhanging place with a rope ladder down it, so that one's arms have more work than the legs all the way down. It was so cold that a raw egg provided by the guide turned out to be full of lumps of ice, and we could find no place sheltered enough to sit in and I was so tired in my arms that they would scarcely grip, but we got down remarkably quickly – $2\frac{1}{2}$ hours from the top to the Italian hut – and here rested one hour and I

74

revived with tea and wine mixed – not a bad drink. It was a fine clear day : M. Viso visible and every other hill in Europe as it seemed. We had more beastly ropes below the hut : it is unpleasant dangling in the air and looking down for miles into the valley. We met two Englishmen toiling up towards us, and passed the time of day, and by twelve o'clock we were on the Italian glacier. We did five more hours slogging mostly over softish snow, across the pass to Zermatt, and got triumphantly in – a long day's walk. The guides were so pleased, and want me to do all the really difficult things in the Alps now. They were nice people, both of them, and told me the miseries of taking people who have to be hauled up and down and cannot be moved along quickly when the *tormenta* comes.

I did no more climbing. It is so horribly expensive and I was only able to do this because Viva had invited us and we had no hotel to think of – but it is a grand sport. My dear Professor came that way two years ago, and I was thinking of him coming down into Italy, and it seems so strange that he should be on the other side when we feel him so near. I seem to be missing him more and more.

Your own

* Sudden death of Professor Ker on 23 July.

FREYA

ROBERT STARK

L'Arma
29 August 1923

Dearest Pips,

I have now been having an awful time here because just as peace was descending on the *vigna* and all going smooth, Nicola falls down and bangs his knee and has been laid up in hospital these three weeks. I am so sorry for Nicola, but I do not see how it is to go on next year : I don't think he has the health or the knowledge to work here on his own, and Rosa makes it hopeless. However we have six months still to think about it, and I hope you will be here to consult. Meanwhile I have a good man pro. tem. It has been hotter here than ever before. I loved it, especially not having to go to S. Remo once a week [for Arabic lessons]. Now however autumn has come with winds and the good time is over.

I am going to start on the garden this very afternoon. It was too hot hitherto; but now I shall bed out the chrysanthemums and hope to prepare for bulbs. The little orange trees are nice and flourishing at last and next year we shall be able to graft the vines and start the pergola. I have had a beautiful invitation, to spend two weeks tramp round Carcassone and shall be there by Sept. 15th. I shall be back by the end of the month in time for *vendemmia*.

Oh it will be good to see you at last.   Your own
FREYA

FLORA STARK   Montpellier
15 September 1923
Dearest B.,

I am just leaving after a sunny morning and walked over the university and saw the gown of Rabelais hung in a cupboard just behind the hall where they give the degrees. The spirit evidently survives, for just over against the door of that solemn apartment is a fresco with four pink students in blue striped bathing dresses drinking champagne by the riverside. I am quite sorry to go: it is real pleasant provincialism. All the people are fat and proud of being so; the dinner last night was a small kind of orgy and I was given a litre of wine without asking for it: here they all realise that food and comfort is what one lives for, and glory in it. The shops are innumerable, huddled in the smallest space, in tiny dark back streets, and you can satisfy every want of life in a five-minute walk. There is nothing austere about this delightful university: I wonder it has only 600 students. When they die they send their portraits, and there are rows of them from A.D. 1300 onwards.

Lots of love from

FREYA

FLORA STARK   Carcassonne, Aude
16 September 1923
Dearest B.,

Venetia [Buddicom][19] only turned up this morning early. The hotel is all right, a dim place on a courtyard, an aged waiter with a sense of responsibility, pretty chambermaids, an attempt to *confort moderne* and divine meals. The people all tuck their napkins over their stomachs. The French bourgeois has everything in life to make him happy except beauty in his wife, and that is a dubious happiness.

We are in the new town – so to speak, for I believe it was founded and laid out by the Black Prince in good straight streets, cobbled, and water running through them, a pleasant tinkle to listen to from one's bed. The town is full of country people in the mornings, and lots of booths – and they are a mountain race already, much keener-featured, with blue eyes often as not, and Basque in their speech I take it.

76

I found my way to the old town, which is quite apart and grim and deserted on the hill. It is almost too good to be true. I do not love it, like Montpellier and the more human places; it is too like a monument and outside of real life, and one has to have guides and tourists all round – but I have never seen so wonderful a place. What would I not give to be transported for a day or two to its best times and see it with its own life and people. The country is wild and beautiful, not mountainous enough to hide the skies, and broken into vineyards and wild uncultivated places. It is a series of lovely open views from the battlements. Of course I should have brought Froissart; he travelled here and I never thought of him.

All this country has beautiful churches rising to immense high square towers above the townships round them, and visible like great symbols all over the countryside.

The people here are vintaging. They wear black straw hats, or sunbonnets – the old women white caps with frills. All the country from Cette to this place is vine, not staked and tied like ours but looks like gooseberry bushes, and all dancing in the wind of the sea. Very good sweet grapes.

Your

FREYA

FLORA STARK   Les Cabannes
                                             19 September 1923

Dearest B.,

Here we are on the edge of civilisation, but rather shocked to find that a caravan of twenty-one English walked this way to Andorra before us. They sprained ankles however and had to be carried so we didn't think much of them as forerunners. We have what looks like the most bloodthirsty brigand for a guide – a fisherman with an eye to business and an adventurous spirit: his name is Antonine. It is a little summer place for fishermen, with a big stream of clear water and all green around, and the Pyrenees beginning most suddenly in abrupt rocks.

We came here about 6 p.m. and spent the time, Venetia fishing and I asking for the guide. Have just been sitting now – after supper – in family circle in kitchen listening to nice but prosy old man lamenting the absence of anything masculine in our travelling outfit – 'même un beau-frère'! We felt more and more depressed as we listened. We have taken tender farewells, and shall wake up with alarm clock and make our own breakfasts and be off by six I hope.

Goodnight and love from   Your

FREYA

Andorra

22 September 1923

Dearest B.,

Here we really are, though it seems hard to believe – and I am talking Spanish of a sort and feel it strange to be for the first time in a country whose language is not familiar. Our guide turned up at six on Thursday and we started with the beginnings of dawn on a cold-looking grey morning with heavy dew; when we left a little village close to Les Cabannes we walked for the rest of the day in almost absolute solitude. They are not high mountains: one col was 2,600 metres, – but long, long valleys, and no villages at all: nothing like the painted churches and towers of the Alpine valleys. Beautiful fishing, hunting – chamois, bear and wild boar, and quantities of birds. We followed a good mule track near upon four hours through woods, and then we climbed through a series of clefts from one hanging valley to another till we reached open pasture and the high ridge of cols – which surround Andorra on every side. We met two shepherds with mules while we sat at lunch and that was all: their beasts were going down to winter quarters next day.

We had no idea whether we could reach the first houses the other side before nightfall so walked all day with only two hours' rest. Had tea in a lovely upland by a clear stream and made the kettle boil, then started on the last ridge – which opened out and onto a large landscape with lonely lake lost in the grass meadows and folds of the hills, and shining in the last light. We got to the ridge at 6 p.m. and looked over Andorra, all wild narrow ridges, and habitations nowhere – a most lonely beautiful country, and made for camping by one of the streams. We raced down and got to Serrat, where an auberge was promised. But that is only a summer place and the auberge was an old woman in a blackened room sitting by her cauldron: – nice old people. They had no candles, but lit up our supper with shreds of pine-wood, – the real old fashion – and talked of smuggling and the poor look-out now with the exchange. We slept on hay in the *grangia* and the next morning took most cordial leave of Antonine who was going back to fish in the streams we had come up by. We loaded our packs and walked along feeling rather weighted by them. But it was an easy day, always following the stream down a mule path and the country getting more cultivated. The churches are old and simple outside, with most gorgeous altar-pieces right up to the ceiling inside, with rows of niches and wooden figures of saints in old dim gold, 15th century I should think – and there are five of these, one over each altar. There is a statue of Madonna and child in the next village to this that I am really tempted to steal.

This is the main valley and we find there is a motor into Spain to Seo de Urgel (could any name be more alluring?) – where the bishop and the shops are. We are going tomorrow, but don't know what will happen as we had not counted on Spanish exchange, or on so long a way round: we are carefully portioning out our francs. Hope to bring back some yellow and green jars, but it is not a good country unless one could rifle the churches.

Your

FREYA

FLORA STARK   Seo de Urgel
                                              24 September 1923

Dearest B.,

I don't know whether this will reach you before we do, but it is such a joy to write this address and put on a Spanish stamp, that I am making the most of the excuse. We are leaving our hearts in this little town. We leave tomorrow at eight – if, that is, we can pay our bill – because we have been buying cord shoes and nice little cakes with cream in them.

We have a delightful tavern: it looks very villainous when you go in, but our room has a brick terrace with the river and hills and moonlight all in front of it and big grapes on a trellis, and we have endless meals and polite people who greet us with new salutations each time. There is martial law in this country just now but no one would guess it – and this morning we wandered over the fort and the garrison posed to me for a snapshot: the gates were open, the walls crumbling, the courtyard planted with beds of iris: anything more peaceful you never saw.

The cathedral is very very early and all great columns of grey stone, very square and simple, and here and there the high gilt edifice of the altars of this country. It is a seminary town: priests as thick as black beetles and very like them.

A pleasant, hospitable country – only I am getting so tired of their asking for the man who must be with us. Even an old unknown woman in the street hobbled up to me and asked me 'No tienen hombre?' Next time we must invent some decent reason: a pilgrimage, I think.

Love to you dear B.

Your

FREYA

79

22 October 1923

Dearest Pips,

First of all I have had to tell Nicola that he is not to stay after next March. He is not up to the work here; I have been awfully sorry to do this, and it took me ages to screw up my courage, but now it's done, and life till next March will probably have a fair number of tempests! The next trouble was Granny: we cannot possibly afford to keep her in any boarding place in England, so I have written and offered to take her out here. I don't think there is anything else to depress you with you poor old Pips – and these are not real depressions after all.

We have been making the wine – not much this year but I hope it may be good. Now carnations are beginning and I hope to pay expenses anyway. We have had no rain yet: I don't know what is going to happen to this country, this has been a three years' drought already.

The really bright spot on the horizon at present is that Colonello Biancheri[20] and his brother have invited us for a ten days' tour in Sardinia some time this winter. How I wish you were coming for that. It is a thing I have dreamed of for years. It depends on Mussolini, who makes the Biancheri brother work hard and get few holidays. You can't think how pleasant it is to live in a country with a sensible dictator. The Greeks may not like it, but here the railways improve, the post office works, and the laws are beginning to be observed. We daren't say much on these topics to Alice Edwards who is hurt in her feelings because of the snub to the League of Nations – but it is worth all that to get a decent government at last.

Your own

FREYA

18 November 1923

Dearest old Pips,

I have just this morning been down to the oil mill to see the crushing of our olives and divide the oil with Nicola, and we have got 45kg. of oil off the six trees, and about as much to follow later. The trees near the house, which we water whenever we have a bath, have bigger berries than any I have seen between this and Menton. It was most picturesque to see the men in the dark subterranean sort of place, with the big stone wheels crushing the berries: they crush them for about three hours, then pack the mash neatly into those fibre baskets we saw at Bevera – do you remember? – and crush out the oil: then pour boiling water on it, and a man with a scoop scoops out the oil off the top of the water : that is for table : they then throw the water and dregs back on to the crushed olives, and repeat the operation for lamp oil.

I made 500 litres (my share) of wine – and the wine and oil together have covered my share of this year's *vigna* expenses. It is going to be a bad carnation year. It is still so warm that the flowers hardly travel and few people buy, and they are all rushing out into bloom.

My Arabic has not got on at all with all these affairs, but I now have a little more time, and our new slavey has the virtuous habit of bringing me breakfast half an hour before her time – at half past six : you can imagine my feelings – but it gives a good long morning, and I can soothe myself by reading all the curses of the Koran afterwards. Biancheri's brother, who is a charming diplomat in Rome, has given me an introduction to the head of the Oriental School there and if I can possibly manage it I will go for three weeks in the spring and get coached for my exam.

Love to you dearest Pips – always – and good luck.

Your

FREYA

ROBERT STARK

L'Arma

16 January 1924

Dearest Pips,

I am going to ask if you think I might have about £25 during the year to spend in carriages for Mama : she gets too overtired each time she goes to Menton or Bordighera and I am getting rather worried about her. I thought if I could have a carriage for one afternoon a week it would solve the problem, but don't see my way to doing it out of my own money – as we are living up to the very limit of my £200. She is not at all as strong as she used to be. Of course I hope that George really will make Dronero pay up fairly soon, but meanwhile I think it might possibly save an illness if I could arrange this for her.

Granny is not here. I am sorry in a way, but glad in another as I think she is more comfortable in England, with all sorts of learned talk going on. I could only entertain her with Arabic verbs or the diseases of carnations.

I have discovered another Old Master for my collector friend, but have not the joy of travelling with it myself : but I think I may get enough out of it to go to Rome on. When quite old and past active work I shall write a lovely smuggler's story.

Your own

FREYA

L'Arma
3 March 1924

Dearest Pips,

I meant to write some time ago and give you L'Arma news – but now we have had another shock and have been through a busy and sad time. Alice Edwards came from Menton to spend two days, was very fit and jolly trotting round Bordighera, and on the day she was to leave had a bad heart attack. On the 24th of March, she had another bad attack and died after half an hour. It was a weakening of the muscle round the heart, and nothing to be done. We wired for George, and he is here now – it has been such a terrible shock and grief to him. We are thankful to keep him for a few days to recover here quietly and then in May I hope he may come out again for a long time.

This has been a bad year. I hope the next may improve. You will get the first gold medal for the Empire and a large sum to be spent on a first class ticket here. Do arrange for next winter in Italy. We do want you so badly. I feel *abandoned*.

Herbert Young[21] left a little while ago. It was nice to have him. He could not understand my wild excitement when the tulip and narcissus bulbs began to come up: his things apparently *always* come up – and he could not see that it was an event to me. It is so cold that everything is late. We have never had anything like it; snow every few days on Grammando and no clothes warm enough.

Mario's business not yet settled: hope it may be by the summer. I must stop now with my dear love dear Pips. Come to us when you can.

FREYA

Rome
13 April 1924

Dearest Pips,

A very happy birthday to you. I cannot wish you anything nicer than to spend the next one here in this wonderful place: I am revelling in it, only retiring now and then in a state of exhaustion from seeing too many beautiful things.

Biancheris, whom I expect you remember, are here and one of them is in the Foreign Office and getting us all sorts of privileges such as a window on the 24th to see Mussolini opening Parliament, and permits into the Vatican, and an audience with the Pope which I am rather terrified of: I am told one may only speak when spoken to, so I can't talk to him about Macugnaga nor tell him that I mean to do his own pet climb up Monte Rosa this summer.

I am doing some work – going four times a week to read Arabic: the lady professor says I have a remarkable talent for Oriental language and compare favourably with a Monsignore who has been learning for five years and gets no further. Prof. Browne, who is the great Cambridge Orientalist, came over to lunch before we left and has invited me to stay there, and will probably discover a teacher for me sooner or later along the Riviera.

Elections here were a great fascist triumph – and the trams and houses are all fluttering with flags. The black-shirts and all the pageantry look extraordinarily in the right place here with all the columns and arches of Imperial Rome. We saw Mussolini talking to the assembled Romans in Piazza Colonna, from the balcony of the Palazzo Chigi: it was really impressive, with flags and the crowd below, and the column of M. Aurelius standing very tall in the half light and Mussolini himself in profile against the pale spring evening sky. The crowd was amiable but nearly killed me all the same, it was such a squash.

When you write, tell me where you used to live in Rome and what your special haunts were. Love to you dearest Pips, lots of it always, from

FREYA

ROBERT STARK   Rome
                                                          28 April 1924
Dearest Pips,

Your letter has come just as I was seriously thinking of settling down to write; I don't like to hear of too much work; it would be nice to have you for a year's complete laziness. We are all a little weary with a strenuous life. It is really a great thing that all should be going so well out there, and all made by you out of nothing to begin with: it is a slow business, to build up, and a great thing to see the result beginning to take shape. But I wish it could leave you to us a little more and I do long for the time when the credit side will be large enough to pay your way to and fro every year. That is far and away what we want most badly and I would give up most sorts of other things for it.

I don't know where to begin about Rome, there is so much about it and all so wonderful. We only had one day out so far, a lovely day motoring by Grottaferrata round the lake of Albano to Genzano, with lunch looking down on Nemi; we went down to the lake after, all the hillside thick with

cyclamen and a little blue or white sort of aster and violets and the lake full
of frogs. It is a secret, fascinating place.

Love to my dear old Pips.

Your

FREYA

L'Arma

7 July 1924

ROBERT STARK

Dearest Pips,

I am really awfully sorry to hear about bad crops. It is very disappointing,
to work so hard for it and then have all destroyed by a late frost. I am busy
getting things fixed for our three weeks' absence. It is so hot one can hardly
move.

I have a lovely book, Curzon's *Monasteries of the Levant* – written about
1830 and full of delightful travels in Albania, Mt. Athos, Syria and Egypt.

Your own

FREYA

Macugnaga

29 July 1924

ROBERT STARK

Dearest Pips,

I have been and done it – that is to say I have been up to the tops of M.
Rosa from this side, which is the most difficult and has only been done once
before by a woman. We left the hut at midnight and crossed the 'Canalone':
it was exciting because the night began with clouds and if it got worse we
would have had to return across the Canalone, which is only safe from
avalanches for a very few hours when the heights are frozen. However the
moon came out and shone wonderfully as we zigzagged up the glacier,
cutting steps sometimes in hard snow, sometimes in clear blue ice, with big
chasms of ice hanging over us in fantastic shapes – a wonderful sight. We
were caught by the sunlight on the last slope and reached the rocks at eight in
the morning. I went with a Belgian climber and two guides, neither he nor
I in very good training (as I am supposed to be living on milk and eggs and
quietness!) – and we were very tired by twelve when we reached the top –
twelve hours' climb with very little rest. Then we saw the whole of Switzerland clear, in a keen wind, every peak showing as if cut in steel. I would
have been fit for the return down the glacier, but my companion was feeling
the height (4,630 metres) and could hardly get along, so we walked along the
crest to the Capanna Margherita, which we reached about 4 p.m.; it is the
highest Alpine hut and I found that I could neither eat nor sleep from the

84

beating of my heart. The wind howled all night and it was cold and we wondered why we had come. At two in the morning we got up in thick mist and came down over an easy glacier the other side, across two passes back to Macugnaga, another twelve hours' good walking – and neither of us apparently any the worse, to the amazement of my doctor-friend Poldores who says that my constitution is an insult to the medical profession. The truth is that the high air is like champagne to me. I feel I could do anything in it. I am so pleased to have succeeded, as I have wanted to climb that peak for three years. Now I have been very good, leading a quiet life and taking milk for all I am worth, and am much better than when I came up.

We go back to L'Arma on 31st – just as well, as the weather is breaking and anyhow I couldn't stand sitting down in the valley much longer. This hotel is full of the noisiest Milanese, the only pleasant people to talk to are the guides.

Tanti baci dearest Pips,

Your

FREYA

ROBERT STARK

L'Arma

1 October 1924

Dearest Pips,

I must send a badly written line just to tell you that I am really better – beginning to eat again (though not much, alas) and feeling a little more alive. It was lovely to get onto the sofa in the garden again and see all the things growing – as I was not strong enough even for much reading in bed and spent my time just lying and meditating. I thought a lot of Ford Park,* and all the walks and rides, and found myself creeping down to the ponds in the wood to see the moorhen come out with all the little ones after her. I have a great longing for the moor just now. If all goes well I think I shall try to get away from all worries next year and spend a few months in England, just doing nothing but getting really strong again; the nurse here says that a good long rest is what is chiefly needed.

The wind is howling and rain slashing down from the north-east and it feels like winter beginning – and just when the men wanted to get the roses in.

Lots and lots of love from

Your

FREYA

* The Starks' home on Dartmoor.

L'Arma
                                                   8 December 1924

Dearest Pips,

I'm afraid this letter is going to be late for Xmas: I sent a book – a good shocker for a wet day – and hope that may arrive in time – and this will follow and bring good wishes for New Year's Day. I was so awfully glad to get your beautifully long letter, and glad to know you had a good crop after all. I hope Mr. Taylor finds someone to buy: it would be a relief to have you safely in Europe, and feel at least that this great distance is done away with. I can't tell you how I long for this to come off; to have you here, and be able to make a nice little life of our own in the sunshine and as far as possible from worries, if that is ever possible. It is always 'one darned thing after another' but I suppose one does come on a streak of quiet weather now and then.

I am not fit at all: I seem to have hit on as slow and tiresome a disease as was possible to find.* It is frantically annoying: I seem quite all right till I move, then – after the most absurd little walk or drive the wretched pain comes back and there is nothing for it but rest again. I have a very good Dr. now who is really doing good (for his own pocket as well as my inside) and I hope that 1925 will be a less depressing year than this: it has really been more depressing than I can say; I am thankful it is nearly over.

I am only £20 out of pocket over the *vigna* this year: that is not bad, and I ought to make it in carnations. I have got in about 1,000 roses and think of putting as many more: also some mimosa trees.

The Dronero thing is going on, but the Italian law is slower than anything I know except my own inside. The lawyer says Mario Roascio is just doing all he can to delay, and the thing gets put off from one hearing to the other. I feel as if I never wanted to see the man again – when I think of all the difference it would have made, to yours and Mama's comfort, to my health, to all our happiness – all in the hands of the wretched little bounder. Well, well.

This must go with all my love dear Pips – and the real hope that next year will bring you.   Your

* Gastric ulcer.   **FREYA**

Ospedale Mauriziano, Aosta
                                                   25 January 1925

Dearest Pips,

You will be surprised with this address, but by the time this letter goes, I shall be well through an operation and on the way to spending a busy

February here getting over it. The good doctor from S. Remo came to the conclusion that it was better to cut away the ulcerated piece of my intestine, rather than face another six months of diet on my sofa with a chance of a relapse if ever I do anything energetic afterwards. We have come here because there is a particularly good surgeon whom he knows, and I expect that by the end of the week the ordeal will be over. I shall have to take things fairly easy this year, and then I hope be as strong as ever again, as the cause of the trouble will have been removed.

We had some charming people at Mortola just before leaving – the son, a young man of thirty, took his wife from Kashmir to Chinese Turkestan over more or less unexplored country, and spent four years in Kashgar as consul, the only Britisher in all that enormous country. He gave most fascinating accounts of a sort of Arcadian life; everything grows there – it is all highly cultivated, and well governed by the Chinese: no railways, telephones, etc . . . but a five-months' caravan trek to Peking. The most beautiful mountain ranges you ever saw, ending in grassy steppes. If Europe turns to a wash-out, let us retreat and be happy in Central Asia! This is a medieval old place, beautiful arches and columns, and the black and white nuns flitting about make it look still more in character.

Your own

FREYA

ROBERT STARK   Ospedale Mauriziano, Aosta
                                                     10 February 1925

Dearest old Pips,

It has been trying waiting here from day to day while the surgeon was making up his mind which particular piece he wanted to cut out of me. Now all is settled, and it will be done tomorrow, and Mama will add a line to tell you all is well over.

They have improved things so much of late years that I don't expect it will be very painful: they will leave the wound almost alone, and avoid the trial of frequent dressings. I hope to be at L'Arma quite early in March and go in April for a good long convalescence in Asolo. Wish you could be there for that: think of tea on the bank there, and the iris round that little figure of Bacchus. I am longing to be there, and my own self again.

I was allowed some walking these days, and the country is more lovely than I have ever seen it here: a snowless foreground of warm yellow-coloured earth and grass – and then the white mountains.

Your very own

FREYA

ROBERT STARK   Aosta
                                                             17 February 1925
Dearest Pips,

Am getting on fine – slept without morphia and hope soon to have learnt how to breathe without feeling wrung to bits. This my first letter writing. I have a little new snow to look at. Your letter came nicely just when I could take notice.

                                                             Your loving
                                                                    FREYA

ROBERT STARK   Aosta
                                                             24 February 1925
Dearest Pips,

I am sitting up – very proud! It is nice to have a new bit of window to look out of at last. There seems a spring-like difference over the brown trees and meadows even in these three weeks.

                                                             Your
                                                                    FREYA

ROBERT STARK   Aosta
                                                              2 March 1925
Dearest Pips,

Mama has left this morning, so you see I am getting on. The doctor motored her to Turin, and promises me lovely drives when this old wound closes up. A little stitch deep down must have given trouble, and it still has to be kept open to let some matter out: not serious, but the opening was so painful that I fainted away on the medicating table and feel ill-used at having this in addition to the operation. I hope you like the New York shocker: it gave me delirium, being read too soon after the operation, and we had to substitute *The Pilgrim's Progress*!

Colonel Biancheri has just sent a huge basket of flowers – garofani, freesias, hyacinths, mimosa: they are such a joy here. Lots of love. I hope to leave about 15th March.   FREYA

FLORA STARK   Aosta
                                                              9 March 1925
Dearest B.,

I still have some fever, but today the Prof. comes back and will open the wound again: he was laid up for two days so could do nothing and I unfortunately took just that moment for this little relapse. It is hopeless without

88

him, as of course there is no real nursing. I am well otherwise and have been on the terrace and do not find the days too long. But alas, shall certainly not be home by 15th, nor till end of month I think.

Your loving
FREYA

Aosta
10 March 1925

FLORA STARK

Dearest B.,

Prof. Massobrio came back last night, not yet very well himself. He says that there are some people who cannot assimilate silk stitches: it is rare, but I am one of them unluckily. He gave me a long medication, over half an hour, Philomena holding my hand and doing the weeping for me. There is no danger, only slowness, as now he has made a deep new cut, and taken out the stitches, the cause of the trouble, and it must heal up on its own. He injected cocaine, so I did not feel the worst of it.

I had a bad time these days, with pain all the time except the short snatches of sleep. Clot's news,* and my fever, and the news of the professore's fever all came in a bunch, and I really felt like throwing up the sponge. However, it is all right now. Will you tell people, so as to explain my not writing – esp. Colonel, as I should write to Rome, but can't manage more than you, Pips and Viva.

Nine days you have been away and I have one letter and two scrappy cards and 9/10's of *those* funerals and death. No news of the people round, no gossip, nothing of Nipper, or cow, or roses, or Joan's baby: nothing of what Massobrio told you as to my possibilities later, nothing of Rome! and you believe in affection to the absent! and I have written every day except one, when my ears buzzed too much.

Your loving
FREYA

* Her mother's death.

Aosta
19 March 1925

ROBERT STARK

Dearest Pips,

I am not great at writing yet, but think I can manage a letter this time. All goes well – my temperature remaining even sub-normal, so that soon I shall have the circulation of a lizard or a frog. I also feel hungry again, and can walk out on to my terrace and there sit in an armchair and let the sun bring me to life again.

As soon as I can I will go straight to Asolo, leaving all agricultural problems till I am strong enough to tackle them on my return. The new peasants appear to be settling down definitely: it has been such a work of diplomacy for nearly a year.

I have no news, as one day is exactly like another and very dull. Crochet, and reading, and the arrival of the post, and the rest of the time spent in a sort of coma. It is a blessed relief to have no pain and soon I hope the wound can be allowed to close.

Am just reading a history of the Popes, and the list of all the old monuments they pulled down to put up their own new ones. Bernini wanted the stone of Cecilia Metella for his Fontana di Trevi, but the Roman populace made a riot and prevented it.

I have wallflowers sent from home, and daffodils and the scent is like spring in the room. One has to be ill to realise what flowers really mean to one, and they look so lovely against the snowy background of my window.

I can't tell you how I long for you here. I wonder if you will soon be able to sell out and come? Or shall I go out to you next year? – if only there was more money in the world – our world! Your loving

FREYA

ROBERT STARK Aosta

26 March 1925

Darling Pips,

I am *dreadfully* sorry about your trees, poor Pips, I can't tell you how much. Don't worry about the money here. Viva has lent me some for the time being, and I can always get a loan from my banker. We have been through worse before this, and when I am once out of hospital and through the convalescence, I shall be stronger than I have been for the last eight years and able to tackle things. Mario will pay up finally: there is no doubt about that, it seems it is only that the Italian law allows itself to be dragged out in this way.

I shall long to hear from you and hope the damage is not too absolute? Oh Pips, I do feel how it is, to see all the long work knocked to pieces.

I am getting on beautifully now. It is extraordinary how long it takes to get over the weakness: I think I could do just anything, and then find myself worn out with a little stroll in the garden. Today it is snowing hard – but I hope to be in Asolo among the iris before the middle of April.

Always your own

FREYA

I am getting fat!

Aosta
15 April 1925

Dearest B.,

The Prof. took me to Cogne yesterday. It is very kind of him, because it is such a struggle for him to get away. I had no recollection what a wonderful valley it is, and especially now with the snow. I didn't see Basile, but sent *saluti,* and we saw an old patient, all the family, four generations, gathered in the stable: five cows on one side, and the big table, sewing machine, bed, cradle, stove and chairs, and all the women in their costumes on the other. It was a Rembrandt picture.

I am much better: I fear I must not walk yet, any fatigue makes me ill at once. But at Asolo I can rest. I have told Vera about Pips' trees. I thought it would not be right that they should not know: if they still keep the money, on their heads be it, but at least they now know what it really means.

With love always.

Your
FREYA

ROBERT STARK Asolo
25 April 1925

Dearest Pips,

I came here a week ago, but the journey was rather exhausting and I have had to go slow again. There are a few changes here, but I think nothing can really spoil it, not even motors hooting through the street. The house is the same, and the garden improved. The grassy path to the little Bacchus is bordered with masses of iris and shut off by a gate of beaten iron. I can't yet go for walks: two months or so of a quiet life still prescribed, and I lie about in the garden and wish I were ready for all the old walks.

All goes well with me, now it is just a question of going very quietly till I strengthen up again. Lots of love. Are you coming soon? I do long for it.

Your
FREYA

ROBERT STARK Asolo
10 May 1925

Darling Pips,

I am getting on, though very very slowly. Everybody tells me this is not to be wondered at and I must allow a year to get over the operation. I get far less pain now however and am able to play a mild game of badminton or

take a walk down the Forestuccio and back by the short-cut. I can also
motor, and my nice friend Poldores is taking us round about – Bassano
and Marostica last time – dear little place, looking as if embroidered in an
old sampler. We went also to Feltre another day. What a jewel of a place,
with the long street of palaces and piazza at the top. We went up by the
Piave and down by Primolano and Val Sugana. It must have been a fierce
war down those mountain funnels. Feltre was taken without fighting, so
luckily escaped damage. All the inscriptions on the old piazza, dozens of
them, have been effaced: but it must have been long ago, perhaps by
Napoleon, or even some Guelf or Ghibelline.

Your own

FREYA

ROBERT STARK Asolo

1 June 1925

Dearest Pips,

There is lots of news: first of all my exciting summer plan, which
consists of a five-roomed chalet in the Cadore (San Vito near Cortina) where
Viva is inviting me for the summer. I shall stay till the autumn, under the
care of my doctor who has a villa there, and in the hope of getting back the
strength which so far is making a poor show: I wish it was a matter of
letting one's hair grow, like Samson.

Vera came up to see me for three days from Milan. It was very nice after
such a long time (without husband) – and we just sat about like old times
here. She was looking very well, and enjoyed it too very much. We have
been reading Trevelyan's last book, on Manin and the defence of Venice in
1849: it is a magnificent story and well told. That, and learning Venetian
embroidery are my two occupations, and then people drop in.

Mrs. Beach is starting a weaving factory* of silks: it is just beginning
with two work people and one apprentice and we are all taking an interest in
its proceedings. They make beautiful silk. That, and Mme Casale's
embroidery school, will make Asolo quite an 'arts and crafts' sort of place,
but as yet no sign of the crankiness that seems to accompany such.

Lots of love

FREYA

* Tessoria Asolana.

S. Vito
                                                24 June 1925

My dearest Pips,

Here I am, with Viva and Herbert [Young] in a very primitive little
chalet out among the meadows (very poetical but full of manure just now).
Mama came up to settle us in, and has now gone back to L'Arma where I
trust she may not find too many muddles: and I am to try and get fat here
till September or October. I am not yet walking and feel rather sad at just
meditating at the mountain-foot; but they are fine to look at, big rocky crests
all round in a circle, and a beautiful upland of wood and meadows below.

I do nothing all day but embroider and read very little and find writing
very hard work. Lots of love dearest Pips.

                                                Your own
                                                FREYA

                            [Posting delayed until] 1 July

I have just heard from Mama about Roascio. It seems that the business
can be settled at the next hearing – in October – by means of a declaration
from you that you did not promise him or Vera the money: he first said it
was part of Vera's 'dot', then that you had promised it when Rozel was
sold: the lawyer caught him up at that and he had to accept a declaration
from you as decisive. I do hope it will be finished with in October; it will
be such an awful problem to face the winter otherwise, as I am afraid I shall
not be well enough to look after p. g.'s after all. I can only just walk a few
steps yet, as it brings on pain and sickness. What a slow weary business it is.

Mama sends good reports of the *vigna*: my new vine plantation thriving
and the 2,000 roses planted: and 22,000 carnations. Our peas were *all* eaten
by rats: what can one do about it?

Write again, dear Pips – and send the declaration as soon as you possibly
can, because it will prevent endless postponements.

                                                Your
                                                FREYA

S. Vito
                                                16 July 1925

Dearest B.,

Do tell me more about Gabriel. Poor man, he is such an idiot, he was
bound to choose badly. He did not want anyone in particular, but only a
wife! Who is she by the way? And is it official, or shall I wait to write?

And is she rich, or beautiful; will they live in Dronero? What a blessing I don't care for Gabriel. That was my first thought, with much relief.

It will be dreadfully sad losing Viva; I don't know what I shall do without her cheerfulness around; it is such a blessed rest to have everything taken off my hands. I feel as if I were able to *relax* the first time for years.

Lots of love to you from

Your

FREYA

                 S. Vito

22 July 1925

Dearest Pips,

This is a short note, just to tell you that the doctor has finally come, and put me to bed for a week to be under observation. I think you would rather know the state of things though I am not telling Mama. There is still some trouble and I am afraid it will be a long affair, though he is quite cheerful about a complete cure in the end. I am afraid it will mean a good while still on my back, living on milk. It is depressing: I have not had a good meal for fourteen months and long to lead a real life again, but what can one do? He tried to cheer me by saying it was neither a tumour nor tuberculosis! I will be here all August for certain and probably September, and then see how things go. Viva has been such a brick: she has been housekeeping and nursing me, and has not let me spend any money, which was a blessing considering my denuded state – and makes it possible for me to see this year through without any more borrowing: so you need not worry about that.

I expect Mama has written about the Mario affair. I hear they are trying to back out of the declaration I told you of, but hope they will be made to stick to it. My own idea is that those Cuneo judges are bribed, they drag the affair out so: but of course it may be Italian ways.

I must tell you the trouble I have been the unwilling cause of. De Bottini, Gabriel, met me in Turin, when I came through, all screwed up to propose to me, and I (with true kindness as I consider) hastened to tell him that matrimony was the last thing I was thinking of just now. He immediately fell into the clutch of a matchmaking aunt who has engaged him to a lady they hardly know: 'Thirty-five – so she says,' Clot viciously remarks. But Clot is so furious with the poor man that she is making his life a burden, and says he should go on proposing till I change my mind – more like Molière than real life.

My darling Pips, I am afraid this letter will worry you. It is nothing fatal however: and I have every hope of being my own self again before I am quite middle-aged.   Your own loving

FREYA

Dearest Pips,

Your letter was a treat, and such pleasure to read that the little trees are not so bad after all. But it is an abominable blizzard to have cut off this year's possible holiday.

I am bad at writing because it is still a great effort to me, though I seem to be getting on at last and now get up for about an hour's stroll in the meadows and then retire to bed again. The doctor hopes to have me well by the winter, but I rather think Monte Rosa was the last of the High Alps for me. What a blessing I did him while I could. I shall never forget that experience.

I hope you are not worrying too much about our finance: my budget will hold out I believe till Xmas, and my creditor is amiable and in no hurry. Also the carnations and stocks promise well and the 2,000 roses are now being grafted and are supposed, poor things, to start work this very winter. I long to get back to the little place, but shall not leave here till Sept. 30th and then go slowly by way of Asolo. Now Venetia Buddicom, with whom I walked in Spain, has come for a fortnight – so I have a pretty good time. Oh dearest Pips, I do love you.   Your

FREYA

Dearest Pips,

I think I shall have to go home pretty soon: it gets very cold in here and the snow is creeping towards us. I think as soon as I can take the journey, I will go to Viva's for the winter: the wretched doctor tells me at least a year of practically invalid life is necessary, and it is easier to manage in her comfortable house. Sometimes I cannot help feeling that it is almost better to have no life at all, but this is nonsense, and no doubt one day I shall wake up with the pleasant feeling that it is good to be in the world after all. I am really much better, only I suppose the ten years of more or less constant strain have told more that I thought, and I cannot recuperate as I used. Doesn't it sound as if I were old and decrepit.

95

I have been walking a little – about a mile, and that is the limit I am not to exceed for the next year. It is extraordinary how much one comes to notice if one's walks are restricted: all the nice little things, beasts and flowers.

The snow is coming very near and much earlier than usual. There is just now a crowd of sheep pouring down from Pelmo after their summer season.

Viva has sent me the *Arabian Nights* in Arabic and I am waiting to get to my dictionary to tackle them.

Lots of love darling Pips.

Your own
FREYA

FLORA STARK S. Vito

15 September 1925

Darling B.,

Your letter has come to cheer me up – such a relief. I am feeling a little less gloomy anyway, but rather sad still at the usual relapse which has got me in bed again. I hope to begin eating and arising again tomorrow.

I am now completing the *last* [embroidery] towel: one more lovely than the other.

FREYA

ROBERT STARK S. Vito

20 September 1925

My darling Pips,

We leave next Thursday for Asolo, by motor: it will be my one glimpse of the country round and I am looking forward to it –but I have taken a strong prejudice to the Dolomites and I hope never to see them again. I don't see the fun of looking at mountains from down below anyway.

What is lovely now are the gentians – not blue but clusters of little purple flowers as thick as stars.

By the way, thank you for papers. I was very glad of them having come to the end of all literature except the Bible. I read the book of Samuel: exciting stories they really are.

We had a visit from W.P.'s friend Mr. James who told us a new story about him which I had never heard. It seems they were discussing claret at a dinner party, and recalling how it used to send people under the table. W.P. looked up in his deliberate way and said: 'I was drinking claret the other night with a literary gentleman in Edinburgh – and at 3 a.m. he thought he was God Almighty. He put his hand on my arm and said: 'It's not their sins that worry me, Ker; it's that I've got so much to do!'

My dearest love always.

Your own
FREYA

L'Arma
3 November 1925

Darling Pips,

This is a long silence again, but we have had a sad time with the loss of our neighbour Colonello Biancheri. He was so good a friend and it hardly seems true even now, till I go by the big villa and see it all shuttered up and desolate. He came across in a boat to see me a day or two after my return, and then got a heart attack, which got complicated with pneumonia and killed him after only ten days: it seems there had been serious trouble for a long time. Altogether it has been most sorrowful and harassing.

I am now busy preparing for London and seeing to things here as far as I may before I go. I think I shall stay over New Year in England and possibly through January. I am *much* better and living nearly like other (quiet middle-aged) human beings.

I have a fine fat book to read. Doughty's *Arabia Deserta*. He travelled in 1876 among the Beduin and gives his adventures day by day in the most beautiful English. I will keep it for you when you come, as they are two fat volumes and need much leisure to get through.

Mama has just told me that you have been able to help us out of the financial tangle. Thank you ever so; I can't tell you the hopeless feeling of having to cope with these things when one feels still weak and incapable. This will help us through the winter. I only hope it does not mean great difficulty for you? I did not want to bother you now that your little trees are not doing their bit.

Oh I didn't tell you the news. Olivier has let *all* his villas to the Begum of Bhopal, the only woman ruler in India and a great swell. Mama is to housekeep for her (I'm rather sorry for the Begum!) and we feel that Mortola is becoming more and more illustrious. At present there is chaos up there; an extra floor being arranged for the native servants, the drive being 'whitewashed' with gravel and a wooden railing to give it a deceitful appearance of solidity, and Herbert as happy as can be. The date of the Begum's coming is very uncertain, and may not take place at all, but anyway the rent will be paid and it has the happy result of forcing H. to make the place habitable.

Lots of love dearest Pips.

Your own
FREYA

11 Grove End Rd.
                                                           November 1925

Darling B.,

I have so little energy for writing that the days go by more than I intend.
But I go out a little now and am quite satisfactory to the doctor and hope
all is going well.

The Arabic goes on. It is a question of whether to take the exam in July
or next January, and I think probably the latter. It would mean coming
back here in October to work. I seem to please my Egyptian, but the work
takes me very long. I believe I have anaemia in the brain as well as everywhere else.

Your
FREYA

FLORA STARK   11 Grove End Rd.
                                                           6 December 1925

Dearest B.,

I am reading Lord Rosebery's *Napoleon: The Last Phase,* a very interesting book. I should like to know how much and how long Mussolini has
studied Napoleon's life and career. The feeling in England is very anti-fascist
on the whole I find: I wish A[gostino] would send me something really
good in the way of a statement of Mussolini's own point of view. There is a
life of him just out, but that I am told is so excessively enthusiastic that,
especially in England, it just acts the other way:

I spent a day and night with dear little Minnie [Granville][22] and enjoyed
it so much in her doll's house filled with oddments. She gave me a charming
time, and brushed my hair, and rubbed my face, and gave me a charming
brown country hat. I feel so like a recluse after two years of not going anywhere – feel as if I could hardly move about a drawing room.

It seems that Napoleon's disease was internal ulcers; I can quite see why
he collapsed through his last campaign.

FREYA

FLORA STARK   11 Grove End Rd.
                                                           10 December 1925

Dearest B.,

It is sad news about my flowers. I do hope something comes of the rest.
I am very anxious to have those 500 every fortnight: unless you do that, I
shall lose half the profits, and cannot afford it this year. So please do make
the effort to be regular.

I went to see Mrs. Trevelyan at the B. Italian League which seems to have turned to a nest of anti-fascist refugees. I shall be going to one of their meetings and will know more about it, but as far as I can see there is very little sympathy here for the present state of Italy. I think the chief reason, or anyhow one of them, has been the sort of person who supports the fascists here – all the Die-hards and the *Morning Post* and ultra-conservatives so that anyone even moderately liberal is thrown into the opposite camp. I spend my time trying to persuade people that the same names do signify different things in different countries, but what is the force of mere reason against sentiment.

I shall stick to my Arabic, and spend next winter here and get my diploma in 1927 and go out: they say I am quite good at it and only need a year's study now.

Your own

FREYA

ROBERT STARK

11 Grove End Rd.
14 December 1925

Darling Pips,

I hoped to send you a nice account of riding or walking in Scotland in a few weeks, but instead of that these wretched doctors have been x-raying me and find there is still some trouble and have put me to bed on milk. I shall try and do Arabic to make the time pass, but one can't be very intelligent on four cups of milk in the day.

It is lovely being ill here compared to Aosta, and I feel that·one can get the best opinion and do all that really can be done. I have many people in to see me. I am reading W. Page's letters (the ambassador here during the war) – that and Jane Austen's letters make a good combination. Then I have the *Arabian Nights* in Arabic. I have fallen on an unexpurgated edition and will have to be careful and see what is coming when my little Egyptian comes to give his lesson. It was already an awful shock to him to be shown up into a lady's bedroom.

Your own

FREYA

FLORA STARK

11 Grove End Rd.
10 January 1926

Darling B.,

I must give you commission for more books *as soon as possible.* They are all in the shelves above my desk: *Al-Fakhri,* a big book all in Arabic with loose binding; then Caetani, a red volume paper bound – I want vol. III;

and Goldziher *La Loi et Le Dogme d'Islam*. It will be an awful big parcel but I would otherwise have to buy them and I will need them if I go in for the exam. It is very doubtful however if I can get it done: if I were well I could manage it, but it is a year's work in six months. But I mean to try.

I seem to get on well and am now up again though not yet out of the house. I now write little essays or translations for my Sheikh who seems pleased with me. I shall hope in a fortnight or so to get as far as to see Sir Thomas [Arnold, at the School of Oriental Studies].

My dearest love to you. Avoid going more than once a week to Ventimiglia: you know that it is quite easy to avoid if you make your plans a little ahead!

Your loving

FREYA

FLORA STARK   11 Grove End Rd.
                                                         20 January 1926

Darling B.,

I am very sad about the disasters in *vigna*. Do give details.

Of course I should be thankful if you could have someone to share expenses with you as it would be an enormous relief. But it is out of the question unless you can bring yourself to devote more time and care to making them comfortable: it means at least two hours of dull spade work and not doing it yourself, but thinking out the maid's work — and I don't think you can bring yourself to do it. Our visitors have never been comfortable, and though it didn't matter for them and they all enjoyed it for other reasons — it would be *impossible* to have p.g.'s on those terms. The chief difficulty is the food and that can only be kept good by ordering ahead (so as to avoid hard meat etc.) and a careful criticism of *every day's meal*. If you felt able to tackle it of course I should be more than grateful and it would be a real help. But it is better not to do it at all rather than make a mess of it and get ourselves a bad name.

Ever so much love,   Your

                                                         FREYA

ROBERT STARK   11 Grove End Rd.
                                                         3 February 1926

Darling Pips,

I don't go out yet beyond Circus Road though I hope to reach Dorothy's very soon. My time is chiefly devoted to Arabic. If all goes well I shall try to come back here for three months next winter and get the diploma which I feel sure I could now manage. It is a brute of a language: imagine a page with no vowels, no punctuation, and nothing to show where one word ends and the other begins, and all this in a language you don't know. My poor sheikh has such difficulties: every now and then we come to some very unexpurgated passage and he has to hem and haw and try to explain and then when I ask questions tell me that 'it is not exactly that'.

Did I tell you of our scare at L'Arma about the road – exclusively for motors, to run right by us and spoil our headland? We got Biancheri to find out about it in Rome and it now seems they will not make it unless the Casinos open in Italy: may they never do so!

I am reading *Robinson Crusoe* for the first time, and very good it is.

I feel very pleased with myself, as Mr. Cornford has just written a most flattering leader about the Italians in the *Post* (far more than they deserve), all to please me.

Your own
FREYA

FLORA STARK   11 Grove End Rd.
                               2 March 1926
Dearest B.,

Viva took me to Harry Lauder: he is too charming, such a really delightful person behind it all. It was an early performance and we got back at nine o'clock and were just at dinner, very weary and dishevelled, when in comes Lord Olivier whom I had asked to call some time ago not knowing that he was a particular bête noire of Viva's – and I like him so much. I think Viva likes him better now however.

Dear old Herbert has written full of joy, apparently under the impression that if the motor road comes we would leave all and go to him. I must undeceive him gently and also tell him I am not mentioning the matter to anyone except Viva.

Lots of love from   FREYA

FLORA STARK   11 Grove End Rd.
                               21 March 1926
Dearest B.,

I have just returned from a night spent at Mrs. Bramley's and enjoyed it very much: it is a mediaeval gate-house with the moat and old leaded windows and battlements intact – and filled with pretty things and magnificent old rugs. She is a wonderful intelligent old lady. I have an idea she did not like me: probably thought me too independent. Her son and daughter-in-law were there and were most charming: they had been building a town in the desert outside Alexandria and hope to go back to it if the Egyptian government allows, and have told me to go and see them there. They are such charming people and you can imagine we talked of nothing but the East. In the morning they took me into Oxford and we wandered round the Ashmolean Museum, full of lovely things.

Lots of love dear B. It will be nice to see you so soon.

Your

FREYA

ROBERT STARK

L'Arma

18 May 1926

Dearest Pips,

It is just a month since I came and I can't think how all this time has skipped by without my writing: but it took me a fortnight to get over the journey which was still rather much for me, and then we have had the house full of masons doing repairs, and really hardly a breathing space. Now your letter of April 23rd has come to rouse my conscience.

I am going to write you all the details of the Roascio suit in a week or so when I have seen the lawyer in S. Remo and heard exactly how things are. Nothing is being done till your affidavit comes, and I hope you will make it as strong as you know how. It is quite true that he sent the man to get the tax out of Mama, on the money which *he* is keeping, and it is too abominable. Unfortunately the Ventimiglia tax collectors are also the Cuneo bankers who finance him; I am very sorry she allowed herself to be frightened, but it will certainly not happen again.

I am morally certain that I have found out the reason of all the delay. Mario is now head of the local *fascists* and the law will do all it can to favour him. It is very difficult for non-fascists to get anything like fair play, and I feel positive this is the explanation: if so I think I shall speak to my friend Biancheri who knows Mussolini, and see what a word from that quarter might do.

I found a lot of muddles here of course, and have had a bad year with the *vigna*. I have a lot of new things in however; a nice plot of 2,000 roses which ought to bring in something, about 20 mimosa trees, peach trees, white broom, and a lot of new vines.

Don't sell out any capital for the Asolo house: I think that English War Loan is the best thing we have and worth sticking to, especially since the glorious victory over the strike. Herbert will be here in a fortnight on his way to England. I shall have to try and get to Asolo next spring. Couldn't you be there too? Wouldn't it be nice to take our old walks round there again? It is a blessed thing to be able to walk again, even a little. I went in and out from Menton and felt like a normal human being once more.

Our neighbour Lady Currie has just lent me Col. House's letters, a thrilling book for all the unknown information it gives. I am doing no reading otherwise and have had to drop even Arabic.

Ever your own loving

FREYA

ROBERT STARK

L'Arma
3 June 1926

Dearest Pips,

The lawyer has been so busy receiving Mussolini and speechifying, I could only get at him on Monday. He seems quite hopeful and tells me that there should be nothing in the way of a final decision in your favour as soon as your affidavit comes.

I suggested that a word from Rome might help matters along, but he was strongly against this and assured me that there is absolutely no way out for Roascio. He will have to pay your £2,000 in full, with the interest. As to Mama's money, that subject has not yet been touched on at all.

Meanwhile, I think I can pull through this year, though I am not quite sure about the winter. The fact is that another £100 a year is really necessary now, prices are still rising and show not the slightest sign of a decrease and unless my carnations happen to pay, it is really impossible to make both ends meet. At present I have enough money to carry us to October.

Now I think that is all the business? I am quite tempted to take to gambling. I went to spend two days in M. Carlo and took twenty francs to the Casino to try a system which I evolved all in my own head years ago; I tried it three times and won 200 francs each time, and feel quite tempted to go on and see whether I lose these ill-gotten gains or make 7 millions, which my calculations point to as the proper end of the speculation. I would rather do without them than look like some of the people round those tables however.

Your loving

FREYA

FLORA STARK Varazze
Friday [July 1926]
Dearest B.,

Vera is seriously ill. She has the best doctor in Genova to look after her and two nurses, but I must stay here till she is through the wood for she clings to me and I feel I can give her more strength than anybody else.

The trouble is, besides her heart, a uricaemia which has now started; also trouble in the liver. It seems she had a miscarriage and this developed after. I have not yet seen either her or the doctor so merely send this news at second hand and will hope to write more definitely tomorrow morning.

Your own

FREYA

FLORA STARK Varazze
Saturday [July 1926]
Dearest B.,

Vera has passed a very much better night and this morning is only 37.4. Heart quite good. The doctor yesterday held out scarcely a hope, but I cannot help thinking this is a turn for the better. He gave an injection of 'Urotropina' which seems to have done the miracle. We will see how the day goes. It has been a fearful shock all round, for yesterday we did not think she would stand more than a day or two: but now I cannot help hoping that she has got the better of the infection.

If it goes well, I shall return as soon as she can be left. It is a matter of a few days the doctor says.

Your own

FREYA

ROBERT STARK L'Arma
14 September 1926
Dearest Pips,

Just a word – only to tell you V.'s convalescence is going on as well as one can wish. She will come along here when she is quite well, so as not to be in this doctorless desert when she might still need attention. I shall not send any more bulletins, as all now is well again.

I have numerous troubles of my own. There has been a general exodus – one peasant's wife and three cooks (including De Poli) flying at a moment's notice without a word to anyone. De Poli very drunk at the time. I am thankful to be safely clear of him as he had taken to threatening Maria with a revolver.

I feel I must have a holiday soon or *bust*. When you come shall we go to Tunis for a few weeks: only a short sail from here. Let us make plans anyway.

Love my darling old Pips.

Your own
FREYA

How are your apples?

L'Arma
25 September 1926

Darling Pips,

Clot sends word of a little relapse of Vera's – we are rather worried and Mama has gone down there. We had been hoping to have her up here with us next week, but it now looks as if it were to be a long affair yet. I will write again and keep you posted. It is the wretched poison which is not yet out of the system and one is always afraid of its localising somewhere dangerous – but she had been gaining strength so rapidly. I hope she may throw it off.

Your own
FREYA

ROBERT STARK

L'Arma
2 October 1926

My darling Pips,

I have very sad news. I wish I could be with you, to have you in my arms and tell you. Dear little Vera died, quite peacefully and without pain, early on Thursday morning. Mama was with her, and she was very happy: no fear, only the thought of getting better and coming away with us to rest. She was very weak, but the crisis seemed over: the new centres of infection were getting smaller, and we hoped to pull her through in spite of all – and then the infection developed just under the heart, and nothing could be done. God bless her, and us too dear Pips. My whole heart is with you – if only I could be near to help you bear this sorrow. Darling, darling Pips, you know how near I really am. I love you so very much. Mama has just come and is very exhausted but all right. She went to Dronero and will write to you. Everyone was so devoted and grieved – all the poor people, and country people, even from far away in the mountains, came down.

Our one comfort is that nothing different could have been done to avoid this. She had the most careful and best treatment and doctors from the first – but it was blood-poisoning and nothing could help.

My dear, I will write again.

Your loving
FREYA

ROBERT STARK   L'Arma
                                                      8 October 1926

My darling Pips,

I have been very busy these days, partly answering crowds of letters from
many kind people, and partly trying to make plans for Mama for the winter.
I feel she must get away from all worries, and so am going to try hard to let
the house and get her either to England or Asolo on the proceeds. I also feel
myself that I must get a let-up somehow. Meanwhile I am just counting the
days to hear from you.

There is very little to tell you dear old Pips. We are just trying to carry on.
I have heard once from Dronero, and had good news of the children. Before the end of the month I hope Natta will manage to finish all the business
affairs.

I have just made half the wine and now it is pouring with rain. We have
been praying for water in the empty tanks for weeks, but it is tantalising of
it to come down just before the *vendemmia* is over.

My own darling I wish I could just fly over to you.

                                                            Your
                                                      FREYA

ROBERT STARK   L'Arma
                                                      8 November 1926

Dearest Pips,

Your letter to Mama was waiting when we came back from Dronero.
Natta and Roascio are meeting tomorrow and I hope the matter will be
closed.

It was sad to go up there, sadder than ever now. The children are darlings,
and cheered us up with their romping and gaiety. They are all going to
Cuneo for the winter as the two oldest go to school, and we will have them
down here I hope as soon as holidays begin. We have let the house for four
months and are going to England. I hope it may do Mama good.

I am longing for a letter from you, dear old Pips – just to say you love me,
for I do feel very lonely.   Your own

                                                      FREYA

ROBERT STARK   Train
                                                      27 November 1926

Dearest Pips,

I am off at last and it has been such an unholy rush, it was not possible to
find even five minutes for a letter. We had three weeks to turn out and

inventory everything, and put an anthracite stove in to make the tenants happy. Then when it was nearly done, the floods came and we had to bail out the water. And when the poor people arrived in the deluge we had to make them think Mortola really nice in spite of appearances. The sun now shines and all is well. I have £90 for four months and am taking Mama to England on the bust, for she needs it very badly.

I have also let the land for six years and hope to find things a bit easier so. But it has been a great job and I am tired out too.

Oh my dear old Pips how glad I was to get your letter. How I wish I could see you.

Your own

FREYA

FLORA STARK

Ben Cruach, Scotland
17 December 1926

Darling B.,

We had a most beautiful drive up here, through two showers and gleams of sun, the Loch more beautiful than ever. And here I am having three very pleasant quiet days with just the two dear old people* excellent company, talking of books, philosophies, and the amenities of life – oh blissful after the starvation of constant practical problems. My only sorrow is that I cannot very politely leave them for a good long tramp round Corrie Grogan as I long to do – but I hope to get four days with Poldores here before going south and to get some ridges and look over them.

I am told that Car approves of me. She is a fascinating creature, full of impetus and discipline, caprice, sense, and unsentimental goodness. I am getting fonder and fonder of her – and she is so human and unpedantic in her understanding.

Let me hear the news from Natta. I would like to know, as, if M. does pay fairly soon, I might just avoid borrowing from the bank again.

So glad to hear cheerful news of the tenants.

Your own

FREYA

* Penelope and Car Ker (sisters of W.P.).

ROBERT STARK

Strathblane, Stirlingshire
6 January 1927

Dearest Pips,

I was just lying in bed this morning thinking that I must write and tell you about my day in Edinburgh, when your letter came Dec. 9th. I do wish

Canada were a bit nearer. If I manage to sell L'Arma, who knows but it might be feasible to go out to you next year for the summer? So far however there is no one wanting to settle under Mussolini.

I am so much better already and quite good at facing the winter. It is what I really like, the Moor country, drizzle and all. I have had a few good walks, about six miles or so, and not very tired.

Edinburgh was a good day. The old High Street one of the finest I have ever seen, and we had sunshine across the water over Fife and the far Highland snow. As we came down from the castle there was a soldier's funeral – six bay horses to the gun carriage – beautiful creatures, obeying the man ahead, who led them by just moving his hand slightly to right or left. And the Camerons were playing their pipes, so that Penelope and I just stood and wept.

I am going to Thornworthy on the 15th and hope for some riding (recommended by the doctor, good man). I shall have to take several feet of cloth off my riding coat – and me having been a pioneer in breeches.

Mama sends good news. She is seeing old friends and I think it is doing her good. I shall not be meeting her again till March, as I shall be nearly all February c/o Miss Buddicom, my travel companion in Andorra. Hope to get riding there also.

Mario has written to Mama saying he was paying 1,000 lire a month beginning in January – so I trust he may be doing so: it will be a great blessing, and also from the point of view of Mama's own feelings, poor dear.

I tried a little Arabic again, but find my brain very poor and am giving it a little longer rest. I was in truth as tired as could be and this let-up is the greatest blessing. They spoil me thoroughly, give me breakfast in bed, surround me with nice books, and do their best to keep me off the hill tops. I had hopes last week of learning to skate, but the wind turned south-west and set into thaw.

Your loving
FREYA

ROBERT STARK

Thornworthy
19 January 1927

My dearest Pips,

I came here on Saturday, and was driven out in the moonlight from Exeter – very lovely over the sleeping moors: and here I found your two letters a great joy to me.

How I wish you were here now – if only to see how all your little trees have grown into forests. You have really changed this bit of country. All the woods above the three ponds are now tall, with avenues between stems. We had a snowfall the day after my arrival, and walked down there: it was most beautiful, the little islands coming out of a thin coat of ice, and the rhododendrons grown very large, and the whole place frozen and motionless like a garden for the Sleeping Beauty.

We took two ponies very carefully yesterday afternoon, and went round by Waye Hill and Holystreet and back by Log Hut. At first I thought I should never get over the shaking; my poor muscles seem to have simply ceased to exist. By the end of the ride I began to get a grip again however – and only hope now to get a good chance of going on. Today it is all solid ice outside, and not to be thought of.

Tenants at L'Arma are staying on till the end of May, so that we shall have time for a month in Asolo on the way back; I think of going there from London about mid April.

I have put away your lawyer's letter, for many many years I hope. Thank you, dear Pips. It is a relief to know that I cannot be mixed up in any more business with Mario. He has now paid Mama's January allowance: may he so continue.

Your own
FREYA

FLORA STARK   Thornworthy
                                                 26 January 1927

Dearest B.,

It was good to have your nice long letter – and to read what you say about Dronero. It is a difficult problem. I think it will gradually come to the children being at school and we standing by for the holidays: I feel sure that would be happiest for them, if Mario can be self-sacrificing enough to do it. One thing you must certainly not think of – and that is to be in M.'s house for more than a month or six week visit at a time. If you are wanted there, and I am away for three or four months, you must take a separate house. *This is worth any sacrifice* for the whole possibility of future peace depends on it. If you are with him, Mario will not pay (or will do so unpleasantly): and if he does not pay then there will be necessarily a break. We must avoid this at all costs.

Personally I think that if you are quietly living somewhere within reach, the children will be brought to you: Mario will be travelling, and glad to dump them on you. If he were to marry again (I think he probably will) we would have them all the more and would be very thankful to have a home and centre ready for them. And I jolly well hope you may live till ninety and, as far as it's in me, am organising our lives so that you may do so with a quiet mind and without feeling a burden to anyone.

FREYA

ROBERT STARK   Thornworthy
2 February 1927

Dearest Pips,

It was very nice to get your telegram the day before my birthday; it gave me the feeling that you were quite near by. It was a good day altogether, with nothing to worry over, a good ride in the morning, and roast duck for dinner.

Yesterday we had a lovely day, Pud and I, riding out across Round Tor with lunch in our pockets, and down along Taw Marsh to Belston. I remember years ago going to Belston with you to see the ponies counted. We had a steady drizzle to ride in yesterday, but not cold – and from Belston took a track across the moor which led us beautifully to a point above South Zeal. I felt pleased with myself at being able to manage such a long day quite easily.

I leave on Tuesday. The time has passed far too soon and I am awfully sorry it is over. I shall have some more riding in Wales and should like, if I can afford it, to have one or two jumping lessons, for I am so very inelegant about that.

I am sending two French papers with Turkestan pictures taken by my friends the Skrines. That is the sort of country I should like to see, wouldn't you?

Always your
FREYA

ROBERT STARK   Penbedw, Flintshire
17 February 1927

Dearest Pips,

I came on here to stay with Venetia, who is the friend from my Spanish tramp and the owner of this lovely estate. It is very delightful to come to anything so absolutely English: – a lovely plain old house with its park and great trees all round it, on sloping land: a long lake with brick walks and rock plants at the back, and formal garden with its little temple and borders of lavender and thyme. Then steep hills at the back of that, woods for pheasants, and grouse moors behind them, and all the mountains of Wales to look at from the top. The house itself is full of lovely things : rugs and panelling, old pewter and books, and delightful French pictures, china and silver, a perfect treasure house. I have it all to myself, Venetia having been delayed in town by 'flu too late to stop me; I feel a little inadequate to such an establishment. The gardener fills the house with flowers, there is a huge log fire for me in the billiard room, my clothes are selected and laid out for me by the perfect maid : in fact I am wallowing in luxury and bearing up quite well, except that the solemnity of meals nearly overcame me, till I started humanising the housekeeper by getting her to teach me Welsh words.

Venetia comes today, and I shall be motoring in to Chester to meet her, and hope she will be fit enough to ride over these hills before I leave. I shall go to Viva's for March, and to Asolo by 20th April for a month or so.

Your excellent Mussolini article has just come. I thought it most brilliant, and shall send it to Agostino Biancheri so that he may show it to Mussolini. Of course the Italians are quite unfit for parliamentary government. What is going to happen however when Mussolini goes, no one quite likes to imagine : – it may be Guelf and Ghibelline over again.

I wish you could be here to enjoy the spring beginning – such a chatter of birds in the morning, such masses of snowdrops and yellow aconite in the grass, and all the birds getting fatter visibly.

Your own
FREYA

FLORA STARK

Penbedw
28 February 1927

Dearest B.,

I had such a good morning with the hounds on Saturday. It seemed like a dream to be seeing it all again. And my little pony went beautifully, except for the fact that it was her first sight of hounds and she kicked all who came in reach (not hounds thank the Lord, but horses). I felt rather unpleasantly conspicuous, but did not disgrace myself, and we had a splendid run, though short, and cut across country and found the hounds while the rest of the field were still away on the other ridge. Venetia looked so nice; she rides like a centaur; all the people knew her of course, and invited her, but she gets so bored with them. It was all familiar; the same talk, the same horsey criticisms of each others mounts; it was like going back to my childhood almost. And lovely to see the pink coats in the bracken, and hounds over the hilltop.

FREYA

Penbedw
                                                      2 March 1927
Darling B.,

I have been so harassed – what with Olivier, and now Martin and the cow, and Carlo and the wine (from whom I can get no answer) and the old governess Pen wants an Italian home for, and today the fifth letter about the Macugnaga affair – and this a holiday.

I am so glad Lady H[orlick] is going to lunch, and will tell you all the Hanbury politics. Do give me a full account. I wrote and asked her whether her friends had a job for me in Mespot. If she talks to you about it, tell her I mind less about the pay than about having a good deal of spare time for Arabic study. I suppose you will make an appoiontment for me, though what on earth I shall *wear* goodness knows. What a lovely pot pourri of a lunch party.

We would be going to all sorts of lovely places if only it would not rain. It is very pleasant all the same, and Venetia very agreeable to be with, and glad to have me I think. She is a lonely creature – and not as happy as I am, in spite of riches, and beauty, and everything – she would be so much happier with about a sixth of her income, poor dear. Do not worry about where to stay dear B. If you feel you would like five or six days more to gad about with me, get Bessie's little room, which is so near and comfortable: I have saved enough to run to that: I have been so very economical.

All news on Monday. What fun to see you dear B. It seems an age. It will be nice to have a nice quiet time in Asolo to talk it all over. I shall begin Six Pillow Cases there!

                                                      Your loving
                                                      FREYA

Penbedw
                                                      3 March 1927
Dearest Pips,

I had three hours with hounds on Saturday. They drew the covers at the back of the garden while we all waited on the moor. We went in-country, trotting down the lanes, a lovely sound of hoofs. It was all like being in a dream, so new and so familiar. They found again and went away, luckily over moor with no jumps. We had a good short run. Venetia cut across the valley and we got up to the pack running above with just one solitary rider in pink, all the field far behind. Then they lost again, and we left them, as our ponies were not up to a hard day (nor we either) – but they had a glorious long run I heard later. There is nothing quite like it in the world.

Your

FREYA

P.S. Your article was shown to Mussolini, who was very pleased to see it.

ROBERT STARK

11 Grove End Rd.

19 March 1927

Dearest Pips,

Mama left on Monday and has got to Dronero safely. I shall be meeting her in Asolo about 12th April, and will be there till end of May: after that back to L'Arma. I find London very strenuous and get much more tired than I thought likely after all these months. It is the noise and bustle. Viva thought it would be good for us to see the new acquisition bought by the Duveen fund: it is [Stanley Spencer's] *Resurrection* – a cemetery with all the worst-drawn figures imaginable getting out of their tombs: bad perspective, bad colour; and all these lunatic critics are comparing it to Giotto.

We looked into Christie's and saw the Russian crown jewels – not very interesting. Some of them had first been offered to Venetia's jewellers in Bond Street who handed them back to the Bolshevik emissary with the remark: 'I can see no blood on them.'

Your

FREYA

ROBERT STARK

L'Arma

18 June 1927

Dearest Pips,

I have had such an awful time getting in to the house and mopping up the tenant's mess that I can't remember when I last wrote to you; the cool sequestered way of life seems as far off as ever. Now however we are fairly straight and only two really serious problems impending – first the water supply, which has vanished and shows no sign of reappearing: I have had to build a new cistern, and may fill it if only the wind blows hard enough and makes my wheel go round: and secondly the fascists, who are becoming insufferable, looting everyone on their beat and arresting or beating anyone who protests. The lot we had before were all right, but these are the kind to show up despotism in its worst form. They come lolling on my garden seat, have carried off my little St. Christopher and front door bell, and spend the night eating the fruit in anybody's property: one peasant remonstrated, and twelve of them lay in wait and beat him one dark night – and no one dares speak. If there are any troubles, this countryside will rise against them like one man. If I catch them eating my peaches I shall go down with my little pistol in one hand and British passport in the other.

I have just finished Lawrence's book and wish I could afford to buy and send it you. It is good reading, especially in blowing up of the desert railway. Who knows but I may be in that country some time next winter: I am trying hard to save up enough and have got hold of a Syrian Quaker who is going to find me cheap lodging in an Arab village where I shall meet no Europeans. These Quakers are at a place called Brumana, 23 km from Beirut – in Mt. Lebanon. I think if I can scrape together £80 or so, I could manage three months out there. I do feel I must get out before I become too old.

I must stop. There is a stream of people always wanting something or other. Ever so much love from   Your

FREYA

FLORA STARK   L'Arma
                                                               June 1927

Dearest B.,
So good to have the infants at last, and hope to colour up their little pale faces very soon. Hope you manage to come down pretty soon. Have told Mario that he must send me *hay urgently* for the cow. Do see that he does it or she will fall ill and what should we do? I am keeping her till autumn on purpose for the children.

Your
FREYA

ROBERT STARK   L'Arma
                                                               29 July 1927

Dearest Pips,
There have been so many excitements lately that letter-writing went by the board altogether. I have been a fortnight in London trying to get a fascinating job in King Faisal's Harem in Baghdad. Someone was wanted to teach the two Princesses English, and I thought I would try, and very nearly got it too – but unfortunately Arabic was not a necessary qualification and a Scotch lady turned up who was not so young and beautiful as me – (as it seems the Queen is very jealous) – and so I had all the expedition for nothing. I am very sad about it, but everybody else rather relieved, as no one quite knows what life inside the palace there is like, and the British Commissioner refuses to have anything to do with the business. I was quite

114

glad to get away from the cold and wet of an English summer to this lovely climate. We are in the sea most of the day, the children not at all anxious to get back to Dronero.

The children are all talking to me, I am writing under great difficulties. Ever so much love,

Your own

FREYA

FLORA STARK   L'Arma
9 September 1927

Dearest B.,

Just getting ready to go to M. Carlo, seeing Minnie off on the way. It feels very sad and autumnal.

We had a grand tea party, to entertain the Duchess of Lante, a Spanish lady with so lovely a complexion that she has to wear long sleeves and high collar to her bathing dress. When I come back from M.C. on Monday I shall be vaccinated and inoculated too, and also have the doctor overhaul me – as I am not too well, but I think it is just over fatigue from the summer. I wish I could sell this; I feel it is altogether more than I am up to.

Lots of love from your own Freya – to Herbert too. Nice to think I shall be with you in less than two months now.   FREYA

FLORA STARK   L'Arma
16 September 1927

Dearest B.,

Rain at last and like most things that are supposed to be good for one, rather unpleasant. With remarkable foresight I have had the gutters seen to in time, so that what with a dry house, a stove in order, and a store of dry wood I hope the autumn may arrive without the usual cataclysm. Have been wandering over the tanks with dear old Herbert, and feeling my hair turn slowly grey under his expositions: I gave him dinner and liqueurs last night on his arrival: I am sure the four fascists who have taken to eating the *fichi d'india* at the gate thought the worst as we sat on the balcony in the moonlight. They skin their *fico d'india* with the bayonet; I wish I could get a snapshot.

On the 23rd I am to dine with Major More and his wife: he is political officer at Kuwait, and has written me not a very hopeful letter about work out there – but I think it is as well to go, on the chance of something turning up later on.

How glad I shall be of a rest!   FREYA

Dearest Pips,

What good accounts of Waterloo you sent me in *The Times*: one never gets over the fascination of those old wars. I don't think our struggle will ever get quite the same glamour: there is not the outstanding figure – unless Mussolini emerges. I have an idea that they open letters sometimes, so will wait and tell you political gossip when safely on board next month. Do you know what I have arranged, with £10 sent me by Miss Ker? To spend a week en route at Rhodes. Oh why, why aren't you to be there also? I am going to save up next year to get out to you, and simply *make* you come over for the winter.

Your own
FREYA

Darling B.,

I am waiting for news,* and dreadfully anxious – having nothing but your telegram so far. Let me know if I should go out to Pips. Hope to know before Mario comes. No news of him so far.

Thanks for money. Such a relief. I didn't know what to do.

Miss Campbell has given me a letter for the provincial commissioner's wife in Jaffa. Pray God I can go and Pips is all right. I hope for a telegram this morning.

Your loving
FREYA

* of F. S.'s father's sudden stroke.

Dearest Pips,

This is a horrid blow. I am now waiting with such anxiety to hear the news, and I hope to hear that it is really improving fast,

The telegrams all came nearly simultaneously, because the two first were sent after Mario on his travels and missed him; I knew nothing except one alarming message from Mama 'Pips better – does not want you' and this made me anxious and caused my inquiry, which must have puzzled you very much. Now however, I have them all and am waiting – not yet cancelling my Syrian passage till I hear more from you, but very anxious to do so if you will let me go out to you, or if you think you could come over and finish the winter in Asolo? Do think it over, dearest Pips. You know that nothing would give the same happiness as to be with you or have you over here after all this time. My boat does not sail till November 18th, so that I will have plenty of time to alter plans after you get this letter.

Your letter was here. Thank you more than I can say. The present will be kept for the Atlantic, either now or next summer. I think I am going to manage to let L'Arma, and that will make me very wealthy – and able to afford my own voyages, or yours, as the case may be.

I will write again later, but want this to go. Berto is scrambling all over me at intervals and sending kisses to you. They are all well and as lively as crickets – very busy now doing lessons, with an imposing array of Latin and arithmetics and all sorts of civilised tortures, which they take very lightly. We are going to picnic on the rock in Maira; the woods all turning colour round about, and beautiful golden days. Do you remember bathing down there? What a lot of lovely days we have to think of dear Pips – and will have more. Let me go out to you; whatever time you choose will be right for me. .   Your very own

                                                              FREYA

ROBERT STARK   Dronero
                                                      19 October 1927
Dearest Pips,

Your letter, written by Mrs. Hamilton, has just come. Such a relief to see your own signature at the end of it. I am so perplexed, wondering whether to go out to you now or in the summer, and which would be best for you. You will let me know when you get my letter, for it will just depend on how you are. You must decide and send me your decision by cable – and I shall keep in readiness.

I hope we can settle things next year so that you can get away much more, and anyway not spend your winter out there. Would you not like Asolo? Herbert wants you to have the house next to his: it only needs a key to the communication door, and is all ready to be inhabited.

The children keep me very busy here. All their clothes have to be seen to for the winter: they seem to devour garments. We are now going to the market: it has not changed since we used to go there to buy knives.

A big kiss dear Pips. I do so long to hear you are out again. I am inquiring about boats in case your cable tells me to go.

                                                          Your own
                                                              FREYA

Dronero

22 October 1927

Dearest Venetia,

Our letters have crossed – and I wonder if you got mine telling you of Ja'far Pasha [the Iraqi Prime Minister] and his invitation to me. I fear it may put out your dates a little, but not very much. I have made out a schedule and you will see, and tell me before you sail, which alternative you prefer – and I will then write to His Arab Excellency.

We cannot do any real exploration if you choose the early date, partly because of climate and chiefly because of language. If however I hear nothing before the end of the month (when I have to write to Ja'far before his departure) I will settle on plan no. 1, as I fear that is going to be your choice! This year is not going to be our last chance anyway, for I hope – if only the Baghdad visit comes off, – that it may open all sorts of vistas for the future. Let us look upon this as our *probationary* year.

I have been for a day in the hills. Such peace and grandeur. I can walk up easily three and a half hours, and six down next day: but I will train my muscles on Lebanon before you come.

Don't you think that if you get a chance it would be useful to learn the rudiments of surveying: enough to make our own maps as we go along? I am making feeble attempts at sketching, but with a deplorable lack of genius. I wish I knew more of the exact sciences – geology, and botany. Life is *too* short.

Did you read *Monasteries of the Levant* by Robert Curzon? I think it would be good on a voyage. And Wordsworth's *Prelude*? There is also a good book about India in 1812, *The Life of Henry Martyn*. My friend Clarmont Skrine has published his *Chinese Turkestan*, but I don't know what the writing is; the pictures are fine. You might have a look at it in the shop and see if it is good for a travel companion. In ever such haste, my dear love

Your

FREYA

I am getting so muddled with all the conflicting dates. Here is a schedule, as definite as I can make it so far.

1st *Alternative*:

Brumana: 9th December to any time in February.

Venetia at and round Brumana: any time mid February and end of March.

Baghdad: 1st April to summer.

2nd Alternative:

Brumana 9th Dec. to mid February.

Baghdad mid Feb. to mid June.

Venetia – home together by Ram – and possibly Sinai.

3rd possibility: Canada. We will not take this into our reckoning, as it does not depend on us. I will know early next month if I must go there or not.

The best of these is no. 2, if you like India well enough to stay, for it would give us camping weather, and I should know the language: both these are indispensable conditions for Ram.

ROBERT STARK   Dronero

2 November 1927

Dearest Pips,

I am wondering how you are, on this lovely golden day – and hoping to hear – for it is nearly a week since your letter came. I hope you will let me have just two lines on a card at *frequent* intervals, just to keep me happy. I sent you a cable yesterday, so as to hear what you think about plans,* as my letter should have reached you now, and I am told that I must let the steamboat people know in good time if I don't go east or I will get nothing refunded! I don't know what sort of answer to hope for from you, for I long to see you soon, and on the other hand would like to wait till the summer so as to bring you back with me. However, you will have decided long before this reaches you.

Olivier and [his daughter] Mary are here till tomorrow. He started painting from the new bridge yesterday, and the zealous commissioner of public safety came rushing up to put him in prison as a spy. Herbert tried to explain that a spy would find it easier to buy the picture postcards of that particular view, but it was only Mario's chauffeur who was able finally to rescue him.

Your

FREYA

*Father's answer came urging F. S. to continue her journey.

FLORA STARK   S.S.*Abbazia,* Fiume

19 November 1927

Dearest B.,

All well so far and very comfy night. They have changed my cabin, as I thought the anchor was falling on my head through the deck.

Only five other passengers. Young Irish couple, talk in whispers only to themselves; young Austrian steamship agent going to Egypt; elderly

Turinese business man, attitude entirely commercial; and a German-American with an impressive domed head. I sit between the Chief Engineer and the Captain, who must have some Turk in him; he is a jovial old boy, with black lips and an immense stomach.

Weather rainy, Sirocco, and the sea looks horrid, full of small angry waves.

Ever so much love to both dear people.

FREYA

ROBERT STARK   Fiume
                                                    20 November 1927

Dearest Pips,

This is the first stage, and we have been stuck here since seven o'clock yesterday morning because of twenty-two truck loads of Hungarian sugar that cannot be loaded in the rain. The boat – *Abbazia* – is only 3,000 tons I believe, and her decks very black with age, and only six passengers (1st class) so far – so that it is rather a family party, except for the fact that one Austrian, one German, one Turinese, two Irish and myself cannot talk in one language.

Yesterday I went along the straight tramline through the town till I came to a canal – quite narrow – and saw Jugo Slavia the other side: there is a bridge, and opposing sentry boxes at either end of it. When we went to the French consulate in Venice for my Syrian visa, we found it guarded with about 100 soldiers in tin hats, and the little consul simply fuming because they had pulled down his flag as a protest against the treaty with J. Slavia. So there is no love lost just now. . . .

It was bitterly cold in Venice: and Mama was late, so that we came in our gondola through the small canals and out against the Banchina di S. Basegio in the dark and saw the *Abbazia* towering above, spitting smoke and steam, and making me and my luggage feel very small and forlorn. At night she ploughs through the sea in pitch darkness, so that one doesn't know where the deck ends and the sea begins, except for a tiny headlight far up in the air: so I have kept indoors so far, and will wait for a starlit night to go on deck.

Will post this in Serbia tomorow.

Your own
FREYA

120

ROBERT STARK   Spalato
                                                       21 November 1927

Dearest Pips,

I wish you had been with me today: you would have enjoyed the market
at Spalato – all the peasant people bringing their eggs and figs and cabbage,
sitting very top-heavy on tiny donkeys and dressed with red tassels on their
coats and the most absurd little round red caps – sort of skull-caps put very
much on the side with a bit of black fringe stuck on at the back. I like the
look of the people, though they might be grim, and I think Italy will do
best to stay on her side of the Adriatic. The soldiers are fine-looking, and
as if they enjoyed their job: harder-looking altogether than the Italians.
We are loading cement at present, and hope to leave by midnight. It is such
fun waking up every morning in a new place, full of surprise and adventure
with no bother of unpacking to go through. If I could only know you
really well, I should be so happy. As it is I am always wondering just how
you are getting on.

There is much more of Diocletian's palace than I imagined here: all the
front of the harbour town is built between the ancient pillars, the Duomo is
the Emperor's mausoleum, with a marvellous pagan frieze – dogs and
chariots – still intact high up around the dome, and most beautiful approach
among columns.

I expect you are being dieted, so I won't rouse your sorest feelings by
telling you what good things I get to eat: but I am actually getting fat at
last, and the menus are the only thing adequate to explain the Captain's
figure.

Goodnight my dearest Pips.

                                                               Your
                                                             FREYA

VENETIA BUDDICOM   S.S. *Abbazia,* nearing Brindisi
                                                       22 November 1927

Dearest Venetia,

What you want in a ruin is that it should give you a feeling of
magnificence passed away, and of the lapse of time – and that is why it is
better not to have too much restoration. The odd columns and arcades of
Diocletian are let in among the fronts and backs of Spalato houses, until
you come to the one clear space where the mausoleum stands very simple
and grand, with a court of broken pillars round it.

The same at Bari. Two marvellous old churches; you could not say
whether romanesque or Byzantine, but huge and empty and fallen, one feels,

on sadder days. The smaller windows still have the carved stone instead of glass: and a marble elephant is leaning happily out of one of the walls, to support a Norman arch on his back. I wish you had been with me – if only to see the colour of the whitewashed piazza in the twilight.

We are now running under the lee of the shore and shall be all right till we cross from Brindisi into the open: after that, I hear a sailor say 'They will dedicate all their dollars to the Madonna.' Besides our cargo of sugar and cement, our decks are crammed with barrels of oil, matches, figs, almonds, and soap, which are soused every few minutes till I expect the soap to lather through the chinks.

I have a good book – *The Medieval Conquest of Greece* by Sir R. Rodd – but I scarce want to read. It is so wonderful to be away, really away: a new land opening out to me every morning. And pleasant to wander in strange places and come back to one's boat all lighted and warm and feeling very like a home.

My dear love,

FREYA

ROBERT STARK

S.S. *Abbazia,* in sight of Corfu
24 November 1927

Dearest Pips,

Can you imagine what a glorious moment it was this morning when, expecting nothing but open sea, I stepped out on deck, and there was Corfu with all its mountains, and behind it the ranges of Epirus with a dark blue sea in front, and the gulls with the sun shining on their backs circling round us. It is a thrill too to think that this is Greece. I believe no other country would give one quite that sense of joy and wonder. It looks wild enough: a few villages here and there where the hills slope more gently, but mostly great ridges, barren of everything except the travelling shadows. We are going very slow – nine miles an hour – because so heavily laden, and there is a little swell which makes me happiest in my deck chair. I should be broken-hearted to have to miss one of these delicious meals. I have not eaten so much at a time since before the war – seven or eight courses, and so far the luck has been with us for we have been eating in port, or just after starting, before the rolling began.

Just getting into Athens – rounding Salamis – and we passed Ithaca last night and waved a hand to Penelope.

Your own

FREYA

ROBERT STARK   S.S. *Abbazia*
                                                      26 November 1927

Dearest Pips,

We lost the Cyclades in the darkness of the night, and these are the
Dodecanese all round us now, and I am thinking of shedding my leather
waistcoat in this good warm sun. There is a bit of a roll, but nothing vicious
– merely life and jollity, and the sea is deep blue like nothing I have ever
seen – the sort of blue that black would turn to if it could. The boat is
getting queerer-looking passengers at every port now: florid gentlemen
who try and suppress their curly hair with brilliantine, and go in for lovely
patterns in socks and ties. I am wishing all day long that you were here with
me. Yesterday on the Acropolis, if only to see the colour of that marble. It
used to be painted a deep ochre, and now there is still a tawny shadow in
the sheltered places, and the rest just the colour of sunlight. There is a
little Ionic temple so delicate it might be lace worked in stone. My Greek
history came back to me in bits as the old names were repeated – looking out
to Salamis, and Phalerum where the old walls went, and Hymettus and the
way to Marathon beyond.

                                                                  FREYA

ROBERT STARK   Rhodes
                                                      29 November 1927

Dearest Pips,

You have no idea of anything like this island: I came back after my first
wander through the streets quite stunned, and feeling that I must get inside
my ordinary hotel bedroom to feel as if I were in the real everyday world
again. Think of the citadel complete in its ancient walls and towers, with
huge battlemented bastions at intervals and the gates letting you in by zigzag
ways overlooked by some arrow hole or catapult emplacement at every vant-
age point. Right through the middle runs the Knights' way with all the old
houses – of France, England, Italy, Provence, Spain, intact or restored so
that looking up the hill from the bottom of the street you can see it just as it
used to be, a Turkish woman or two in white, and only the Knights themselves wanting in the pictures. If I knew more about fortification I could
describe the walls to you: they are immense, built to a great width round the
city and filled in with earth so that you can walk along a causeway about
thirty feet broad and look over all the roofs and minarets inside. The Jews
and Greeks and Turks are all in separate quarters, with narrow ways like
Venice, only far brighter from the universal whitewash, and the charming

pavements of the little courts and living rooms, all patterns in bright round pebbles black and white, and kept spotlessly clean.

Yesterday the Governor's A.D.C. here took me and some English at the hotel to the second town of the island and we visited one of the Greek houses and saw their beautiful Rhodian pottery – about thirty plates, Persian designs and colours, hanging on the walls and kept as a dowry for the girls of the family. The plates are now practically unobtainable: the modern ones cannot get the colour or anything near it (the old red is made out of powdered coral). They also had a marvel of old embroidery, and a lovely rug spread over the chief bed high up in one corner. The daughter of the house produced a big tray with quince jelly and spoons, and glasses of water, and little glasses of vermouth, and sweets, and stood before us while we went through the rite – first a spoonful of the jelly (very good), then a sip of water, then all the Vermouth, then a sweet.

The local *Maresciallo dei Carabinieri* gave us lunch. I had to talk such a lot, as nobody else spoke Italian. They were all very pleasant, and arranged a divan on their little terrace in front of the view – the great castle walls red-dish gold like their cliffs, and blue sea, and beyond another lonely little promontory where Cleobolus (who was one of the seven sages) is buried with nothing but sea and rock about him. There are a few olive trees, otherwise this is a hot bit of the island – up to 120 degrees in summer – and the wretched people in Rome refuse to authorise their Carabiniers to shed their hot black uniforms or to wear topees. There are seven of them there, and they seem on the best of terms with the people and spend their evenings teaching them Italian. All the peasants along the road stretch out their arms in a fascist salute, which seems to go with the country. In fact one feels here how excellent this form of government is for a primitive and ignorant population. How much better than our foolish talk of liberty for the natives before they have learnt the rudiments of it.   Your own

                                                                                    FREYA

FLORA STARK   Rhodes
                                                                              30 November 1927
Darling B.,

The Governor received me very charmingly and talked for three-quarters of an hour, chiefly about Rhodes and his work here, but also about Turin and Dronero which he knew well. My entrance missed fire a little: when the two flaps of the door were to be thrown open to let me in, one of them stuck, and there were His Excellency and I separated by a crouching menial who could not get the thing to work. We both waited, but it was no good. I was finally asked to deign to accept only half a door, which is I believe 'la Petite Entrée', but quite sufficient for my figure.

After my interview, I was handed over to Signor Benetti, the A.D.C., to be looked after and provided with all I can possibly desire. Every morning I am asked what can be done for my amusement. There is an English Air Force couple here, regular service people, on their honeymoon, and very pleasant in a conventional way. Benetti invited us all to motor half across the island to Lindos, which is its second town. It was a long day – from 8 a.m. to 6 p.m. – over every description of country and roads. I rather believe that what I enjoyed most was dashing across the island and all its ridges on a road which is not yet made, but only planned out, with all its angles and gradients still in their crudest stages: it had all the delights of a switchback with the most amazing landscape to look at between the gasps. It was an old dream of mine, which I now see was only a premonition; I find myself in a car on the brow of a long hill, and the road has suddenly turned to a mule track and goes bang down at an acute angle, and I can't stop. I never come to any harm, and neither did we. The only difference was that here we had an excellent chauffeur instead of myself at the wheel, and that is why I am alive to write. Mr. D. turned round to his wife at intervals. 'See that corner coming, my dear?' he said. But Mrs. D. was very pale, and said nothing in a heroic way.

It was lovely country, and a windy day with shadows. We climbed up on to a high rocky ridge, the island backbone, among cool fir woods, old lichen-covered trees where the air struck cold. The anemones are in bloom, both the white and the bloodstained ones of the legend; and leaves everywhere of asphodel and narcissus. And all is absolutely lonely. The peasants live shut up in villages, which you come upon with startling suddenness, glittering white, low and flat-roofed like clusters of boxes.

We came out to the coast, running by white and blue bays of sand. Round a sudden corner, Lindos appeared, an old Acropolis above the sea. The little white town is on the neck of the promontory, the red rock over it, not a tree in sight. It belongs to the archaic days, but only fragments of walls and columns are left, and what remains is the fortress of the Knights, its wall and great stairway, and the sea far below. I can't tell you what magic of the earliest ages lies on this place; the Knights have gone, but the spirit that still lives here is long before their day. It is all mystery; but a limpid mystery: the sun and sea and the clear light of the islands; there seemed to be no sadness in these lost ages.

Your own

FREYA

S.S. *Diana,* at anchor in Rhodes
3 December 1927

Darling B.,

I am away again, feeling that some months in Rhodes might have gone very happily. I had a pleasant morning wandering among the Turkish graves, and home through the old streets, and met a flock of turkeys being herded through the middle of the town, with a melon seed thrown now and then before them to encourage them in the right way. I plucked up courage and walked into the mosque which was once Santa Maria of the Knights; very restful now and dilapidated. The sun streamed in through little round panes of blue and yellow glass and two sparrows were chattering in the dome. I sat down on a seat and looked at the walls where the peeling plaster is never renewed, and at the untidy sabots strewn about for the feet of the faithful, and at the absurd grandfather clock, and wondered why it was all so harmonious.

I have been looking out at the hills of Anatolia. Benetti says they would shoot any foreigner at sight who should land there. I doubt it. But the Turks keep it all closed against the Italians, who are looking that way with obvious appetite. All that I have known to come over from Smyrna since my arrival is a travelling circus, and you will be interested to hear that the lion died of seasickness on the way.

I came out to the *Diana* from tea with the Governor's wife – such a clever little lady, with quick movements like a mouse and a mouse's long nose and narrow face and bright, kind little eyes. I was the only lady to tea with twenty-five students from Italy and a number of stout official gentlemen; and as I was standing just behind Her Excellency my hand got kissed twenty-five times also, on false pretences. It was like an ode of Hafiz to come up to the house, for it was moonlight already, and one approaches it through a formal garden full of roses with a fountain splashing.

The *Diana* had meanwhile anchored outside the harbour and had to be telephoned not to start without me. It was very unreal rowing out in the night under the fort and the windmills on the pier – three large vessels at anchor floating like bunches of stars in what looked like a deeper sky below them. The moon was riding through big white clouds over the ramparts.

We have just started now and I am going to bed.

Your own

FREYA

S.S. *Diana*, Cyprus
5 December 1927

Darling Pips,

I dont know whether this will be a long letter, for the boat is ploughing along with great slaps of water banging her side and a tinkle of spray at intervals, just the noise the splintered ice makes when you cut steps in the glaciers. At breakfast I had to retreat to the open air, and looked at Cyprus with a jaundiced eye, only wishing that the wretched island would stand still for a second. It was a kindly land however, for it got between us and the 'Greco Levante', and gave us a smooth sea till we turned this last corner. Now there is melancholy howling in the rigging, and the engines going heavily, and three objectionable Greeks in the cabin.

We had great luck yesterday, and put in to Adalia to deposit a cargo of sugar. The Turks are none too anxious to encourage foreigners, and very few ships go there now. You have no idea of the magnificence of Taurus, rushing right out of the sea in wild peaks to anything between one and three thousand metres – all desolate: no villages, no cultivation, as you slip by for hour after hour, and simply long for some sign of life. At last the ground slopes down more gently and runs out in a long flat red cliff making a huge bay of level fertile land with these magnificent mountains at the back. At the bottom of the bay is Adalia – a clustering, neglected little place with old Venetian battlements crumbling down into the water and a sandy cove where the boats are drawn up, all painted a lovely dull red. The only smart objects there were the Turkish officers, who, much to everyone's surprise, let me go ashore: a huge old Turk seized the mail bags, and beckoned me, and off we went, rowing to the quay.

It is quite a large place and centre of a big country, and the markets simply marvellous – three or four streets of them, all open shops, full of business and colour, with all the gimcrack produce of Europe and every colour of the east. Donkeys, and men with sashes, women tramping along in very sensible trousers, fascinating saddlebags and stirrups, and fine-looking country people, much more serious than Italian or Greeks, but good-natured (apparently). I tried snapshots, but was promptly stopped by a man in uniform: they are very nervous. After one of Mussolini's more aggressive speeches one of the Lloyd Triestino boats was stopped as she was heaving anchor because they thought the ultimatum was on its way and that they might as well collar as much loot as possible.

I saw not a single European inscription in the whole town, and the only signpost I understood was over a photographer, and that was an angel with large wings dropping portraits on the surprised gentlemen in bowler hats below.

I went down to the harbour after an hour or more and waited for a boat. I got the same Old Turk and sat in the boat with an amiable young Turk in spats and Homburg hat who offered me cigarettes and told me in bad German that he was director of commerce. I said his markets were very fine and we shook hands cordially on the gangway, and I paid five piastres less to the boatman thanks to his presence.

Your loving

FREYA

VENETIA BUDDICOM

S.S. *Diana,* Mersin
7 December 1927

Dearest Venetia,

This is all enchantment, the names alone are enough to satisfy an average mortal. I have seen Taurus from the sea, and turned the headland of Paphos with a sea so blue Venus might have been born that minute.

Rhodes is already a dream in the past: it was a perfect week and must be repeated with you some time: Adalia too with old Venetian ramparts crumbling down into the sea. You have been rolling along in the luxury of passenger liners and cannot think what a lot of incident is brought into one's life by a cargo that has to be dumped out of or into lovely red and yellow lighters at every port.

Here I have seen the last of my fellow passengers depart and am now all alone in great state with the Captain and Chief Engineer on either hand at meal times – and rather looking forward to a day or two's solitude for I have never been so much talked to in my life before and feel that the Eastern Mediterranean is simply *crowded* with friends!

Tomorrow I hope to come into Arab-speaking country. I feel I have seen so much and such various things that a little dullness and steady work at Arab grammar will be good. I hear Brumana is over 2,000 feet up, and I shall probably freeze.

Ever your

FREYA

CAR KER

S.S. *Diana,* off Alexandretta (Iskanderun)
8 December 1927

Dearest Car,

You must hear about this morning, for it was the last of your present, spent riotously and most successfully on a pilgrimage to Antioch all by myself (I being the only passenger now on board) with an Arab chauffeur and a boatman who refused to be shed at the landing stage. Great thrill to find my Arabic adequate for getting what I want, and even for a limited admiration of natural objects, though my adjectives are painfully monotonous.

We went high up; how high I don't know, but the Turkish wind came like a knife round the corners and there was ice in the ditches. We stopped at the first village to look at a khan – the proper sort with gloomy arches and animals tethered, and people stooping over fires in the small side chambers. We went on, up the pass, through myrtle and oleander, and here and there a tree, past a long string of camels, a glorious sight against the sky; then down in loops and at a great rate, with the lake of Antioch lying as it were in the middle of a shallow saucer of marshy, fertile land with hill horizons on every side. Nothing moving in all the lonely country except black outlines of oxen ploughing.

It was astonishing after all this loneliness to find Antioch, with a ruined castle crag above and the muddy Orontes before it, swarming with life. Streets of red leather shoes; streets of carpenters, blacksmiths, weavers at their looms with the goat whose hair is being woven into saddlebags tethered to the doorpost. Every kind of costume and colour worn with every degree of casualness. The countrymen who travel with their donkeys wrap up their heads so that the first impression is a population all suffering from toothache and nothing like the dignified turban of the *Arabian Nights* but it is the *Arabian Nights* all the same.

The mosque was a place of peace. A little enclosed piazza of marble, mellowed by ages of sunlight, with four orange trees laden with fruit growing between the slabs of the pavement. Inside, the sun was streaming on to white walls, and the arches just touched with green and yellow in a simple pattern, and the carpet floor blazing like a ruby. My chauffeur hesitated about taking me in: but my Arabic was too bad to understand objections; and there was no one inside but an old Sheikh in a corner who woke up with smiles at my offering for the poor.

Ever so much love from

FREYA

FLORA STARK
S.S. *Diana,* Tripoli
9 December 1927

Darling B.,

An awful night last night. The wind comes howling down the empty funnels of these hills, and the poor *Diana* simply staggered under it. I followed its three separate melodies most of the night, the high piping in the rigging, the tramp of the engine working hard, and the slap of the seas which sent drops of cold water on to my face through the closed deck window. I shall be glad of dry land.

Did you have an eclipse of the moon last night? The Captain called me, and the stars were like new pins and the moon smoky dull red, her left side just beginning to come to life again.

I should like to paint our cargo on the lower deck: a crowd of patient, unhappy sheep with drooping heads and long sad ears, and eleven black bullocks. The men, too, loading and unloading, with their baggy trousers and red tasselled tarbooshes, looking just like Sinbad the Sailor as I met him in the picture-book on my ninth birthday.

Your own

FREYA

VIVA JEYES Brumana
11 December 1927

Darling Viva,

My hostess, Mlle. Audi, is a gentle little thing with a sort of refined and faded youth still clinging to her, all alone with one maid in a little square stone house with whitewashed rooms, very clean and full of plants in pots. Stone-tiled floors and a stove in the sitting-room which, however, she says smokes in cold weather. I can't help wondering whether it will be considered rude to sit in my fur coat.

Mlle. had a teacher all ready waiting called Salehmy, who is to teach me from 5.30 to 6.30 every day. Mrs. Fox at the Quaker Mission seems to have her doubts, but the head of their school is also going to see me, and between them they will no doubt hustle me along the paths of knowledge.

The time-table is almost monastic. Breakfast 8; lunch 12.30; tea 3.30; supper 6.30; bed 8.30.

Mrs. Fox has been here for years and followed Allenby's advance through Palestine with soup kitchens. She says the Turkish corruption is outshone by the present administration (I hope they don't censor letters here).

Your loving

FREYA

ROBERT STARK Brumana
12 December 1927

Darling Pips,

You would like this place, though it is not exactly the Gorgeous East: no ladies veiled, and dozens of little sedentary tidy villages with red roofs doing their best to make Lebanon look bourgeois. But then you come home in the dusk and the jackals are barking in the valley below, or you pass a tavern and three men inside are playing on instruments invented long before the time of David and singing their curious wild monotonous verses. At the end of every verse the audience gives some mark of approval and encouragement: I pleased them very much by joining and saying *taìb* (good), though not catching the meaning of the song. I can hardly make out a word in fifty so far, but hope it may come fairly quickly. I have a charming-looking young man, immaculately European except for his red tarboosh with a tassel to it, and he is coming every day at 5.30 for £3.10s. a month. Now that I have made it clear that I am a poor student and not an eccentric millionaire, Mlle. Audi has undertaken my protection and is planning all sorts of things for me, not all of them exactly what I should wish for.

Your own

FREYA

VENETIA BUDDICOM

Brumana

14 December 1927

My dearest Venetia,

I have taken my map and a compass out this morning, and sat under a pine tree looking at Lebanon, and thinking of you. Brumana is a glorious village, a long ridge of neat stone houses with red hillside and pines and stones running straight down to Beirut and the sea. Even from here one can see where the civilised fringe ends and we should get into lovely country inhabited by jackals and Druses.

Goodness knows how much of this impossible colloquial Arabic I shall be able to manage by the spring. I have a charming young Syrian professor every day, and a beautifully clean lodging with excellent food – and kind landlady with nothing to complain of except the most acute cold. it is all right while the sun shines, but then there is an interval of absolute numbness till I reach my nice warm room.

When I came here (four days ago) Mlle. Audi rather appalled me by telling me that there was 'quite a lot of society in Brumana: Bible classes, Y.W.C.A., and reunions for reading and improving one's mind': so far however this terrible vista has not been filled in as far as I am concerned, except for a Quaker service on Sunday, all in Arabic, and Arabic words to some familiar hymn tune; all which I found most improving, though not in the manner intended.

Ever your

FREYA

Brumana
                                                          22 December 1927

My dearest Viva,

The Mission school gave its entertainment on Tuesday night and we all went. Such a funny mixture. They had eleven boys, each with one letter of the word BROTHERHOOD pinned on to his chest. They stood in a half circle, and each boy in his own language repeated a sentence to say that the world is one great family and his own nation a member thereof; it was English, French, Italian, Spanish, Portuguese, Greek, Hebrew, Armenian, Turkish Arabic, Egyptian Arabic, Syrian Arabic.

Salehmy has been telling me that tigers used to inhabit the Ras el Meten valley where I was so happily wandering. I think this is a delusion, and that anyway he means panthers. He tells me such strange details about the domestic habits of the hyena. He says the hyena lures you into its cave, then *tickles* you till you die, so that it may eat you dead. (His French is poor, he may not quite know what he says.) 'Why does one follow the hyena to its cave?' say I. 'C'est par la sympathie,' says Mr. Salehmy, very solemn in his effort to explain. He tells me however that Miss Cook is wrong in affirming that the hyena walks under our windows every night. What we hear are the jackals, careering in the valley with piercing little barks and shrieks that sound peculiarly evil.

Your loving

FREYA

VENETIA BUDDICOM   Brumana
                                                          Xmas Eve 1927

My dearest Venetia,

I feel that Baghdad is bad as a tramping centre: and I have discovered a new and conclusive reason to make it unsuitable and that is that the Iraqi Arabic is completely different again from the Syrian, so that it would mean starting with no knowledge of the language at all (for speaking purposes). As for this Syrian, I am distinctly hopeful. The difficulty is to get accustomed to a language which pronounces hardly any of its vowels: but I can now put three words together and understand them when spoken and really feel rather pleased with myself. I long to have you here for just a look over the landscape and the map, one more alluring than the other. The essential is a good Druse guide so that we may not be drawn into religious troubles. With enough Arabic to talk to our guide, who will be able to make it clear that we are English and not French, there should be no trouble.

I have not been about at all yet, for the weather is abominable, and I have to take so many short walks just to get warmth into my body that the whole day has gone before I know it. I do four hours' Arabic, and then try to afflict my companions with as much conversation as I can. It is miserably cold: the only time out of the twenty-four hours in which I am warm at all is the latter end of the night in my bed or when the sun shines for a few hours into my room. I must have something Stoic mixed with the Epicurean, for I can't help feeling pleased through all the discomfort at living as it were among the real things: the sun not a mere ornament in the heavens, but something on which your day's happiness really hangs: and the spring looked forward to with all the feelings which you can see in the old writers who came before the days of comfortable houses.

It is all such a funny mixture of French culture spread rather thin: I trot along with Miss Audi with her high-heeled little shoes and shingled head, and meet the tall shepherds striding down from the hills with an air about them unfettered by any of the conventions the French have been able to establish.

My love to you my dear.

Your

FREYA

MRS. ROBERTSON   Brumana
                                                            25 December 1927

My dearest Mrs. Robertson,*

This is really 'between the desert and the sown', for we are still among vines and mulberries and Beirut is a painfully Frankish town, and we go calling on each other in high heels and the Parish fashion last but one. But we look out to where the prosperous villages stop and the bare ridges go up to their watershed, and peasants come down from this country with gay beaded mules, sitting in baggy clothes on embroidered saddles, with a white cloth round their tarboosh if they happen to be Druses, and the rifle which the French have carefully eliminated obviously missing from their natural outfit.

I have been trying to think why it is all so fascinating, and have come to the conclusion that it is the feeling of a life not merely primitive – we have that in Italy – but genuinely wild. The Christian who has lived for centuries on the edge of massacre; and the Druse who no doubt still fills his winter evening with tales of the Old Man of the Mountain[s] – no amount of French education can cover this up. If I happen to be talking French as I stroll along the road with my landlady and catch a glance of hatred from

133

some white turban passing by, it gives a feeling of the genuine original roughness of life, which is worth the pilgrimage.

I have been received with great friendliness and the village is doing its best to teach me – only too pleased to find someone who has come neither to improve nor to rob, but with a genuine liking for their language.

You will be amused at my Christmas Day. A Maronite mass at 8.30, the ceremonial like the Latin, only set to the *wildest* Arab music, with a fast fierce gaiety about it that made the oddest contrast with all memories of masses I have ever heard.

Then our Quaker meeting, where we sing Syrian hymns to the tune of 'God Save the King', and rows of scholars from the Quaker school – Turks and Armenians side by side, Iraqis, Syrians, Greeks, Egyptians – listen politely while someone tells them that the world is really one harmonious family. This conglomeration of scholars is due to the motor car, and I am wondering whether Mr. Ford has not done something for the peace of the world after all.

The best of wishes, dear friend,

Your loving

FREYA

* A friend in Bordighera – Bismarck's niece.

POLDORES THOMPSON [MACCUNN]

Brumana

27 December 1927

Dearest P.,

They are all Christian here – about six different sorts. The Druses come in from the hills, undistinguishable except by a white wrap round their heads, and a fiercer look about them. I am trying to induce Venetia to agree that our tramp should be through their country (quite safe, I think, if we have a Druse guide and if only I can speak a little). Meanwhile I shall do no sightseeing but work and save up. I live here on 8s. 6d. a day including everything except postage stamps (my lessons are included).

Oh, my dear, you can hardly imagine what a joy it is to be free all day long to do my own work; this alone was worth travelling across the world for. I sit in my little room and feel as if I were Queen of the Universe, and the fact that I have to get up and do exercises every half-hour to keep the circulation going makes no difference.

Your loving

FREYA

Brumana
                                                       1 January 1928

Dearest Pips,

I am sure you must have misunderstood about my wanting to settle you
back in Italy, for I know you would not care for that. I had only thought
you might take an occasional winter off, possibly somewhere here in the
East with me, where (if ever I can live as I like in this world) I shall probably
end by finding some little cranny. I quite see that it will take me till well on
into old age to know Arabic only.

I think in April I shall get Venetia to join with a mule and walk among
the Druses. They are quite distinct; live in separate villages or quarters of
village, and wear white head-gear – the women not allowed to show their
hair.

                                                       Your
                                                       FREYA

Brumana
                                                       1 January 1928

My dearest Olivia,

The very happiest of New Years to you and Ernest. What am I to begin
about now? I think I shall just tell you my good day in the country last
Thursday. Such a good day it was, and I thought of you, and W.P., and
many many happy things, walking along under the Lebanon pines, which
looked for all the world like a gentleman's park, or perhaps like the less
cultivated corners of the Garden of Eden with the wild outer world arranged
as a background.

You should have seen the agitated circle of kind Syrians at Mlle. Audi's
tea party the day before, begging me not to go. Finally a much-worried
youth told me he would take his gun (for crows, not Druses) and see me as
far as the bridge in the valley.

It was very like Villatella country zigzagging down among myrtle, pine,
and oleander and an incredible variety of thorns. A good well-marked track,
stonier than anything in Italy, however. And, of course, a mule harnessed
with beads (blue, against the evil eye) and cockleshells, and a driver in red
sash and turban are more interesting than our sober people.

When I left my guide I began climbing the other side in the shadow.
These valleys are so deep, the sun never gets at them I believe; you look up
and see a rim of sunny villages about 2,000 feet over your head, and you
walk in what looks like absolute solitude until the voices of woodcutters
shouting out to each other the news of one solitary female wanderer make

you feel painfully conspicuous – the sort of feeling I remember in the war when being suddenly focused by a searchlight.

When the track divided I was stymied, of course, and sat down to consider; then Providence provided a young man, who afterwards told me he 'had run over a half a mile to see my interesting person at close quarters. He took me along through delicious woodland, his French and my Arabic being equally bad – till we finally came to his village and I had to be explained to the assembled relatives. I was invited into the house, and sat on a long divan admiring the beautiful clean whitewash and mats, and trying to answer questions about my clothes. The sister sat beside me with her arm round my neck, and the mother brought out their new dresses to show me. We then drank coffee, and I was asked to stay a month, or ten months, or a year, or at least a day; and finally I left with many kind words which I could not understand. My language does not yet run to sentences, and I get hopelessly tied up over the fifteen different ways of saying 'good-bye' and 'thank you'.

After this adventure I found my way easily and got to the village (all Druse) by lunch time, and was given a second lunch at the mission, which is perched in an old Druse castle with all the hills of Lebanon round it. Two Syrian boys accompanied me home, giving me scraps of Arab poetry or playing on their reed pipes, joined with wax just as Theocritus has it, and filling the wood with the wild sad sound as we walked along.

I was home by four, and had not walked over six hours actually, but it is hard walking for I must have been up and down over 10,000 feet, much of it like stairways. My heart went like a hammer all night.

Your

FREYA

FLORA STARK   Brumana
                                                               1 January 1928

Darling B.,

A Happy New Year to you! I was so pleased to get your letter when home from Beirut last night. It is an hour's hairpins, quite amusing with everyone jumbled into the cars: reminiscent of Mortola.

I had enough Arabic not to lunch in the hotel but found a ragout, sweet, and coffee for five francs (French) cooked for me over a primus stove in a lowdown little place without tablecloths. The gramophone was set going for my amusement.

But this is a sad people. Neither Arab nor European. They could not stand independently of Europe against the Moslems of the interior. And if they hang on to Europe they are made the tool of every disgusting politician. I believe there is nothing they can strive for with any hope of success. They are a fine-looking people, too, magnificently built men, and women with eyes like stars. And hardy they must be, or they would all be dead. It seems a waste.

Your own

FREYA

VENETIA BUDDICOM

Brumana
4 January 1928

Dearest Venetia,

I have just been taking a rest from perpetual Arabic, looking into Graves' book on Lawrence. Save us from our friends! I begin to feel the man almost unbearable. This attitude of continually saying 'I would like to be modest if only I could' is ridiculous and probably not at all true to the poor man. If only I can get to Baghdad, I have a letter to Mr. Woolley who worked with him on the Euphrates and should be full of interesting information. I see with pleasure that it took four years in the country to teach him Arabic: it makes me feel less painfully stupid. I now begin to follow the drift of conversations and to attempt ambitious subjects like Doughty's Arabian travels in my efforts with Miss Audi at lunch. There is plenty of practice: every afternoon we pay a lengthy call (about two hours) and sit on a divan talking gossip interspersed with one of the sixteen formulas of politeness which I have collected so far. After a while a large tray is brought in with all sorts of delicious sweetmeats, wine, tea; we take a little of each – (fearfully bad for my inside) – and say 'May this continue' as we put down the cup: and the hosts say 'May your life also continue', and then we leave. I believe there is no feeling of class in this country at all: you are divided by religions, and as you see nothing practically of any religion but your own, you never have the unpleasant feeling of being surrounded by people who are hostile and yet bound to mix up their lives with yours.

I am very popular here – the one and only person who has ever come to learn Arabic *for pleasure*.

Your loving

FREYA

137

Brumana
                                                                7 January 1928

Dearest Viva,

Some day, when I can get away and if I am still alive, I must come for
a whole year and get the language into my bones. I shall not be happy till
I can *think* in Arabic.

So far no one understands me except Mlle., who is so like Miss Matty
that I sometimes feel I am wearing a crinoline myself here. She is not
pretty, but has dainty little hands and feet and clothes, and inexpressibly
refined manners; and is always fluttering with emotions, which she lives on,
I believe, for she never seems to eat.

I envy you your mild weather. But that is all I hanker for, and I am not
lonely – not more than one is anywhere in the box of a life. And happy to
be at my own work.

Ever so much love from

                                                                FREYA

Brumana
                                                               14 January 1928

Dearest Pips,

It was very nice to look down through the field glasses two days ago and
see three big boats in harbour – and then sit expecting letters – and sure
enough there was a fat bunch of *Times* and your good note. It is good to feel
you getting on: it is bound to be long, and of course it will mean being
careful. I have also had to get accustomed to the feeling that all this pleasant
world may suddenly and at any moment come to a stop as far as I am
concerned – and it doesn't seem to spoil things, does it? Rather gives them
a peculiarly valuable flavour: a sort of enhanced gambling feeling – and
I hope we may have this feeling for ever so many years.

                                                                Your
                                                                FREYA

Brumana
                                                               14 January 1928

My dear Margaret,

The East is getting a firm grip. What it is I don't know: not beauty, not
poetry, none of the usual things. This place is a grand scene with all the
details neglected. Of course it is not the genuine Orient, only the semi-
European fringe full of French ideas second-hand and second-rate, and
European clothes and furniture peculiarly unadapted to the casual Eastern

silhouette. And yet I feel I want to spend years at it – not here, but further inland, where I hope to go as soon as I get enough Arabic for the absolutely necessary amount of conversation.

The village is kind, at least the Christian part, for we all live in separate compartments and have little to do with such people as Druse, or Greek Orthodox, though we may live next door. My landlady speaks of the Druses as Napoleon used to be spoken of to naughty children in England.

I find the people just as human here as anywhere else: and one great interest in such a different civilisation is that it gives you a sudden fresh view of your own; the nearest in fact to getting out of the world and examining it as an object. The only people I don't care to study are the uncivilised. Here it is too much, not too little, civilisation that is the trouble. That, and an incapacity for forgetting. Mlle. Audi talks of iniquities of Druse governors two hundred years ago as if they had just happened. It is amazing to see all the primitive feelings coming through the refined convent breeding.

Your affectionate

FREYA

FLORA STARK
Brumana
14 January 1928

Darling B.,

A little less cold these days and feeling of spring in the air: I took a long walk and got beautifully warm, but not yet feeling very well. *Much* better here than in most places, however – good water, healthy air and people, and Mlle. simply living for my food. I have the same sort of happiness as a man with a devoted and domestic wife, and sympathise with his contentment.

A kiss to you from

FREYA

VENETIA BUDDICOM
Brumana
18 January 1928

Dearest Venetia,

I've come to the conclusion I don't like missions: I don't believe they are in any real touch with the people here, and feel that they could have done so much better by just existing as a Christian school without the pretension to improve the heathen. It is extraordinary to see how little they manage to share the life of the place: I believe I am thought painfully eccentric for preferring to go among the Syrians rather than to these little Englands outside England which might just as well be at an hour's distance from London so far as any influence of the East upon them goes. They will tell you where to get silk scarves, and all about Armenian servants – and then the gossip of the British colony. The Syrians are all so charmed to find anyone genuinely interested in their language that I feel the real way to be a missionary would be to come to learn rather than to teach.

Your

FREYA

ROBERT STARK

Brumana
21 January 1928

Darling Pips,

I wonder what you would say to the *antiquarios* here? There is most lovely old glass – said to be dug out of the tombs of Baalbek and Byblos: probably faked, but it looks as if the light of the lost centuries were still shining on it: I wonder how long I shall resist temptation and remember that I really will have to get home and have nothing with me to pawn.

The Druses love us just as much as they hate the French (and that is saying a good deal) – and I am told that when Venetia and I go travelling in their villages we shall find them very friendly. Last year, however, one could not go even to the next village with safety, and Mr. Oliver – who runs the mission at Ras el Meten across the valley and is adored in all the countryside – had to drive with a Union Jack on his car, as the habit was to shoot first and ask after.

Dearest Pips bless you. How I wish it were nearer, without Atlantics in between.

Your own

FREYA

VIVA JEYES

Brumana
22 January 1928

My dearest Viva,

I have your letter, and am grateful to think of warmth and comfort on the way! Just now there is a spasm of mildness, but I am told it is quite a mistake to think the worst is over, and that the elders of the village usually, if they are wise, go to bed in February and reappear in March.

I went this morning to the Greek Catholic mass. The service was a family affair, rather pathetic. The mustard-yellow check overcoats of the two young men who did the singing spoilt the general effect. The mixture of absurdity and solemnity, reverence and triviality, one feels so strongly in all these Christian sects. They have existed just on the edge of massacre for centuries, and this does give a certain dignity to their absurd differences.

Today I was stopped in the road by the owner of the public house, who told me that till I came he had never liked a European lady! This had to be translated, being, I am happy to say, out of my usual repertory, and I was rather uncertain which of my sixteen polite formulas to use in reply!

Your loving
FREYA

VENETIA BUDDICOM   Brumana
                                                    22 January 1928
Dearest Venetia,

Just a line *–very sleepy –* in case my last goes astray – to give you all the news and advice I can for your coming. I forgot to mention among the necessities (such as strong boots or shoes, puttees, warm woollens, and shady hat) a basin with a cover guaranteed to keep insects out of one's sponge etc. The disinfectant apparatus I have and all else, I believe.

When we end up at Damascus, and if you feel like a week or so there, I have a letter to a lady who will find us a room in the Mohammedan quarter and we will have nothing to do with Palace Hotels.

Is this all going to come true? Life is very strange. I am glad to be going through it on the whole.

Your loving
The muleteer is being inquired for.   FREYA

CAR KER   Brumana
                                                    26 January 1928
Dear Car,

You are a fairy godmother. Such a wonderful birthday present! I shall take it down to Beirut next week and promptly fall into every temptation I can find.

Some of it shall be devoted to a comfortable donkey. Venetia comes in March and I mean to get her to look at Druses with me, as many of them as still live this side of Damascus since the French bombing. I think it would be about a fortnight's march, taking it easy and sleeping in villages, and I was just thinking how much more comfortable it would be if I could afford half a donkey to fall back on when tired, and behold, here the creature is – or as good as, for it is just finance that does it.

I am longing to try my Arabic with no other languages about. The hill talk is nearer the classical and altogether pleasanter than this untidy town talk. The hill people are the right sort wherever they may be.

I went yesterday for a long cross-country exploration with lunch in my pocket – quite unnecessary, for everyone offers food as one goes and what I actually ate turned out to be delicious – dried figs wrapped in the local bread (which is thin like sheets of coarse brown paper) and pulled by a gentleman by the wayside from somewhere in the region of his tummy, inside his big red sash – inside everything he had on, I rather suspect. However, it was all wrapped up in a clean white handkerchief and tasted remarkably good. I gave chocolate in return.

He found me in the wilderness, for I took a short cut and found a wood-cutter's path. There I met the man and was told that no lady had ever been seen here before, and was I married? This is always the first and most interesting question; I suppose they think a husband should keep me safely at home.

It was good walking in the solitude with the cyclamen and blue anemones blossoming all to themselves in little glades. The valleys go up steep as stairs from their river beds till you reach the first shelf: then up from shelf to shelf of good wide, level ground, till you find mulberry patches, and vines and villages on the third or fourth ledge where the sun can shine all day. There are no people down below except wood-cutters and charcoal burners. Now and then in the stillness you hear their axes and look and look till something gleams and moves among the tufts of trees and grey rocks. I don't believe even the winds get down into these deep valleys. One feels as if one were surprising a secret as one goes down – and it is almost as pleasant to come up again and meet the first cows or donkeys browsing about on the other side.

Your loving
FREYA

VIVA JEYES   Brumana
                                                  30 January 1928

Darling Viva,

I have never been anywhere where it is more fun to have clothes: everyone is so interested in them, and if I put on a fresh hat on Sunday mornings, it is with the agreeable certainty that it is going to give pleasure to the whole congregation.

When there is anything new, the etiquette is to show it to all your visitors. Today we paid a morning call to some people near by and were shown, first, the new coat and shawl sent from sons in America; and next, the new W.C. We went in procession, husband, wife, daughter, son-in-law, and the chain was pulled with solemn pride – only no waterworks followed. I rummaged among my adjectives for something suitable, and finally brought out 'healthy' with what I consider creditable discrimination.

Did you know that camels in the evening bring bad luck? Eight of them came padding past our door at dusk as we came up the steps; rolling along like waves in the half light. They have a very soft footfall, as if they were treading on dust. I don't think it is only my romantic mind that clothes them with mystery. Mlle. told me of the ill omen and was reluctant even to pause and watch as they rolled by.

She told me today how she watched the Allies entering Beirut from her little balcony up here. There were two 'fregates', or three (she can't remember): one was British, and the other French. The French flew an enormous flag, and the British waited to let her pass first into the harbour, right up against the quay: and Mlle., looking through her glasses, realised that it was to be France in Syria after all.

Your loving
FREYA

FLORA STARK   Brumana
                                                              2 February 1928

Darling B.,

The School has started evening classes for the village, much to the annoyance of poor Salehmy, whose only time for improving his own mind was the evening. He came yesterday, filled with annoyance and amusement because, instead of a rise in salary or an hour off in the daytime, Mr. Fox had merely added a special prayer on behalf of the evening teachers. All these rifts in the lute are coming to light as I am getting adopted by the Syrians!

Your
FREYA

ROBERT STARK   Brumana
                                                              3 February 1928

Dearest Pips,

It has been *hot* the last two days (such a pleasure): the sea seemed to be gathering steam, and gradually condensing into clouds, and now at last the rain has come and is pouring steadily.

My teacher, Salehmy, and I are going through a regular course of politenesses. First he sent me two *beccaccie* (is that snipe?) – very good too. Then I invited him for a motor drive and picnic with the Manassehs and Miss Audi: now he is giving a soirée of Arabic music in my honour.

The picnic went off very well. We zigzagged down to the plain – feeling rather like an aeroplane just on the verge of looping the loop – and ran along between the sea and the banana groves along the Tripoli road (full of holes), till we came to the Dog River. It is the old way of all the conquering armies: not a particularly high defile, but very steep, and the grey rock is forbidding; and every conqueror has left his story cut in the face of the rock. As we climbed up, I came on one solitary flowering asphodel: rather impressive there at the entrance of the valley, facing the heroic inscriptions – the earliest Assyrian – bearded kings (Sennacherib I am told) with noses very like those of the present inhabitants: then down through illegible Greek, to Marcus Aurelius in good permanent solid Roman capitals; Saladin, Napoleon; and two British. All these very sober and plain: it only remained for the peculiar bad taste of the French to put the largest inscription of all with bronze helmets and palms – apparently for the exploit of chasing King Faisal from Damascus.* We finished the day by going to the one Lebanon village where they weave: three little looms in a shed, and a shop across the way where the splendours of the East unroll in lovely dressing gowns and *hideous* cushion covers. It was great fun helping Professor Salehmy to choose a wine-coloured gown with pale gold pyramids down its back for his party wear.

It is good to think that spring will be here so soon, and then summer, and then you.   Your own

* General Sarrail in 1926.   FREYA

VIVA JEYES   Brumana
                                                              10 February 1928

Darling Viva,

I hope my birthday greeting will not go to you from a bed of measles. The Spring has started like your infantile essay – cholera in Baghdad, smallpox in Damascus and Beirut, and measles here.

We are all supposed to be re-vaccinated and not allowed in Beirut without fresh certificates. Unfortunately, the doctor has lost the vaccine. The doctor's cousin, Miss Bennington, has just come out from England and is very restive under what she calls 'their slipshod ways'. My Italian training comes in useful: I find myself quite placid under trial. I have managed only one bath since I came, and have to wash in cold water every evening, and my room has nothing but pegs and a table – and it is all quite bearable.

Venetia wires she is not coming till 15 April, so I shall stay in Damascus first.

The world is all almond blossom and anemones.

                                                                Your own
                                                                FREYA

Brumana
                                                                12 February 1928

Dearest B.,

We picnicked at Deir el Qal'a yesterday, an old temple to Jupiter of the
Dancing Floor and some Phoenician god before him. It is high up on a spur,
and the Phoenician blocks now enclose a small garden belonging to the
Maronite monks. The almond flowers hang out over the old smooth stone,
and there is a good snowy amphitheatre of hills standing well away across
the valley. We saw a white tip, and Salhemy said Hermon, but people are
liars about topography.

It was a very ill-assorted party: Miss B. normal British; Mlle. disposed
to flirt with M. Alexandre who was placid but bored; and Salehmy whose
French is so peculiar. I found walking between him and Miss B. trying,
acting as *trait-d'union* between what refuses to amalgamate. Mr. A. made a
determined effort to walk back with us, but Mlle. has all the obstinacy of
the People of Feeling, and collared him. I should have liked time to wander
among the old columns and lovely yellow stone. It is a great building
country; the stone seems easy to work and hard; the colour of it simply
delicious. We came back by the rough road, made out of sight of the coast
by Turks for their guns; a gun and some old trenches are still there below
the monastery, derelict.

                                                                Your own
                                                                FREYA

Brumana
                                                                12 February 1928

Dearest Dot,

What I find trying in a country which you do not understand and where
you cannot speak, is that you can never be *yourself*. You are English, or
Christian, or Protestant, or anything but your individual *you*: and whatever you say or do is fitted to the label and burdened with whatever misdeeds
(or good deeds) your predecessors may have committed. And then of course
your sentences, intended with just the shade of meaning you desire, come
out shorn of all accessories, quite useless for anything except the mere pro-
curing of bread and butter. How glad I shall be when I feel that the country
is really *mine*, not the mere panorama to the stranger. Meanwhile the world
is open. I feel that my seven years' patience is rewarded with Rebecca
straightaway, and am very happy.

                                                                Your loving
                                                                FREYA

Brumana
                                                          14 February 1928
Dearest Venetia,

It appears that the theory here is that I am a spy for the British. I am entertained, only hope the same bright thought won't enter the French heads too and bother us while travelling. We shall be all right this side of Damascus, but probably find difficulties if we want to go south at all.

Don't come a day later than April 15th, or it will be too hot: the climate seems as unsafe as the Syrian dog: he comes wagging his tail and at the end of your petting bites your hand off. Mine was saved by my coat sleeve.

                                                          Your
                                                          FREYA

HERBERT YOUNG   Brumana
                                                          19 February 1928
Dearest Herbert,

What a lovely time you will be having in the garden now – everything just beginning. Here also one feels the spring, though when the north wind blows it is like a blast of sheer ice. This country is just like the psalms – the same sort of violence about it, the good and the bad. I regret more than ever I was not properly and thoroughly brought up on the Bible. Who were the Amalekites and the Hittites? And what happened in Bashan? The latter country I really want to find out about, and I am going to add a P.S. with the name of a book and beg you to see if it is procurable at a reasonable price and if so to get it sent to me in Damascus.

Ever, ever so much love,

                                                          Your
                                                          FREYA

P.S. The book is Porter's *Giant Cities of Bashan* – an old book so I hope not expensive. I should also like Cook's handbook to Palestine and Syria – but this not indispensable.

ROBERT STARK   Brumana
                                                          23 February 1928
Darling Pips,

We had an earthquake last night; quite slight, but enough to give a gyrating sensation to one's legs. It had been pouring all day (it still is) and we were sitting after supper, Mlle., my teacher Salehmy and I, over our little green table by the fire when a noise came rushing along – an inorganic sort of roar. I wish I had been paying more attention. I was not thinking, and only knew what it was from Mlle.'s paralysed expression, and when I tried to get up found it quite difficult to move – for less than a second – because of the wobbliness of the room. I have often wondered whether I should be one of the people who say 'Après vous' in fires and shipwrecks. The truth is, I was halfway to the door to see if it would open, and then remembered Mlle.'s chronic need of moral support and nobly waited to hold her hand into the passage. By this time everything was long over, and we devoted ourselves to eau de Cologne and ether for her fluttering nerves. I was so pleased to feel what sort of a movement it is. Only hope it does not mean any destruction somewhere round about.

Your own
FREYA

ROBERT STARK   Brumana
                                                 1 March 1928
Darling Pips,

We thought – we really did think – that we should wake up to a fine day this morning and when Marie the maid told me that it was snowing, I thought it a joke. It was the *Padre Eterno*'s joke however, and we are still going on with our third week of bad weather – everyone looking a little pale and worn. All the goats are being hurried down from the higher villages: they are nice animals, mostly black, with long drooping hair with a silky wave to it and curly horns.

The French have just published a decree condemning a number of Druses to death. I am told they are all well out of reach and safe, but it will not make for friendly feeling, and I do wish they had waited till Venetia and I have done our little wanderings.

When the north wind blows here it turns the sea to the most beautiful varied colours of old turquoise and green and yellow where the sands are – almost too beautiful to be outside a dream one thinks. I am feeling quite sad to be leaving in ten days' time, and feel as if it were venturing again from a pleasant safe corner into the big world.

Ever so much love dearest Pips.

Your own
FREYA

Brumana
                                                         1 March 1928

Darling B.,

The clothes sound lovely, and you tell me they will *wash*. That is indispensable, in case I go in third-class carriages or among the Beduin poor. As for the silk, I can't imagine ever wanting anything cool to wear any more.

We are still alive, though wizened. Miss Audi thanked me today for suggesting the shutting of the sitting-room door, which has been open through all these winters till I came!

Mr. Edmunds lectured on Russian yesterday. He spent a year and a half there doing relief work, and it was pleasant for a change to listen to someone whose thoughts are well arranged with a thread running through them. He has a taste for ideas, which is pleasant. I do like people who have not yet made up their minds about everything, who in fact are still *receiving*: taking up new impressions, and assimilating them, and adding bits to the philosophy one builds up for one's old age. That is youth really: not a matter of years.

                                                         Your own
                                                         FREYA

Brumana
                                                         3 March 1928

Darling Pips,

I am so glad to have news – though it is not so good as might be. I can't help wishing I had got out to you first instead of after this journey – though it would be sad now to have my visit ending. If you feel you would like me to come *any time,* let me know, and I can always manage somehow. Otherwise I thought of starting some time in August (as I shall then have the money for the voyage) and try and clear three months ahead of me to be with you, over Xmas.

At present I can't get to Damascus because there is still so much snow. The train goes, but ten hours with no heating is a fearful thought with this north wind, and I have no news of my room yet.

I had a good day yesterday. We went down to the sea and Byblos – now Jubail. It used to be one of the flourishing Phoenician towns placed in a kind of low amphitheatre of sloping land between the real hills and the sea. Just a little place now with one pleasant sleepy bazaar street up whose stone-flagged length you look through one of these arches – neither pointed nor round – that give dignity to all the buildings here. The real sightseeing is in the Phoenician graveyard where there are huge sarcophagi cut of one stone with monolithic lids with knobs sticking out of them for the ropes (I suppose): very like cast iron art and giving one the feeling of what an unpleasant unimaginative people the Phoenicians must have been. The remains of their goddesses (I believe it was Astoreth at Byblos) are just as repulsive: though there is a forlornness about them – feet and bodies broken off at the thighs and roughly hewn in stone, the floor and walls of their temple still traceable among debris and weeds – giving a melancholy picture of a dead religion waiting for its non-existent worshippers.

The castle, which is just beside this temple, is far more cheerful – with the body of it still intact, the bridge, and the moat, the guard room, and the banqueting hall, and the secret passage to the sea all visible; and narrow steps to climb, and a flat grass-grown roof to come out upon and look at the surrounding world.

We came back to lunch at the River of Adonis. It was flowing clear green, and strong – not red, as it should do in winter: I suppose we must take it that the spring is here. It was like spring too down there: the fields among the banana trees were filled with deep red poppies. I insisted on the sacrifice of our flowers from the Roman bridge and we saw them floating down, gleaming like rubies in the sun on the green water – the first offering Adonis has had for a long while I expect. And it was pleasant to see the Syrian headmaster of the Friends' Missionary School sacrificing to his ancestral gods. I long to hear you have warm weather, for that should do both of us good.

Your own

FREYA

FLORA STARK   Brumana
                                                          3 March 1928
Darling B.,
   Yesterday I went to the Municipio to help in the vaccination of the village. As it turned out, there was no help needed except the occasional buttoning up of some small infant; but it was amusing to watch the various types – so very various, blue eyes and black, from the rather loosely put together northern features to clear portraits from the old Assyrian; occasionally a streak of negro; occasionally good aquiline. The method of strengthening people by starvation and murder seems absurd, but there is no doubt it appears to work here. They are as hardy as can be. When you think of them as compared to Italy, it is like thinking of iron and earthenware: you feel these people are hard *all through*. I imagine that what is wrong with them

is just what was wrong with their Phoenician ancestors: they have no imagination; therefore no ideals, or not sufficient to make them really do something. I am reading about Phoenicia, and it seems that all their genius went into practical things and manual execution. And so, in a degenerate way, it still goes on, and the Syrians spread over the world, America, Australia, no matter how far, making money and thinking about money.

People are kind, and say they are sorry I am going. I am sorry too, and feel as if tearing up roots.

Always your loving

FREYA

FLORA STARK   Brumana

9 March 1928

Darling B.,

I called yesterday to say goodbye to Salehmy's mother and found a banquet prepared, a table heaped with good things. I find that the only way out is to seize on whatever is portable and say you will take it with you.

So many calls to pay. Four yesterday, and ended at the teacher's tea table at school. Tomorrow some people from the Central Friends' Committee will be here and we are all asked to tea and to see football after. Shall I wear my nicest frills? I do feel I have been good for so long. Luckily Mrs. Fox so approves of my respectable introductions that she swallows me as well. She has been really so kind; and I feel I must have been a trial, landing here from the blue without knowing a soul; and everything I do, the most ordinary things that everybody does in any sensible place, gives them electric shocks all round.

Next letter from Damascus, I hope.

Your own

FREYA

FLORA STARK   Brumana

11 March 1928

Darling B.,

This is my last letter from Brumana till May, and I am feeling so depressed, like a waif starting off into the unknown again, now that I have been settled here so long. Everything seems to have swelled itself out too, like a pony when you saddle it, so that I can't be contained in my boxes.

The guide however is found, and his name is Najm – star – surely a good omen. He is middle-aged, sturdy, with lively brown eyes, a moustache with a twist to it and a red sash round his middle; and he promises to see to us, body and soul, till we are safe through the Druse country; and will show us all the old castles and the modern ruins by the way. May it go smoothly!

I had a pleasant day yesterday with charming Mr. Edmunds, who turned his back, in a lovely blue coat with brass buttons, on all the Sunday ceremonies and came wandering. He is good at walking, only he had never been off a road before, and discovered with surprise that Lebanon paths are stony. I enjoyed talking like a human being again after nearly four months' starvation; I suddenly realised how long it had been! We had egg sandwiches beside the stream – rushing green water now, and no skipping over stepping stones like last time.

We found a real tree, not merely a pine, and sat in shade, and watched an eagle turning its great flat head slowly in the sun and, after a long time, flapping across the valley over our heads. The river is a long way down: we were made excessively aware of it by having to rush up the hill at speed so that he might be back by five – and we did it with one minute to spare, but my heart was pounding like a hammer all night: I must be getting old. Two goatherds, also, we talked to; they looked so well in their old red jackets and muffled up heads among the black browsing goats and speckled shadows. One of them came up with the first black kidling in the crook of his arm, born that day, a little leggy anatomy, soft as silk.

I must finish off the packing.

Your own
FREYA

ROBERT STARK

Train to Damascus
14 March 1928

Dearest Pips,

I had to put off my departure because of the snow – still very heavy on the passes. We are now crawling up at an incredibly slow pace: it is about 150 kilometres and takes 9½ hours. I have a Syrian family with me: we spend the time eating. The last station they dashed out and brought leban, the milky cheese: this station it is onions. My Arabic works well – and I have just been hearing them explain to the only French lady in the carriage that *everyone* in England knows their language. People who want conversation stroll along the outside of the carriages and look in at the windows as we crawl along. The sun is getting very hot already, but it is the good burning sun of the hills up here. I have seen the first black Beduin tents pitched among the olives and the poppies.

Later

We are now down across the ridge and on the stretch of flat valley between Lebanon and Anti-Lebanon – Mount Hermon south-east – not a mountain really, but the culmination of the ridge. A river winding towards the south, with broad pebble bed, like Italy but for the solitary camel. When we came to the top of the pass there was quite a lot of snow: great snow-balling at the stations, and the passengers kept a little store to throw balls at unsuspecting labourers down here in the plain. The Syrian lady told me that seven years ago she was blocked on the pass: the train could go neither back nor forth, and all the passengers had to spend six days in the tiny little station building – there is no village up there. I saw the Oriental attitude to women very plainly: the poor little girl could do nothing right – 'sit down, get up, do this, do that' – but the little boy was allowed to slap his father's face and was king and sultan over the whole family.

Did I tell you I saw the storks? A whole army of them flying overhead and wheeling towards Turkey.

Your own

FREYA

FLORA STARK House of Khalil 'Aid, Damascus
15 March 1928

Darling B.,

I haven't been out yet, but the East has been coming home to me quite busily. Imagine one of those little backyards in Venice as the entrance to my home. You climb up rather rickety stairs, through the lower litter of garments, saucepans, old shoes and flower-pots, to a pleasant room with seven windows; where, unless, you are extremely careful, everyone can see you while you dress. I really think the bed is all right: I have found nothing alive anyway: in fact what I complain of is that everything smells as if it were dead. The children's clothes were bundled out of my room, and various necessities like jugs, towels, mirror, rug, brought in at intervals while I sat rather dismal on the bed. That has a lovely yellow quilt and two long hard bolsters. I do manage to get hot water in the morning. But there are so many smells.

I had breakfast with the family this morning and felt how much I am still fettered to the lusts of the flesh. We sat round the primus stove beside the washing-up bucket, and I tried to anchor my mind on the fact that nothing much besides old age can happen to the inside of a boiled egg.

The landlady is pretty and looks tired. Her name is Rose: she is at this moment blacking her eyes at my mirror; and she uses my powder, which I do so dislike. If she did not wear incredibly sloppy European clothes she would be quite ornamental. There is no particular sort of privacy here, except that the men are out of the way most of the time. It will be splendid for my Arabic, and I believe I can stand it. The best of it is a roof to walk on and look at the other roofs, and the minarets and the red hills. The desert comes close: just red rock, not a shimmer of grass on it; the cultivated land washes up to it like a wave and stops as suddenly. It gives one the feeling of being in prison.

Later

I have been out with Sitt Rose, and discovered a European side to the town, tramlines, avenues and shops: it is what they are proud of, of course.

I found Mr. P., the Vice-Consul, in that district. He was evidently very pleased to have a new English person to talk to, but I did not like him very much. He has invited me to dinner, and to go walking, but I hardly think I shall do so. He does not know a single Syrian here. He thinks it impossible I should stay in my native lodging, but says there is no alternative except hotels.

I was so glad of letters. I have been feeling a little depressed.

Your most loving

FREYA

ROBERT STARK

Damascus

16 March 1928

Dearest Pips,

It is not all joy living with a native family. I had my first lunch with them: I was given a plate and fork – the rest just dipped their bread in the dish. It is very rich food, pepper, onion, grease, all the most deadly things. I have confessed to being an invalid and eat just the milky things, and even so am wondering how the experiment will get on. The family is mother, aunt, and three nice children, full of life and spirits: the father only appears in the evening, when we gather in one of the bedrooms and sit round, callers coming round and the gentlemen handing each other the hubble-bubble. It is certainly not the East as the average tourist sees it. I wish I understood more – all the really interesting conversation escapes me.

Your own

FREYA

Damascus
                                                              16 March 1928
Dearest Venetia,

The plan is to ride from April 17th to the end of the month, and then have a fortnight's rest in Brumana before going home through Palestine: I can't delay beyond the end of May, and don't think I could manage the ride, and the return by Palestine, without the rest in between. If it succeeds it should be a gorgeous tour, the flowers all at their best and the weather not too hot. May would be hot I think.

I have a funny little room in a native house. I am trying to think I don't mind about cleanliness: if one could make oneself independent of these physical things, how easy it would be to travel. I haven't found anything alive in the house however; and I try to read Dante and not look at my meals as I eat them.

It will be so good to see you.

                                                              Your own
                                                              FREYA

LADY HORLICK   Damascus
                                                              17 March 1928
Dear Lady Horlick,

This wobbly letter is from a bed of sickness in Damascus. Not a long one I hope: the prospect of being ill in a native household is too terrible.

I only came two days ago. A wonderful journey down the Barada valley; it is just a green strip between desert walls of red rock, as mad and fantastic as the landscape of dreams. You can take one stride from the rich garden land into the desolation. The valley suddenly opened, and there in the after-noon sun was Damascus, yellow as an opal, the river running through between straight banks like a willow-pattern plate. There is the exact description in Chaucer somewhere, of Simois 'like an arrow clere' flowing through Troy, and I thought of it as I came along, and before the railway station turned the East to mere untidiness.

If I feel strong I hope to make journeys from here. It is all a question of food: you offend people if you refuse their hospitality, and you die (or I should) if you accept it. Perhaps you die in either case: I have not tried offending a Druse!

I have been introduced to a delightful Moslem Sheikh who will show me Damascus free from tourists. He is part owner of the most beautiful house in the city and belongs to an old family of Albanian Turks who became Arabicised about four generations ago. I admired his good manners, for he came to call and was welcomed into my *bedroom* by the assembled family before my Arabic could rise to the occasion – before I had time for anything except to clutch the nearest dressing-gown. He sat talking with charming equanimity, though I am sure it is not the usual way in which to be introduced to a Moslem.

I was not able to reach Baghdad after all. Ja'far Pasha, who invited me, resigned, and is now sent as Minister to London.

Much love and remembrance to you from   FREYA STARK

FLORA STARK   Damascus
                                      17 March 1928
Darling B.,

It is very annoying. I have been quite upset and ill. I tried to think it was imagination, but finally sent for the English doctor. Wonderful nation we are! He never asked a question, but gave me a prescription, talked about food (and well he might) to the lady of the house, and went. I was just longing for a little bit of moral comfort and felt this rather chilly. But I am glad it is nothing requiring energetic attention. I shall be all right living on leban and eggs.

My room is quite nice and quiet in itself, and the sun comes in. I get a cypress tree and bits of roof, and the children bring me flowers. The landlady comes to borrow stamps and envelopes. I feel that it is rather hard on the poor people that their first European should be such a trouble. They are very obliging in their casual way. They come offering me raw salads to chew in bed as if I were a rabbit in a cage.

Luckily I got some books from the Mission. I dragged myself there to tea yesterday, but it was stuffy.

                                    Your
                                    FREYA

FLORA STARK   Damascus
                                      18 March 1928
Darling B.,

I am up again, languid but much better. I had to send a wire to V. (who has put off her coming till May) and reached the very edges of exasperation at the slowness. When the old man began *reading* my postcards before sticking the stamps on (with a queue of people waiting), I snatched them from him and gave a general shock to Oriental feelings.

                                    Your loving
                                    FREYA

Damascus
                                                    18 March 1928

Dearest Venetia,

I hope there may be no more telegrams, for it means an hour of irritation
in this country to get them off. I have wired 'Come May'. It can't be helped
but it is sad! It would be poor fun for you, however, to have me sick among
the Druses, and I am rather uncertain of my own strength.

I don't like my landlady here. She borrows my soap, and, whenever we
are out together, she gets into a carriage which I have to pay for: and I dislike carriages anyway, because you never see anything but the coachman's
back. The trouble with travellers – and this includes missionaries – is that
they come into contact with only the third or fourth rate people, and that
gives no impression of *any* country.

I have been to see some charming Mohammedans: a young doctor and his
sister (dressed in the latest French and beautifully shingled). The doctor took
me out after the call to look at Damascus outspread at our feet, its groves of
blossom stretching away to the hills in the sunset. He swept his arm around
one side of the landscape and said: 'This belongs to my family.' It is
wonderful rich land, irrigated by the seven rivers, which lose themselves in
swamps full of duck and wild boars: all round are low volcanic hills. In
spite of dust, noise, tawdriness, ugliness of detail, there is a magic: not to
be understood in a day or even two!

                                                    Your loving
                                                    FREYA

Damascus
                                                    19 March 1928

Darling Pips,

I have just been living in the *Arabian Nights* all day – wandering in the
bazaars this morning: sitting on the ledge of the little shops while the mer-
chant in his long gown spread out his silks before me and the merchants
opposite, squatting in their little shops, with their amber beads like rosaries
clicking through their fingers to pass the time, looked on at the rival trans-
action. The Moslem ladies have to lift their black veils to see the stuff they
want to buy: you see them bending over, with one hand to their veil and the
other holding up the garment: or trotting away with the porter carrying
packages behind them – just as the story has it.

This afternoon we went into the narrowest blackest streets, with overhanging rooms and a slit of daylight: I say we because I had a charming,
and so handsome, young Moslem cavalier to whom I had an introduction.

He belongs to a good family here, and came along in the flowing brown and gold cloak given by Ibn Saud to his brother. We wandered by Saladin's tomb, close to one of the marble water basins in a little garden of orange and blossoming almond. Then through the ruined town: sad and horrible. They say the French áre going to rebuild it, and I think it would be as well, for it must rouse a lot of vindictive feeling.

Tomorrow is the last of Ramadan. Everyone is saying their prayers at a great rate, in the big Mosque cloister – big as a piazza, full of people coming and going. There is so much; such a jostle, and variety of types: fair blue-eyed hill people, the real Assyrian, every degree of black, and the Beduin in their rags and big strides swinging their rough cloaks, their dingy little tattooed women behind them, donkeys with panniers jostling among the people (sometimes with skins of oil, not at all pleasant to be near), camels in long strings; occasionally a horse with handsome red and yellow tassels and blue beads; and all in the half light, for the bazaars are roofed over, and the little shops open on to them about two feet off the ground, like the rooms of doll's houses – or a row of boxes at the theatre.

Your own

FREYA

FLORA STARK   Damascus
20 March 1928

Darling B.,

Ramadan has just ended at sunset. Such a business in the bazaars, shopping for the feast. It lasts three days. We went on to the roof to hear the muezzin: it is extraordinarily moving, voice after voice ringing out from the high steeples to declare the greatness of God to the people below. The flat roofs of course give a wonderful advantage to the minarets. God is the *Master* here: not the Comrade and Teacher of our churches that stand clustered amid their flock.

Your loving

FREYA

ROBERT STARK   Damascus
21 March 1928

Dearest Pips,

I went out this afternoon with all the family to see the arrival of the new Vizir – the head of the government, though under the French Commissioner. We went at two and sat on somebody's wall just in front of the triumphal arch which was made out of long poles and carpets flung over–very effective, especially as there was sword dancing going on underneath, to the beating of two tom-toms. The way the swords are twirled about, so fast that you can't see the movements of the wrist at all, is very fascinating. In the other hand they hold a tiny brass target: they move their arms about, first very slowly, then gradually faster with the music, moving and suddenly springing and getting nearer and nearer – always keeping in harmony with each other – till they close up, twirling the swords about so that it seems impossible to avoid being hit. At the close one of them brings his weapon neatly horizontal between them and they kiss above the blade very prettily. I was told the Vizir wouldn't arrive till four, so I left the family and walked along the road, and then branched off and found myself in actual Paradise – flat country all grass or brilliant green corn, all filled with running streams and speckled with shadows of olives and blossoming fruit trees. The old Moslem peasants were saying their prayers, their spades stuck into the ground, their coats spread out, and their shoes beside them while they knelt with their face to Mecca; it seemed a good and pleasant way of praying. There was nothing to disturb the picture: the villages all flat, baked clay – a lovely ochre; and the women in their bright clothes, like Tanagra come to life, the beautiful line of the draped head and shoulders, and their little blue or red frilled trousers showing underneath. One group was so lovely that I peered round their courtyard door and they all came and showed me the baby – not a month old and its eyes already blackened for beauty. I remembered just in time to say 'In God's name' before praising it, so as not to cast any evil eye on its poor puckered face.

When I got back at 4.30 the Vizir was just arriving: a huge green banner in front, frantic singings and brass bands, soldiers, drawn swords in the air, and he himself a young man, quite round and amiable, with a turban and about two hundred motors behind him – all the old Fords of Asia it looked like.

Your own
FREYA

FLORA STARK   Damascus
                                         21 March 1928
Darling B.,
   The older lady has just been in to tell me tactfully that Moslems are not to be trusted. 'Even if a Moslem smells like musk, do not put him into your pocket' was what she said.

Yesterday I was asked if I was Arabic. It was only on the strength of two words, but imagine my joy.

Your own

FREYA

FLORA STARK   Damascus
27 March 1928

Darling B.,

I am going to get up today and try to get out. I hope to be well by the end of the week – but I fear the donkey trip will have to be given up. It is heart-breaking, everything being propitious except my own self.

A kind American lady came yesterday and brought me soup: the first food I could eat with anything like pleasure these twelve days. I lapped it up, and was then prayed over, which was also kind and made me feel rather like the Deserving Poor.

I have asked if I can meet Mr. Edmunds by car, and perhaps see one or two of the most accessible Hauran cities: but what a way of doing it!

Your own

FREYA

FLORA STARK   Damascus
1 April 1928

Darling B.,

I had tea at the Mission yesterday, but did not go for a walk as intended, feeling too ill. I do find those ladies too suffocating. Even the young ones seem to have all natural interest in life and buoyancy taken out of them and think of nothing but their own narrow little bit of path of righteousness.

To feel, and think, and learn – learn always: surely that is being alive and young in the real sense. And most people seem to *want* to stagnate when they reach middle age. I hope I shall not become so, resenting ideas that are not my ideas, and seeing the world with all its changes and growth as a series of congealed formulas.

Your loving

FREYA

FLORA STARK   Damascus
2 April 1928

Darling B.,

I was able to be out this morning and enjoy my walk through Damascus slums, trying to find the 'four great gates'. I had an adventure which might really make the Mission hair stand up, and gave me a nasty qualm. I fell into it because it was so like the *Arabian Nights*. An old man with a venerable beard came up as I was strolling along with my camera, and said, just as anyone would expect: 'Follow me, oh lady, and I will show you a beautiful place.' So I followed. He told me it was an ancient bath, unused I supposed: and turned down a very narrow dark passage which went below the level of the street. I did hesitate, but he said 'Have no fear', and it is not so easy as it seems to change one's course when once started. We came to a heavy studded door, on which he knocked. Ten centuries dropped from me by magic: I should not have been at all surprised to see the Caliph and his two companions on the other side! The door was opened from the inside. and there was a great vaulted hall, lighted from a window in the roof, and with a cistern of flowing water in the centre. There were alcoves with carpets on a raised platform round three sides, and various men lying about on them with their heads wrapped in turbans and nothing much except their big bath wraps on. I did feel I was not in at all a suitable place! They gathered round me in an instant. Then I heard the door clank to behind me with a horrid sound as if a chain were dropped.

I had an unpleasant sensation as if my heart were falling – literally a sinking of the heart in fact – but I did remain outwardly calm; only I put my back against the wall so as to face them. I said to the old man: 'Oh my father, wilt thou hold my gloves while I take the picture?' and got my camera ready with complete disregard to the rules of photography. They had all come up so close to me and I thought them a villainous-looking crowd. Someone murmured to the old man: 'French?' 'English,' said I hastily: 'we are your people's friends.' This had an extraordinarily soothing effect on the atmosphere. I asked if they would mind moving away from me for the picture, which they did in silence. When I had taken it I thanked the man who seemed master of the bath and turned to my old man to have the door unfastened. This also was done in complete silence, but just as I was stepping out two or three of them asked me to turn back and look over the baths. This you may imagine I did not do. I was very glad to have that door open, though I suppose it was all really quite all right. I wish now I had taken the picture with more care, for I don't imagine any European has been in that particular place before. I am not mentioning this episode here, for as it is I am being almost shadowed by the family, who are evidently fearfully anxious. Think of it! My landlady has never in all her life been even into the Great Mosque.

My Sheikh has taken me over the Great Mosque, a wonderful, beautiful place to pray in. It was almost as S. Marco for its atmosphere of peace. It is immense. The richness and colour is in the carpets. All the detail is lovely: the Imam's niches, doors, pulpit, worked in marble and mother of pearl, and old blue tiles outside under the columns: but the general effect is absolutely simple; there is nothing to take the eye or the thoughts away. The people wander in to pray, or talk quietly. All the political plots were hatched here. There are platforms, where they read the Koran, swaying backwards and forwards as they chant it in a low voice. In one corner there is a marble basin with flowing water. And there is a pleasant silence, since everyone goes barefoot on the soft carpets.

Your

FREYA

FLORA STARK

Damascus
4 April 1928

Darling B.,

Do you know that my living here comes to less than 6s. a day, and I am so rich I don't know what to do with myself.

Yesterday we went up to Salahiye – my Sheikh and I – to look at Damascus in the sunset, her gardens getting greener day by day in the plain below. We met his cousin, H. E. Hakki Bey, a charming old man who was governor here four years ago. Chairs and coffee were brought us, all out in the open country, very pleasant. These well-bred Moslems are very agreeable, and just as easy to get on with as well-bred people the world over. Of course, one cannot become intimate unless one knows enough of their civilisation to be able to see from their angle. If you think what we would be if we lost *all* our Latin and Greek roots together with their derivations, and substituted quite a different culture which most Europeans know only by name, you will see that one does not need a great divergence of character to explain the difficulty of understanding between East and West. I don't believe there is any more fundamental reason why one should not know a Syrian as intimately as anyone else who is not of one's own race.

I have most illuminating times discussing religion and politics with my Sheikh, and he talks quite freely, finding me interested. I told him that I have long thought of Mohammedanism as one form of Protestantism and far nearer to the spirit of Protestantism than the forms of Christianity here.

He is convinced that the Koran is superior to the Bible, just as he is convinced that Arabic poetry is superior to the literatures of Europe. This is all interesting in someone who has been in the hands of the missionaries for the *whole* of his education.

Your own

FREYA

Dearest Pen,

Yesterday was a wonderful day : for I discovered the Desert!

One must not believe people when they tell you things. They told me I could not see desert unless I went to Palmyra which is too far this time. I looked at the map, however, and decided on a lonely ruin marked where the Damascus streams lose themselves in lakes, and the villages end. Nothing beyond but names of hills and water-places and the road trailing away south to the lands beyond Jordan. My Moslem friends came with me bringing their guns, which we had to hide whenever police came in sight. The pretty sister wears a black veil over her face, but she throws it back in the country.

Such a road! It was sandy and smooth at first, running through avenues of walnut just coming into leaf, and the green corn on either hand. Then we began to wade streams, water well up to the axles : then on to banks at absurd angles. We began to meet Beduin : their black tents were dotted here and there. The country got poorer, the corn thin and uneven, the trees stopped. For some time there would still be a clump of shade by the villages – then nothing – just the mud walls baked yellow sloping up one of the strange solitary little hills that rise out of all this country like dolphins' backs.

We were taken along a road that melted into invisibility, then found ourselves on hard sand, thorns and desert rushes brushing against the wheels. The country looked white like chalk here, all gentle lines and travelling shadows; and, half lost in distance, a glimmer of snow from Hermon, and the Damascus hills.

And then the wonder happened! Camels appeared on our left hand : first a few here and there, then more and more, till the whole herd came browsing along, five hundred or more. I got out and went among them to photograph. The two Beduin leaders, dressed gorgeously, perched high up and swinging slowly with the movement of their beasts, shouted out to me, but the Beduin Arabic is beyond me. I can't tell you what a wonderful sight it was : as if one were suddenly in the very morning of the world among the people of Abraham or Jacob. The great gentle creatures came browsing and moving and pausing, rolling gently over the landscape like a brown wave just a little browner than the desert that carried it. Their huge legs rose up all round me like columns; the foals were frisking about; the herdsmen rode here and there. I stood in a kind of ecstasy among them. It seemed as if they were not so much moving as flowing along, with something indescribably fresh and peaceful and free about it all, as if the struggle of all these thousands of years had never been, since first they started wandering. I never imagined that my first sight of the desert would come with such a shock of beauty and enslave me right away.

Love to you both always from

FREYA

FLORA STARK   Damascus
9 April 1928

Darling B.,

I had just given up Mr. Edmunds and made up my mind for a lovely four days' trip towards Leja and Bashan, when I got news of him, aggravatingly saying he will come *either* tomorrow or Thursday. I suppose it is not bad for my health to be quiet, though so dull. I can't tell you how bored I am with the poems of Browning, and I read through the whole of Dante.

I am learning how necessary it is to keep one's own standards and one's national standards for one's own use, and not to judge other people by them. Another thing I have noticed is the absolute lack of all historical sense among these people. No *perspective*. What happened five hundred years ago has the exact vividness of yesterday. It came upon me with a shock when a child here was reading out some of the more gruesome massacres in Kings: I decided on the spot that I should leave the Old Testament out of the curriculum if I were a missionary, and stick to Christian charity and the New. If you come to think of it, the Old Testament is the worst literature possible for these races: with that on the one hand and the Koran on the other the reign of toleration has very little chance.   Your own

FREYA

FLORA STARK   Brumana
17 April 1928

Darling B.,

On Thursday Mr. Edmunds arrived: I was more glad that I can tell you to see a normal human being of my own kind again! It was rather amusing: M. Paul Alexandre chose the same afternoon to appear unexpected on my doorstep. The two gentlemen's unhesitating verdict was that my lodging was Impossible, and they urged me to return in their car. It is only now that the effort is over that I realise how great it was!

My Damascus home was really rather unspeakable. Poor Mr. Edmunds! He bore up very creditably, but he will never know how much, *much* worse it might have been. I went upstairs when they were supposed to have prepared his room up on the roof, and made them do it all over again from

163

the beginning. And I kept him carefully out of the dining-room, which was enough to make a quite strong man faint away.

M. Paul was rather a bore because it meant that I had to speak French, English and Arabic alternately all day long, and also he gravitated irrepressibly to all that was European and seemed to be drawn by a magnet to things like tramlines. And I had to bargain for such atrocious objects on which he set his heart. We spent a morning in the bazaars. The two were just like infants buying new toys; I enjoyed it so much.

Next day was more or less taken up by business. I had to pack, and pay good-bye calls. I went out a little with Mr. Edmunds, and we strolled about among the little shops, watching their crafts: the tinsmith polishing his coppers by standing *in* them on a pile of wet gravel and then swirling himself from side to side at such speed that the gravel polishes off every stain in no time. Then the weavers weaving striped silk for waistcoats – a nice Mohammedan with a beard. Then the man who presses tarbooshes under a heavy brass press heated by a primus stove. Then the man who lives in a little dark shop cooking rice in milk all day long. Then the makers of sabots; they chop them neatly out of pieces of tree trunk with hatchets, and give them their slim shape with a couple of clever strokes. Then we wandered into the jewellers' *suq* – a gloomy place they lock at night, and filled with great iron safes.

On the Sunday, our last day, we went out to the lake where Barada ends. Luck again: for we found the Beduin. The black tents were dotted round. It was a happy place; open sky and the river moving slowly, quite deep, through the grassy plain. The Beduin came towards us and we strolled to the tents. I think I was well inspired. I asked for the Sheikh's tent, and this seemed to be the right thing: it was the biggest of them all, open along the front and divided into wattled compartments, and we were taken to the largest compartment where the two coffee pots stood in a hole in the ground and the Sheikh himself lay fast asleep beside them. In a corner at one end all the tiny lambs were huddled safely.

A rug was spread for us: we squatted down, and looked across at our sleeping host, who began to come to himself very gradually. He finally came to a sitting posture, in which he remained meditative for a while with his eyes on the ground, looking magnificent in his flowing garments and grey beard. He then spat, reached out a hand to the man nearest him – a fierce long-faced Arab with two long pigtails – and began murmuring in quite incomprehensible language which did not sound particularly cordial. I made a feeble attempt at explaining our existence, but one can't carry on small talk with a Patriarch, and the correct thing seemed to be to sit silent.

After a long while, the Sheikh stretched his hand to the coffee pot, and poured out a few sips into two little cups which he handed to me and M. Paul (I was surprised at the woman being first served!). M. Paul then offended by refusing the cigarette which the kind A.D.C. had (literally) just licked into shape for him. He made it up by offering his tobacco pouch, and the atmosphere began to thaw. 'Oh daughter of my heart,' said the old Sheikh to some question of mine: after that I felt all must be well.

I went and sat a little among the women in the next compartment and was warmly welcomed there. They were much interested in my clothes and tremendously impressed by silk knickers. I looked at their thick saddlebags and weavings. The women were charming: one or two truly beautiful, with small, delicate straight features: every movement was graceful and full of ease and dignity. They are tattooed all over their chins up to the lower lip, and their head-dress is of the same colour, and wraps the face round like a nun's: and the whole effect with the long blue gowns and silver bracelets is very dignified and beautiful.

They told us of their wanderings. In winter they find grazing five or six days' journey in the desert: the old Sheikh told me the land there is full of ruined cities. Finally, as we got up to go, they said they were preparing our meal. This was an awful prospect: certain death for me, anyway. I explained that we had already eaten the meal in our hearts, but that we must get round the lake before nightfall and could not wait, but would eat the fatted sheep next time. This was a brilliant linguistic effort, and successful. They watched us into our car with interest, but no vulgar curiosity.

That was the best of the day, though the rest was good enough. We skirted the rushes, the lake full of herons and duck and innumerable strange birds catching the sun on coppery wings. The space was immense. We lunched in the shadow of the car with the warm wind singing round us. To the north and east, small sandstorms were whirling along in high columns: and we saw mirages, blue waters so unmistakable that we were taken in, and finally came home in the late evening light along the Palmyra road. In spite of all, Damascus has been well worth while.

Yesterday we came away – a lovely drive by the green Barada water, then high along the desolate ridge of Anti-Lebanon, all red earth and rubble, with Hermon on our left striped with snow. I shall never forget Hermon as we climbed and looked across the green spaces to where he lay like a great wave asleep in the sun crested with white. We climbed into the crisp air, good breath of hills: reached snow: here they have built houses to pack it for Beirut's summer ices. We lunched among the Lebanon pines, feeling very much like coming home.

We have left the East behind us. This is not Europe: but it is Mediterranean. Very lovely. A thin film of vivid green from young corn and mulberry leaves is over it all. The last snow just melted off Sannin.

Miss Audi embraced me. And gave me a bath. You never saw anything so immaculate as my bed-curtains. I found myself *stroking* their lovely whiteness!

Your own

FREYA

VIVA JEYES

Brumana
18 April 1928

Dearest Viva,

I have left Damascus. In spite of all I still carry the Enchanted City in my heart. We had one scrumptious breakfast in the hotel lounge before leaving, but even while revelling in the softness of those cushioned chairs, I could not help pitying all the poor misguided tourists from the very bottom of my heart!

My second day in the desert was even better than the first. We had coffee with a Beduin Sheikh – Ghassan of the Rualla was the name, I think. It was impressive: and might have been 4,000 years ago. I don't know what they made of us, but it all became very friendly before we left. The last we saw were the tall figures standing with an indescribable grace on the short desert grass. It alone was worth three years' Arabic: like looking through a window on to a life completely unknown, and strange and beautiful from its fitness: an immense sense, too, of space and freedom. It was a shock later in the day, when we had rounded the lake and were running at a fine pace over the hard sandy earth, to see another car and be told it was the son of the Sheikh Nuri Shaalan returning to his tribe.

Lebanon is delicious now and I am warm. I am busy trying to get fat again.

Your loving

FREYA

VENETIA BUDDICOM

Brumana
20 April 1928

Dearest Venetia,

Joy to get your letter. I can't tell you how I long for May 1st.

I had two days in the desert: only the fringe of course, but yet it was freedom, limitless more than the sea, for you felt no shore to it. Oh, indescribable. I saw a Beduin waving to his horse and the creature come to him from quite a distance, galloping, a beautiful sight. If you wave your sleeve (they wear very long trailing ones), it is a sign of friendship: this man made us the signal, a draped figure standing in that loneliness as our car jolted over the rough ground. We found a Roman fort, nothing of it left but walls, still square and sharp, the waste lands round it. Behind us and already out of sight ran the last eastern road, old as the Druids and trodden always by people on the watch: no peaceful harvests or leisurely strolling there. We ate our food with little clouds of Roman sand blown off the hewn stones, and thought of the fragility of things.   Your loving

FREYA

FLORA STARK   Brumana
30 April 1928

Darling B.,

After lasting for nine days the sirocco has gone, and I had a long walk on Friday in a soft damp mist which seemed all out of place in this landscape. It made the flowers look very bright and I found quantities – dog rose and hawthorn, cystus and orchids, and many strange ones.

It is high time I left. I had a delightful Sunday out with Mr. Edmunds yesterday, but we counted that it was the fourth spent in some reprehensible way that meant absence from Church! Mr. Fox dares not remonstrate for he leans on Mr. E. for the whole management of his school, but it must be a strain.

We found a lovely walk. Took the car to where the road cuts the valley and stream and then followed up the water – a gentle stream with pools and ripples, and the valley wide and like a cup for sunlight, coming down in pine ridges, range upon range, with something of a park about it, and something Arcadian. One went on and on round each corner, impossible to stop. We found a little side valley for lunch, and made salad and cooked the coffee, and then strolled down to the river to wash up and sat and looked at the water, which is always the most entrancing occupation in the world; and then found patches of cool pine-tree shadow to fall asleep in (I did anyway); and then made tea, and found we could not reach our car again till forty minutes after time and could only just manage to be home in decent time for supper. It was the most beautiful valley I have yet seen here; so remote, and yet friendly, for there was an old bridge, half ruined, and vines and olives here and there, and just a house or two – exactly like the old romances. It was a happy day altogether.

Your own

FREYA

Brumana
3 May 1928
Darling B.,

Venetia is here, looking very thin but pretty. It is good to have her. We shall be leaving the day after tomorrow, and wandering, and only know that we must reach Jerusalem by May 20th. I hope for letters there.

Crowds of people coming to say good-bye. I feel it hard to believe that in two days' time Brumana will be in the past.   Love to you from

FREYA

ROBERT STARK   Hotel Palmyra, Baalbek
5 May 1928
Dearest Pips,

It seems strange to be writing from anywhere but Brumana after all this time. One feels, when one goes away without thinking of returning, as if what one leaves were suddenly being shut out of the world, and it seems strange to think that really it is all still existing – tea parties, gossip, heart burnings, politics, and the sunsets beautiful over Beirut, just as if I was still there to see. We left this morning in a car all to ourselves – after vainly inviting the two pleasant young men and successfully avoiding all the elderly ladies who wanted to come with us, and we had a hot drive down to the valley and up Lebanon through summer green and masses of lavender, cystus, rose and rhododendron; down the bare red side where the hills all go in streaky strata, and along the flat piece between the two ranges, Hermon out of sight and everything hazy and dusty and hot sun and cold air beneath it. And we came here and have a room with the ruins just opposite – big square blocks and six immense grand columns against a ridge of snow and hill. We are going after tea to look: one should take one's ruins carefully in small doses between meals.

It is quite different seeing things from a hotel: they become just objects at once, instead of being all part of the *Arabian Nights*. But it is only till Wednesday – for I do believe the adventure will come off and we are going among the Druses. Our beds and kitchen and Najm the Druse and his son, and one mule and two donkeys are to meet us Tuesday morning in Damascus, and we hope to go out by the west on Wednesday morning into the wilderness, early and as inconspicuously as possible in case the French think us dangerous and stop us. We have one letter of introduction and two guns (Najm and son) with 100 cartridges – only for quails I hope. We have to buy a water skin, as all the water is bad there, and presents instead of money to pay for hospitality.

We were up early this morning, managed to shake off the guides, and had a good time among the ruins: we found sunny corners, and sat there to meditate, watching the lovely colour of the old stone, tawny and red and black, exactly like the hills behind it.

There is a wonderful sweep of Lebanon to the north, one immense ridge with zebra streaks of snow, and there was a long curly dragon of cloud lying on it throwing a deep blue shadow, then the red country rolling down to where the Baalbek oasis begins – for it is an oasis of trees in the shaven landscape – poplars and fruit trees and corn, all brilliant green. One can still see how one came up to the great temple, through courts and porticos with niches (in Adam's style) and wonderful steps cut out of solid blocks, six or seven to each block. Not as good as the Acropolis, not so fine; a little more lavish decoration, just the difference between Greece and Rome: all immensely massive, and the guidebook says that the three biggest blocks of the west wall are the largest ever used in architecture. There is one beautiful square door, immensely high: this temple is nearly perfect too, all but the roof, and there the little hawks were flying with very sweet shrill little cries and the black outlines of feathers clear round their white bodies – or they looked white against the sky. Swallows, and hawks, and lizards, and little figures of tourists clambering – all small busy lives running about these immense ruins which seemed to belong much more to the land than to anything human in it, as if the worship of Baal, and then Helios, and then Jupiter, and then Theodosius's temple, and then the Moslem walls, were all inherent secrets which had flowered one after the other in that wilderness of broken stones.

We left after lunch against a strong west wind, the plain and hills all colours under the sun and clouds, and came spinning along the lonely Damascus road, nothing in sight for a long while till we saw two fair-sized beasts and one tiny donkey, the smallest you can think of, trotting behind on his neat little feet. When we got there we saw Najm and his boy with our luggage under them, already looking perfectly oriental. We waved and felt much exhilarated, though how that poor little mite of a donkey is to trot along with the others I don't know: and I shall have to be the one to ride him.

In the hotel at Baalbek we met Miss Newton, who is a great Arabist and to whom I had an introduction. She was very discouraging and said we shall most certainly be turned back by the French, though I can't believe they would be so inane as not to see our innocence. I wish I could make you see it all, the colour and the wonderful light and all the strangeness of it. I am getting to love these huge empty landscapes where you seem to live with the sky as much as if you were at sea.

Your own

FREYA

FLORA STARK

Damascus
7 May 1928

Darling B.,

Only a note, for I am so tired after a chaos of a day, and we are off, or hope to be, at six tomorrow morning.

I went shopping all the morning, for food and lanterns and useful things. Then a wearing time after lunch, with Najm, bargaining over saddlebags and presents suitable for Druses. Such a funny mixture: four razors, five pocket-knives, four pieces of white cambric for the gentlemen's heads and the same for the ladies, five mirrors, one pair of scissors, reels of cotton, needles, buttons, and five small rubber balls with landscapes on them for the children; besides a box of Damascus sweets for the chief to whom I have a letter. Najm bargains with a look of innocence. He has nice brown eyes with flecks in them like the skin of a trout, and a good martial moustache. His profile, when his headgear with all its tassels, etc., is on and his rifle slung behind him, is quite fine, except that his figure is skimpy and he wears yellow boots. Najm's rifle is kept among my underclothes at present: I discovered it there when I went to look at things in the khan. What a magnificent feeling it is to go and see one's beasts feeding in the khan among the sheep and camels and muleteers and drivers! One needs a microscope to find my donkey, but there it is with new gilt stirrups.

Tomorrow is all before us. We are going to meet our equipage outside the town so as not to hit the policeman in the eye. They say the Jebel Druse is closed country.

Your own

FREYA

ROBERT STARK

Jerusalem
22 May 1928

Dearest Pips,

It has been such a time, twelve days, and we have crowded it with every sort of adventure except being taken prisoners. We got taken for spies by French Intelligence and discovered that Jebel Druse is under martial law; we spent two days as guests of the Druse High Priest; we assisted at a Druse wedding in the Leja, the very wildest part of their country; we had escorts of Druse cavalry yelling war songs round us, and we rode on their peaked embroidered saddles, and visited Beduin who danced their wild native dances to amuse us. We visited one of the rebel chiefs, just returned from exile and camped in his large Beduin tent with him and his family beside their ruined village. We then went east to the last citadel before the desert, Salhad, and heard the news of the raid the night before, a few hours' ride away, with twelve Beduin and thirty-two Druse killed. We learned how to sit for meals round their basket-work mats and dip our bread as a lady into the common dish; we saw most wonderful ruins. We think we know now something of desert hardships, riding in dazzling light over the stony waste lands, without refuge from the sun: when the wind came off those stony slopes it was like the opening of an oven door. There were lots of birds, eagles, and larks, swallows in the houses flitting in and out; also gigantic green and yellow frogs in the great tanks near villages.

The sight of a living stream came to us as sweetly as music after our wandering. There is a stony wilderness south-east of Damascus: the Black Mountains, the Hills of Brass, their very names tell you how grim they are. The river Pharpar flows there, but after that you come on practically no water except the village tanks which the Romans built and which still feed the inhabitants with yellow water out of their depths of black hard stone. The life is grim too. The people come down from the rocky plateau of lava where the villages stand – solid rock about thirty feet above the plain, on whose dismal edge nothing grows at all – and they sow the stony plain, and hope for rain. This year no rain has come, or little, and the harvest is practically withered: we went through a dead land and saw the people pulling up the yellow wheat which had turned to straw long before it could ripen. They have no doctor: when they fall ill they die, but they do not often fall ill, and look very handsome and strong: fine fighters. Now there is a lull – the whole country is policed under French martial law – but normally the Arabs raid from the desert and every village has its posts where guards are set to give warning of approaching Beduin. Even as we rode along the eastern fringe we had a curious feeling that it was the very edge of settled law: and our guide was careful to be very ready with a greeting for all we met on the road. 'Peace be upon you.' 'And upon you be peace.' The men have fine straight looks and ride finely, their headcloths wrapped round like helmets covering mouth and nose from the heat; their old tattered cloaks falling magnificently round them. When life is so precarious, and held by one's own virtue always, there is great dignity with it. Their manners as hosts were perfect, rich and poor alike.

171

We had no real danger till we left our donkeys and drove through Transjordan down here with the most incompetent chauffeur imaginable: just stopped him in time on the edge of a ravine near Jordan – he was tilting us over into it in the dark, having mislaid the road.

Shall be in Asolo in three weeks' time.

Your own
FREYA

FLORA STARK Jerusalem
25 May 1928

Dearest B.,

We shall both be rather glad to leave Jerusalem tomorrow. What with packing, mending, finding our luggage, getting money, etc., we are being reduced to the harassed state of mind of the ordinary tourist.

We had a pleasant time for tea this afternoon, going to call on the Bentwichs. He is legal adviser here, and they were both agreeable, and told us that we might have been murdered any time on our trip – which is always pleasant to hear . . . afterwards.

My mind now turns to things like clothes! I am not sure I ought not to spend the day shopping in Venice when I arrive. *A hat* is indispensable: also I rather think shoes; and a parasol.

Love to dear Herbert: tell him I am longing for badminton.

Your own
FREYA

ROBERT STARK S.S. *Palacky*, steaming up the Adriatic
7 June 1928

Dearest Pips,

It hardly seems believable that I shall be in Venice tomorrow, and my Grand Tour over and done – and except for a certain thinness and insatiable appetite due to starvation in Damascus and J. Druse, no bad effects are visible. I rather enjoyed Cairo: things like public gardens with well kept grass and tidy flowers were very restful, and trees along the boulevards, and tarred roads and beautiful shops. Venetia had only three weeks of the unadulterated East, but after five months the charms of civilisation are extraordinarily charming. The Pyramids leave everything else in shade in the matter of mere massiveness. They are so massive in fact that one can only think of them as one would of hills not built by men, and climbing up was very like the last rocky ledges of some Alp, the yellow desert ridges stretching away like lesser peaks from Matterhorn or Rosa. I think too that it was more dangerous to me than many another climb, for my muscle has not come back after the dysentery, and it is a good climb to the top, 410 feet and over, and the steps high: the wind blowing, too, strong from the desert, and the desert itself a loveliness of colour, as if a rosy fire were burning inside it. We climbed down in the twilight, then waited till the moon came up and wandered out among the huge straight slopes, and sat and looked at the Sphinx with her great lion paws that seem too big and give an extraordinary animal feeling to her. There is a sense of vigilance, of repressed motion, about her: in the moonlight now and then the shadow on her neck seemed to move, and if it had really done so I should hardly have been surprised. And as she is exactly the same colour, built of the actual desert, she seemed its very embodiment. All the miserable traffic of tourists, and donkeys, and guides cannot spoil all this: and somehow it seemed merely suitable that eight or nine of them should fall off the Pyramid and get killed every year: an offering in the old style.

There is one lovely mosque* in Cairo, a square thing with four high pointed arches round a court, immensely high, and the interior decorated with very simple slabs of coloured marbles, pale greens and white and black and yellow with little beadings of gold. We didn't think much of native Cairo, after our life in the real East, but we did have a good afternoon the first day of the feast going to the Cemeteries with the whole population, male and female, women in black on carts, crowds of children, with palm leaves, camping apparatus, tea baskets or the equivalent, all going to sit in the family tombs. The Cemetery is a town of narrow streets with small square domed houses each containing its tomb or more of them, and it was a curious mixture of cheerfulness with the natural loneliness of its uninhabited streets. We went to see the Sultans' tombs, all shut up together with the 360 (if that is the number) Mamelukes whom Mohammed Ali first murdered and then politely buried in his own Mausoleum.

Corfu was lovely in itself – an immense bay with Epirus over against it: visions of blue hills in every gradation of distance – and we drove through Venetian olive woods planted by the Republic three centuries ago, to the Austrian Empress's villa, a pseudo-Grecian mid-Victorian atrocity spoiling one of the loveliest places in the world. We smelt green growing grass for the first time again for ages, and good it was.

We have very dull people on board – and I am now longing to reach Asolo and just sit quietly and think for a while.

Your own

FREYA

* Of Hassan.

Asolo
23 June 1928

Dearest V.,

I am still dreadfully sickish – can't think why. It is having a depressingly stodgy effect on my literary style.

I do wish I could discover the statistics of military and civil expenditure in J. Druse these years: the budget in fact.

Just had a note from Mr. E. in Brumana. He says we have left 'a trail of surmises and not a little dust.'

Your loving

FREYA

ROBERT STARK Asolo
2 July 1928

Dearest Pips,

The easiest for me, if it will suit you, is to leave in October and stay over Xmas with you. Will that be all right for you? And don't you think I could manage without having a room built? I could do with a sofa bed in the sitting room or kitchen.

We shall go down to L'Arma in August and I hope have the children for a longish spell.

Asolo is hot now. Very nice for sitting in the garden, but one gets awfully slack. I have been busy writing an article on French politics in the J. Druse, but I think it is far too truthful for publication. They are all so terrified of hurting the French feelings, though everyone out there knows what a mess they are making of things.

Your own

FREYA

ROBERT STARK Dronero
29 July 1928

Dearest Pips,

I came here yesterday after a very strenuous time in Asolo trying to get everything ready and also taking a three days' tour through the Dolomites. It was Herbert's treat, and we motored up to Cortina, and thence to Lago Misurina: and then we motored back over four passes, Falzarego, Pordoi, Karersee, and Rolle, to S. Martino di Castrozza and down by the Brenta to Bassano. I had a prejudice against the Dolomites after that miserable summer trying to convalesce at S. Vito, and was glad to get rid of it by seeing them in their full glory.

It is dreadfully sad to me to come to Dronero – it seems so lonely : but nice to see the infants. They don't leave one a moment's peace in the day.

I shall get to you some time in the last fortnight of October, and bring all my warmest clothes. It will be lovely to see you dearest Pips. I feel as if I am always being pulled in all directions with everyone scattered over the earth.

Your own

FREYA

ROBERT STARK L'Arma
25 August 1928

Dearest Pips,

I shall sail by the *Athenia* from Glasgow to Quebec, leaving October 19th. I don't know exactly when I arrive, but I suppose about the end of the month. I have a Tourist third class ticket and second class on the railway. What do I do if I am stuck for a day at Quebec or Montreal? Is there any particular hotel or have you any friends there? I am quite nervous at the thought of the long journey.

Your letter of end of July has just come and it is nice to think of my room being got ready. I shall be with you over New Year, and it will be lovely to have a Xmas together again at last.

Your own

FREYA

ROBERT STARK L'Arma
4 September 1928

Dearest Pips,

I have most thrilling news for you. A long article on French politics in Syria which I wrote in Asolo has been taken by *The Cornhill* – so you will actually see your daughter's words in print. Not only, but it has elicited a charming letter from the Editor.

Your own

FREYA

MR. EDMUNDS [a disciple of Rudolph Steiner] L'Arma
7 September 1928

Dear Mr. Edmunds,

I am very grateful for your letter – more than I can say by just saying thank you. It is what can be most helpful. I shall try and answer as well as I can. It is difficult for me to get things put into words unless they deal with images of people or objects.

175

That I have confidence in you is very certain. I would not otherwise have told you about these problems at all – which so far I had kept to myself. I don't think I am unreasonable enough to dislike a theory because of the person who holds it: but I know that I accept ideas more easily if they come from people I like. I mean that I know, quite independently of you or anyone else, that your way is in the direction in which I want to go. If the fact of your being a friend makes it a little easier to follow, is there any harm? I suppose you mean that one should not take one's ideas ready-made from anyone? I think I would never do that, for on the whole I respect ideas more than people: but when it is connected with a person, it becomes much more valid to me, and easier in that way. Even when I read a book, it is usually with the thought of someone who would enjoy it also.

I agree most completely with all you say about the goal to make for; I have long felt that there is a Purpose for us, and that if one could know it, recognise it I mean and be convinced, the whole of life would fall into a proper proportion and would become independent of circumstances. So far I have felt that the other plane is there and that our greater teachers have lived in it. But the roads they went seemed to me not our roads – or at any rate not for most of us, because it meant shutting oneself practically out of life. There must be a way, not of renouncing, but of accepting the world and transmitting it to its greater possibilities. I don't think I could renounce this beautiful world: I love it all, from the frills on my tea gown to the Alps, and I love everything that is living on it, just because it is alive. I feel it is part of me too. One cannot say all this is vanity and scrap it. There must be a way of *interpreting* it all. I think you can. If you can I shall be very deeply grateful. I explain myself so badly. It is not the goal I am in doubt about: it is the way of getting there – as if our life were the pebble which is to be turned to gold. We have it in our hand and we know what we want to make of it: it is the instrument, the alchemist's recipe, that is missing. To get control of one's will and thought and feelings seems the proper – indeed the only way: to become conscious, in fact. If you start me on the exercises I will try what I can do and tell you.

FREYA STARK

P.S. I had just been thinking about what you said of the Syrians not being able to appreciate the poetry of the North – I don't see what there is in a poem like Shelley's 'Skylark' or 'Kubla Khan' that they could not grasp? Not to speak of battle pieces. If you ask your advanced boys to compare some of their old poems say with the description of Flodden in *Marmion*, or

176

of the fight in 'Sohrab and Rustum', it would be most interesting to hear the result. It would be rather fun to hand over an English anthology and see what the boys prefer.

FLORA STARK   Dronero
                                                            19 September 1928

Dearest B.,

I have just got your letter and must answer at once, for there are two things I really need to make clear. One is that I do not grouse in the sense of worrying over the past, *except as regards the future*: I should not have bothered to mention that the business with Mario ought to have been settled this year, except that I am anxious not to find it going on next. I think I have settled the business for I saw to it that he went to S. Remo (which he had no idea of doing, now or ever) – but otherwise I knew that unless I spoke strongly the matter would be just where it was when I left.

The second point is that one can't change one's nature 'entirely', you say. One can hardly change it *at all,* and not without a degree of ruthless honesty which is most exceptional. So that the best thing to do is to see that one's life runs so that one's nature does good and not harm, don't you think? In other words, it is infinitely preferable that you should make scarves which you do well and enjoy doing rather than do housework and p.g.'s which you dislike and consequently do remarkably badly. What one does badly is no good to anyone. It seems to me that what you have to do is arrange things as pleasantly as you can in Asolo, see that your own job (of Mario) finally stops being a source of misery all round, see if possible that next summer is organised, well beforehand, so as to leave you more freedom than this year and allow a little holiday for us all: and then you will have done your own job quite nicely. And if I could know that you were doing your own jobs well, I could really face my own lot with a far larger share of strength.

The children are still a problem. I don't quite know what will happen but can do very little about it. Mario of course wants me to stay here; but then I feel I should be doing just as you if you took housekeeping at L'Arma: I should be forcing myself and so lose all usefulness really. And it is children and not grownups that they need. They are all well and jolly. Please do not waste emotion, canalise it to whatever your object may be in the future. You have the luck to be doing the work you like. It is not basking in the sun, and still it is a *great luck* and worth sticking to. I have not yet got it, for I have to do all the jobs I don't like in between and shall not reach my own work until I am about forty : I do, however, hope to reach it eventually, if there is anything of me left.

Ever so much love dear B.,

Your
FREYA

FLORA STARK   Bellegarde
                                                          27 September 1928
Dearest B.,

I was sorry to leave the children and particularly troubled about Bébé. She *must* go to school, or she will be quite quite spoilt and nothing later will ever be able to make up for it. I have spoken out to Mario as strongly as I could and shall write again. Perhaps you can do something when you go. I suggested Switzerland, if he wants languages and does not like nuns, and you *might* be able to carry the matter through and take her yourself after Xmas for the winter term? I will gladly find the money for the journey for a matter so important.

It is lovely being here in the grey northern light again – a nice damp morning, smelling quite different from the other side of the Alps.

FREYA

HERBERT YOUNG   Glasgow
                                                          18 October 1928
My dearest Herbert,

I must send a little scribble on my last day in Europe, if only because I have delayed so long. I have been trotting like the donkey with the hay tied to the pole in front of it, never catching up. Now everything – except my correspondence – seems finished, and yesterday we took my trunk down through the tunnel under the Clyde and up the other side to where the *Athenia* lay. She looks huge, and they say is not at all crowded.

I have lots of books, the *Odyssey* among others, and a charming book – the letters from an Austrian Ambassador to Constantinople in 1550 (Busbecq).

Ever so much love dearest Herbert. I am always thinking of you, even when letter writing gets submerged.

Your loving
FREYA

T.S.S. *Athenia*
                                                        26 October 1928

Dearest B.,

Tomorrow we shall be crossing the Straits of Belle Isle and a blessed thing
it will be to see anything in the way of land at all. The Atlantic really is an
objectionable ocean: 'How shall I meet thee? With Silence and Tears' in
February. Everyone practically has been ill; we had two blizzards, one
decent morning with a rainbow, and the rest damp rain. Now it looks like
fog for the St. Lawrence.

The third accommodation is perfectly comfortable and the stewards most
kind and obliging. The only real advantage in first class is the people; the
effort at pretending to love your fellow creatures for nine days when the
boat rolls about and they are all so dull and with so many babies, and one
feels so uncongenial. They are all good – Scotch of the very petite
bourgeoisie – city folk, with lots of virtues, only not trimmed up.

There is a cold air coming off Labrador, but not so bad as Syria. The sea
is grey, exactly the colour of the sea gulls with the white under their wings.
They are still following us – lovely creatures. I have the joy of the *Odyssey*:
it made me forget even the roll of the waves, such is the triumph of beautiful
words. It is a revelation – to think that I reached thirty-five without reading
it.

The orchestra is on its first sea voyage, with the result that when not overpowered by its sensations, it plays the same three tunes over and over: we
always clap.

I think of dear Asolo and you both.

                                                        Your own
                                                        FREYA

T.S.S. *Athenia*
                                                        28 October 1928

Darling B.,

We are in Quebec. The ship standing most harmoniously still. The sunset
up the St. Lawrence last night was very grand, the blue sheet of water
rushing down in a cold clear light. For a long way only one coast was
visible: the right bank, all very bare and simple lines, and here and there
sparse villages and pointed spires. On the other side, there was a cold
rippling sea, and a green and pink sky, very cold, and the air cold and thin
from Labrador, with the taste of ice in it and crisp and exciting: it was so
clear even the little waves seemed chipped out and frozen in little sharp

ridges. Then we had a round moon in the middle of the smoke-trail of our funnel, and an evening star over New Brunswick.

Quebec has not shown herself till just now in the dusk – strings and clusters of lights and spires here and there piled up in the grey of the water and the evening. We came up to her through thin rain and sleet, and it was too miserable to want to see anything at all.

Thankful the voyage is over.

Your own
FREYA

HERBERT YOUNG
Creston
4 November 1928

Dearest Herbert,

I was glad to arrive, with a vile cold produced by the meeting of hot radiator air and the icy current off the window panes – but now I have had two nights' rest and am spending a lazy day indoors with the big stove going, and two puppy dogs lying about like woolly mats, Pips' gun in the corner by the door, and all the genuine atmosphere of the Wild West – except that I haven't got to cook the dinner. It is a cosy little log hut, four rooms and a veranda, and we look downhill to the roofs of the barns and stable, and little three-roomed hut where Tom and Alice now sleep – all cedar-wood slats, very neat in the landscape – and then across a low undulation of cleared land, brown and yellow stubbles, with patches of forest here and there, to the wide valley: they call it the 'Flats' and the mist lies there in the evening, and the Selkirk range comes out of it steeply, with the sunset straight behind it, for we face due west. There is a little powdering of snow fallen last night on the tops, and a filmy grey sky drifting over the blue, and smoke from various fires going up in long streamers. Pips himself came to meet me at the station: he is very stiff and cannot raise his arms much, but he can walk quite well, and it was lovely to see him, looking as if all these years he had been busily growing more and more a bit of the landscape; at a few yards distance his dear old clothes would just melt into it invisibly. He has a few books (nearly all I sent at various times) and a gramophone, a bath, a stove, and some Chippendale chairs he picked up from a man who was leaving, and a geranium in a tin on the window; and these are all the luxuries – except the telephone, which seems very out of the picture, but is indispensable.

The village is hidden behind the hill and has two shops. There are seven or eight neighbouring ranches visible from our window, and nearly every one belongs to a different nationality – Swede, French, German, English – they are all mixed, and Nature is such a big enemy that all the rest become insignificant.

There is really no means of describing the immensity of this great lovely country. This is comparatively inhabited, and Montreal is a very fine city, with handsome buildings. It is all beautifully organised so as to rest the jaded city-mind and avoid unnecessary trouble. Then your train starts and soon you are out in the endless flat stretches of woods and lakes, solitary as anything you can imagine. The train slips along for two days, and it is always the same: the long stretches of water where the ice is now forming at the edge: the thick pines and white birches, and here and there a sandy road with perhaps two lonely little square boxes of three or four rooms, or some shanty by the water's edge with a canoe drawn up for the winter. People get lost in these woods and can never find the way out again. They go to shoot moose, or fish in the lakes. The monotony of it adds extraordinarily to the sense of remoteness and of the valiancy of men's effort who live here and make the land habitable.

After these two days we reached Winnipeg and the prairie, and came through what might have been a desert sunset over the rolling yellow stubble land. Here there is never a tree: it seems they can hardly live through the gales that sweep from the north and east. The towns are springing up like mushrooms, and more hideous than one can easily imagine: and the people seem a hard prosperous lot, with a dollar-lined smugness beginning to spread itself over the rugged pioneering virtues. While they are fighting to tear a living out of the unknown, these people have something very attractive, free and self-reliant and keen: but when it gets money and comfort, it is not so pleasant any longer.

Your loving
FREYA

FLORA STARK   Creston
                                                              9 November 1928
Dearest B.,

I am depressed, for Pips refuses to think of anyone else to help. It is a hopeless position. Will see what the doctor can do: he is away now, and ill himself.

Going to a dance this evening. It is all very like Bret Harte.

Your own
FREYA

Creston

30 November 1928

Dearest B.,

Your letter came just as I was leaving for Nelson, which is our only comparatively near city (six hours by train and boat). I spent a night in the hotel there, and last night on the boat, and am now, just after breakfast, steaming back along the lake, the hilltops hidden in the cold snowy mists, and one lonely wooded snowy promontory after the other unwinding slowly. The landing stages are little wooden platforms floating in a framework of great poles, like huge bunches of asparagus half out of the water: as the snows melt and the lake rises, the platform rises too till it reaches the top almost of the poles. The steamer is one of those shallow draught paddle boats that they adopted for the Tigris during the war: it can lie right in with its snout on the beach like a crocodile and back out again into the deep water.

I went to Nelson to become acquainted with Pips' lawyer Mr. Garland, and found him a charming Cornishman, most friendly and amiable and with a mind of his own. His wife came to the hotel, took me out to tea (to the Church bazaar) and then home with her to dinner. So pleasant to have a starched tablecloth and silver and such trappings of civilisation.

I was glad to hear prospects of L'Arma sale – for I shall need money badly if I have to come out to Pips at frequent intervals: and this will be inevitable. Thank goodness I foresaw it in time and managed to get at least partially ready for the emergency, for he of course can do nothing in the matter or in the way of finance: in fact I very much doubt if he will be able to suffice for himself later on: however, sufficient for the day.

I am trying to write another Druse article, but not getting on very fast. Pips has no particular occupation indoors, which is fatal for any concentration in our little sitting-room. Also there is always some ancient rancher or other dropping in. Indeed there is none of the buoyancy of prosperity in Creston: everyone is hard up and a little wistful. The energy and *joie de vivre* of the young country seems only to flourish in the towns. The country seems to rise on stepping stones, not of its dead selves, but of its dead pioneers, and the first lot who do the clearing and the real hard work seem usually to succumb: then their successors get on.

Your own

FREYA

Creston

3 December 1928

Dearest Herbert,

This is exactly timed by your letter and Mama's, so that it *should* arrive on Xmas Day. We shall be thinking of you, and wishing for that magic carpet — at least I shall — for though I like the interest and excitement of a new and empty country, I do feel myself *European* to the very bottom of my heart: or at any rate I feel that I belong to the Old World — partly because of the climate of the New, which is twenty-two below freezing this morning, and twenty-six below zero just a little east of us. Yesterday I came home just about supper time with the big planet of the moment (whatever it may be) shining like a bonfire over the western range, and a cold green sky: the road hard with wide frozen ruts of solid ice: and it was so cold that I had no sensations at all below the knees.

I am so depressed, having tried to write a second article — which has been born as flat as a pancake: which just shows that I am not really meant by Destiny for an author.

A long kiss to you.

Your

FREYA

Creston

14 December 1928

My dearest Herbert,

It is very kind to write, for one does feel *very* far away out here, partly because, with the exception of Pips, there is absolutely no one with whom to talk of anything but apples — except Canadian politics, which seem to be rather messy.

I must describe a dance in the Wild West to you. It is really rather fun. Imagine a cold clear night, Orion swinging up over the pines: the mud frozen hard, and me with overshoes and a flashlight, all warm in furs except where an icy zone encircles my silk stockings, making my lonely way through the wood to the Parish Hall. It is not more than half a mile away, all built of pine planks and cedar, and already very cosy with a roaring stove and red paper streamers down the windows: two gasoline lamps buzzing from the ceiling, and the orchestra tuning up. Mrs. Lister, the wife of our provincial M.P., runs the orchestra; she has thin ankles, and a short white skirt, and striped blazer coat, and carries on with immense verve till any hour of the morning. The piano-player's husband is said to have swindled his uncle out of a coppermine just above us on the hill. And a fair young man with a blue shirt and intellectual forehead plays the banjo and also owns the garage here. We slowly began to collect, sitting ourselves in one long row. We all wear home-made dresses and pink stockings, and really look very pretty especially when the colour we bring in from the out-side has stopped interfering with what we so carefully applied before start-ing. The young men don't come up unless they happen to know you, so that your social status can be gauged by the darkness of the coat or the amount of polish which has been given to the shoes that come up to dance with you. No sitting and flirting in corners: it would be difficult anyway in a bare square room. I was then taken to sup with the orchestra and acted umpire while the drum and the lady pianist played dice with the sugar lumps. It was very like the proper Wild West out of the movies looking through the smoke and the gasoline lamps to the young women with their shingled curls and the young men in the tartan shirts. At two we broke up, and packed ourselves back into furs and galoshes and snowshoes. Some kind person offered to see me home, but they all have to get up early, so I resisted and came by myself through the snowy stillness of the pinewood – very lovely.

I manage to do my Arabic every day. Have also started shooting with a small rifle – great fun but not easy. It seems strange that half my time here is up.

Your

FREYA

FLORA STARK   Creston
16 December 1928

Dearest B.,

Pips is teaching me to draw – with no very marked success so far – but he makes me do a memory sketch every day and it is amusing. I can't do anything in the way of study because there is so much interruption all the time – also I have nearly come to the end of my books.

I am fairly all right, and Pips too – though with him one cannot tell: he is not strong at all, and yet not ill. I feel that I ought not really to leave him, but what can I do? Love to you dear B.

Your

FREYA

Creston
                                                          21 December 1928

My darling B.,

It was nice to get your little note two days ago and I was glad to hear that
L'Arma may really sell. It is very necessary, though of course I shall be sorry.
It has so many good memories, in spite of many difficulties.

The snow here has all melted, but it is freezing and I am going out skat-
ing again for the third time today. I sat down four times yesterday, but am
beginning to feel a little safer on my feet.

We have asked the only lonely man we know to share the goose on Xmas
Eve – he is deaf, but we play bridge after.

Yesterday we plucked five geese and the whole house swam in feathers.
Xmas is a hard time on one's domestic pets. The week before it was the
amiable pig – quite a shock to find half of him lying on the kitchen table
when I went to make tea, and the other half across the pantry by the bread
bin.

My drawing is getting on. I do my memory sketch every day and Pips
guarantees that a year of that will turn me into an expert sufficiently to jot
down all notes I require to make.

                                                          Your own
                                                          FREYA

Creston
                                                          Xmas Day 1928

Darling B.,

Your letter couldn't have hit it off better, for it came last night and was so
nice to get. The Arabic letter was from the landlady in Damascus, with a
warm invitation to me and my 'female parent' to spend the spring there. It
did make me feel quite homesick: in spite of all those discomforts, I think
of Damascus with more longing than any other place.

Do let me see all that comes out about Syria and the Near East. My
Oriente Moderno ought to come in and I hope you keep all the numbers
carefully for me, for I shall want to get *au courant* again as soon as I get
back.

                                                          Your
                                                          FREYA

Creston
                                                                Xmas Day 1928

Dearest Herbert,

All the snow has melted, or very nearly, and the landscape was brown except for the white places where the lakes and ponds had frozen, – and then this morning at about 1 a.m. it began to snow in big flakes, and I had to break the trail through the little wood to go to church this morning. Lucky I had my high rubber boots. The fir trees looked lovely with the fresh snow, all so silent. Now the wind is south again – they call it Chanook – and it is thawing.

Viva sent me a delightful book of Persian sketches, so I am well supplied now till I reach England again. And that is a stage towards Asolo, which I feel so homesick for.

Your

FREYA

FLORA STARK   Creston
                                                                1 January 1929

Darling B.,

I am not *at all* pleased with Mrs. Beach's Xmas present to you. My ticket is second class, and is just as comfortable as first, the only difference being that one has the disgusting rich instead of the decent poor and more to eat at meals (wasted on me). And it does go to my heart when I think that such a large sum would have bought a new frock or even a typewriter.

I am very sorry to hear of your continual colds. Can't you do anything to prevent them? If you are concerned for me, you will see to it that *you yourself* keep really fit and well. Don't think it is altruistic to neglect your own health – because *it isn't*.

I hope to hear of the children's Xmas, and that the parcels arrived in time. You never saw such a mail as comes to this place. Six men loaded up with sacks on Xmas Eve. It is rather pathetic and fine to see the trouble they all take over their Xmas.

To live here means a total absence of anything like intellectual life beyond what your own household provides; but it is no good lamenting this all the time, and makes the British very unpopular. A young man told me last night how much the Canadians appreciate it when people come from the old country and are not 'superior'.

Your own

FREYA

Creston
6 January 1929

Dearest Herbert,

I feel it quite hard to write, for I shall now be leaving in little over three weeks and it already seems as if the unsettled feeling of departure were beginning.

I am re-reading Gertrude Bell's *Syria*, and comparing her route with ours. She however travelled with three baggage mules, two tents, and three servants: so I consider we were the more adventurous. She also says that the water in the J. Druse 'is undrinkable by European standards', so I suppose our standard cannot be European: or perhaps an Italian education has hardened us?

Your loving

FREYA

FLORA STARK Creston
19 January 1929

Darling B.,

It is two below zero today, and my window is thick with ice in beautiful fern-like patterns. It simply curls up my poor insides, but otherwise is lovely because the sun is bright, and it is a blessed thing to see the sun.

I have said I will come out again next year in the summer, and Pips is beginning to talk about it and make plans, so I hope it may keep him happy meanwhile.

He took me out for a sleigh drive into the valley flats, a lovely day. We were ferried across the Kootenay, a narrow channel hacked out of the ice across the river, which is about 200 yards broad, with trees on either bank, and all now in a smooth expanse of snow with tracks of wild animals across. The ice was strong enough to carry a man, but most winters a team and wagon can drive across, though the stream is immensely deep and swift and the end of all if you go through. There are in fact quite a lot of ways in which you can come to sudden ends out here: and that is perhaps why most of the women never move from their households.

I am feeling dreadfully depressed about things in general. Leaving is bad, and staying also, and the whole thing seems a hopeless dilemma. Poor darling Pips I believe thinks it very heartless of me to be leaving at all.

Your own

FREYA

Creston
23 January 1929

Darling B.,

I skated yesterday, and my hanky froze stiff in my pocket whenever I blew my nose. You have to avoid touching metal for fear of sticking to it, and your breath freezes on your fur collar so that you feel as if you were in a spiny hedge of icicles: but this is *nothing* to the prairie.

I am busy seeing people – returning calls, etc . . . such a waste of time; with all this leisure I feel I should have done something but I just can't and it is hopeless. I don't think it is possible unless one can sometimes have some-one interested in the same sort of thing to talk to. It can't be helped. I may get to my own job sometime in my old age.

Well, I shall be back in Europe next month: it has gone strangely fast and pleasantly if it were not this feeling of all these chunks of life taken away from what my own life is.

Your own loving
FREYA

Canadian National Railways, Winnipeg
3 February 1929

Darling B.,

Here I am on the way home again, in the middle of the snowy prairie. Nearly thirty below zero, but it is so dry one does not feel it more than at Creston – only has to look out for one's ears and nose, etc. I feel I am quite lucky to have kept my nose. I felt it going rather queer and rubbed it hard in time, but Mr. Palfreyman the grocer had his ear frozen that day and says he came home with it drooping like a spaniel's ear.

It was rather miserable leaving. I hope all may be well till I return next year and possibly find Pips well enough to come back with me, though I rather doubt it. He came down to the station, and Mrs. and Miss Hamilton came, and the bank manager, and the Italian shoemaker with a bottle of rum wrapped in newspaper as a parting gift.

I had the train more or less to myself. One is nearly suffocated by heat in the trains, and frozen outside, and they are a wonderful sight, huge heavy engines and carriages, the lower part where the steam comes out all con-gealed in blocks of ice, and a long sort of beard of icicles all the way down dripping from the roofs so that they look like inventions for Xmas cards. They go along clanking a bell, to frighten away cattle I suppose; but it has a most lugubrious tolling sound. Your own

FREYA

ROBERT STARK   11 Grove End Rd.
                                                10 March 1929

Darling Pips,

I spent an agonising morning trying to listen to gramophone records with
fox trots going on all round, and finally sent you four in desperation and
hope they may be attractive when you get them by themselves.

You will be pleased to hear that I have just been vetted by two medicos
who pronounce me fit for ordinary life, whether in Canada or deserts or
whatever it may be. Rather satisfactory. I never told you, but I had the
gloomy prospect of an operation all winter and had really to hurry back for
that reason: but when they x-rayed more carefully, they discovered there is
nothing to operate, only some medical treatment to put up with. So that's all
right.

                                                Your own
                                                FREYA

ROBERT STARK   11 Grove End Road
                                                15 March 1929

Dearest Pips,

I really do think that you are the most robust member of the family after
all. All the infants down with 'flu, Mama ditto in Asolo, and Mario turned
out of his motor and damaged (but doing well considering). I am waiting to
hear whether I am to rush off to any bedside, and if so, which; or whether
to stay on here and let the doctors go on experimenting with my own
insides.

I have been busy at the B. Museum, looking up old Roman roads in
Transjordan; they had a line of forts far east of the present inhabited line. A
wonderful people: their trace seems to be everywhere. Last night I went
with Viva and H. van der Weyden to the Royal Geographical Society to
hear a man called Crawford who has been doing archaeology from the air.
We saw the photographs of Babylon, and Ur and Nineveh with all the plans
of the towns showing very clearly in faint straight lines. New York seems to
carry out the earliest principles of town planning: the idea of straight streets
at right angles seems the most ancient of all. It got untidy in the Middle
Ages. I think one might find an amusing connection between despotic
governments and neatly planned streets.

                                                Your own
                                                FREYA

Lighthouse End, Lowestoft
22 March 1929

Dearest B.,

Such a nice time here. Miss Doughty is delightful – full of energy, character, and fun, with the most charming smile, and an interest in all sorts of things. She lives all alone with a maid, and runs local politics. She is a magistrate and sitting on the bench now, after taking me to the fish market, which I enjoyed; looking at the yellow trawlers and the grey North Sea behind them, and the pretty brown backs of the fish slithering about the place.

Yesterday we drove out in a sea mist, which cleared before we reached the Doughty village of Theberton, the old house very deserted and lifeless among its park and trees: Italianate columns, bad taste but rather nice, speaking of leisure and comfort and the humanities, and the old church built of little flints (for this country has not stone) with a fine round tower, and the window to the young Doughty V.C. killed at Gallipoli. The family are all naval people, and Charles was heartbroken because his sight was not good enough for the Navy. Miss Doughty herself would make a splendid admiral: she has the clear sensible gaze and the long upper lip and square chin of so many sailor types.

Her housekeeping most casual and one of those vigorous people who are always warm without fires: and as this is the easternmost point of our island, I feel half frozen. But it is rather nice strong air all the same.

Darling Minnie has given me such a becoming hat, very simple with a beautiful seven guinea simplicity.

Your own
FREYA

Thornworthy
7 April 1929

Dearest Pips,

I have been having such lovely rides this week: one day round Batworthy Mire to Round Tor and back by Wild Tor and Watern. I wasn't attending, cantering along, and Whitesock the pony shied me off by a piece of bog – no harm but humiliating. Then another day by Grey Wethers and yesterday to Belever – and all lovely days with sun on the distance and the gorse just coming out.

I will tell you a piece of news – a secret. Another article accepted by *Cornhill*! Called 'Canada and the Odyssey' but you are not to tell anyone at Creston because I don't want my friends to feel they are turning into copy when they come to call. It is just a fancy sketch really more about the *Odyssey* than Canada, and I hope not too inaccurate as to the latter.

Your own

FREYA

FLORA STARK Thornworthy

12 April 1929

Dearest B.,

I have been thinking over an important matter and made a plan to suggest to you based on the assumption that Mario has been paying 1,000 lire monthly, and that they have been accumulating so that we should have about 10,000 lire by June. I thought we might manage to spend a little of this to pay half a year's schooling for Bébé? He might be induced to pay the other half, and then the great step of getting her started would have been made. I don't think we can ever do anything more truly useful for the child, and it is now and not later that the good can be done. Let me hear if you think this is all right and if so I could broach it. I will also try to get at least Bébé to come perhaps with me, or else to come to us in June to the Dolomites: I could pay for that for her.

Your

FREYA

ROBERT STARK Paris en route Dronero-Asolo

1 May 1929

Dearest Pips,

I left London rather worn out this morning, having had a perfect whirlwind of a week to get all done, including a little necessary reading in the British Museum: tea with my editor, Dr. Huxley, who was charming and talked of Alps; lunch with Ja'far Pasha and his wife who are giving me native introductions in Baghdad; then an interview with a lady who runs a thing called the National Political Union, which is trying to keep Palestine out of the hands of the Jews: it seems it is a question of the Dead Sea potash which will make whoever gets hold of it incredibly powerful; then all my shopping; toys for the kids etc. . . . and Herbert Olivier on the very last day getting me to translate letters about his roads to Ventimiglia engineers, which will certainly get him into troubles. This is only a selection.

I do hope to get out next year, if only to tell you all my winter adventures which promise so nicely. I only wish you could share them with me. But I still hope to lure you as far as Cyprus or Rhodes sometime.

I had great fun looking into old travels round Arabia, fifteenth to seventeenth century. Apparently a man called Pitt from Exeter got to Mecca in 1680 or thereabouts. But the first European to leave a record of it was a Bolognese, called Lodovico Varthema, and he enlisted with the Mamelukes and left a full description.

I spent my last pound on a prismatic compass – a lovely toy : I hope it may be useful. It shows the course by night too.

Your

FREYA

ROBERT STARK Villa Freia, Asolo
11 May 1929

Dearest Pips,

It was a great relief to unpack at last and I need make up no new boxes for some months to come. I got here on the 8th and Mama and Herbert came to Castelfranco to meet me, both looking very flourishing. It is too late of course for those Turkestan tulips, but I saw the last, the very last one, of your daffodils, a very fine yellow fellow.

I got four days with the children, and found them all well and happy, except that Angela really needs to be with her own age and I am anxious about her and only hope to be able to keep Mario to his promise of leaving her here for a month after her exam at the end of June.

The garden is full of nightingales : they woke me up, they were shouting at each other so loudly about four o'clock last morning.

I will send you a charming book about Kurdistan, if you can let me have it back again quite soon, for I shall need it in Mespot : but it is a very good one.

FREYA

ROBERT STARK Villa Freia
25 May 1929

Dearest Pips,

I myself am just now busy trying to turn my diary of Druses into a light sort of travel article : will see what happens.

I also have a good subject for the winter, if only it hasn't been exhaustively done already, and that is to combine a sort of history with travel notes to the fortresses of the Assassins, who were the followers of the Old Man of the Mountains, and had a series of castles between Aleppo and the Persian borders. I am very vague about it all, but am trying to find out some more before going out. It seems to me rather promising: although it may all have been done by some thoroughgoing German already.

Love from all here

FREYA

ROBERT STARK   Villa Freia
                                                   2 June 1929

Dearest Pips,

I have an amusing Arabic book – a traveller who wandered all over the place as far as India in the eighteenth century. He was in Damascus one day and saw a small servant boy carrying a plate and drop it, breaking it to smithereens. The poor little boy was very distressed, and a sympathetic crowd gathered: one of the men there told him to go to such and such a place, where a special charity was instituted to give a new piece of crockery for all the broken ones that were taken there: this was a special charity to benefit servants. I wish someone would do the same here.

Your
FREYA

ROBERT STARK   Villa Freia
                                                   22 June 1929

Dearest Pips,

We are up for a few days at S. Martino di Castrozza. There is a magnificent wall of lacy peaks on our east. I have been up the smallest of them, leaving at six and getting to the top at nine, after an hour on the rope up very nice spiky rocks. I felt all right after the first twenty minutes, when I seemed paralysed with pure terror and thought I was going to faint or be giddy: however I set my teeth and by concentrating on the slab in front of me gradually lost the unpleasant sensation that I and all the hillside were going to topple over together. I felt fine while up there, but rather upset ever since; so no more this year; but I think I must give the climbing another chance and go at it more gradually next year, before deciding that I am 'past' it. Alas!

Lots of flowers everywhere now. Fields of columbines, yellow and white lilies, and what looks like an orchid, with a big yellow bay and brown petals. The alpine rose and gentians just out too – and the air is lovely, only coming up from Asolo we shiver with cold.

At the top of this valley is the Passo di Rolle, and there are still the old trenches and shell holes. The whole place was blown to bits at the very beginning of the war, and has been rebuilt more hideous than you would believe possible.

Your

FREYA

ROBERT STARK   Villa Freia

30 June 1929

Dear Pips,

This government is getting beyond anything. Our sale of L'Arma hinges on some people living in France and the man doing the business cannot get a passport to go and consult with them because he happens to be anti-fascist. I don't think any other people would sit down under it. Apparently Toscanini has got into trouble with Mussolini because he got tired and refused to play the fascist anthem whenever a prominent fascist came into the Scala in the middle of his operas. I don't know how it will all end.

Am having lots of trouble trying to get Mario to pay. It seems rather hopeless, and makes one quite sick. He is a dreadfully dishonest little man, and I think he will end by being in serious difficulties all round.

I shall be leaving for Baghdad end of September, and hope to be able to make something out of it this time – if only I could write with more facility. Here, what with the bothers of Mario, and L'Arma, I cannot get a thing done.

Your own

FREYA

ROBERT STARK   Macugnaga

14 July 1929

Darling Pips,

The Kers wrote and asked me here, so I took it on way to L'Arma, an unexpected visit to the haunts of my youth. Five years ago was the last time and then I went up M. Rosa – which now seems an incredible feat looking at its immensity. It is lovely to see it all, and take little pottering walks in the meadows with Mrs. Ker, and see young Edwin Ker off for the real expeditions . . . but makes me feel quite elderly. Only I rather think, if I stayed long enough, I would be doing some little peak or spur, or at any rate trying.

Mario has bound himself to pay the yearly interest to you or Mama, and failing that, to fork out the capital: I have asked our own lawyer if this is all right, and he says it is safe. Of course it means that you lose the capital, but that we had agreed upon before and Mario can have it so long as he pays the interest. He tried hard to charge you with the taxes, and deduct them from what he has to pay Mama, but I told him very plain that he who has the capital pays the taxes, though we will do what we can to help him out of his difficulties. I have got him to pay up the arrears, but it has been altogether very trying.

Yesterday we motored down to Lake Orta – very hot, but lovely, and rowed in a boat with a yellow awning across to the island which looks just as if it had walked out of an eighteenth-century picture or one of the Paolo Veronese backgrounds. S. Giulio is the name, and the Santo apparently arrived there floating on his own cloak, and all the snakes and dragons came out to meet him : at least that is what we gathered from a *basso rilievo* in the church.

Your

FREYA

FLORA STARK Dronero
19 July 1929

Darling B.,

It was very sad leaving the peace of the valley and the dear Kers. They were so good to me. It was all too happy, and such a safe and peaceful atmosphere; one feels that they are just true and steadfast like the hills we were among. We had a great day going up to the Alp below P. Bianco and then down to Belvedere across the bit of glacier, and thought we could never get Mrs. Ker so far over loose boulders and things. But she stuck to it and we were out eleven hours and walking about nine – not bad for an elderly lady near seventy.

Your own

FREYA

CHARLES KER* L'Arma
14 August 1929

Dearest Mr. Ker,

You are a brick! But I don't think I ought to have any more presents (for the time being). Not school books, which one ought to buy out of one's pocket money. May I deal with that bookseller of yours? I am so pleased you were able to make him find the books for I shall now be able to think seriously of the Assassins, not on the way out but possibly on way home next spring. What fun. I think they must live somewhere north of Hama, all very rugged fine country, and a few of them still left, though not of the active sort.

Will you tell Mrs. Ker the latest story of 'the Housekeeper' [Mussolini]? His car broke down in a small town, and while it was mending, he strolled unrecognised into a cinema and saw himself making a speech on the screen. All the audience stood up to applaud, but he remained in his corner till the attendant came round and said to him, 'Look here, you probably think as I do about all this, but it'll be better for you if you stand up with the rest.'

Your loving
FREYA

* Brother of W.P.

CHARLES KER
L'Arma
August 1929

My dear Mr. Ker,

I was just sitting down to write thanks for snapshots, when the postman came with parcels, F. Walpole and the Koran. It is very dear of you. I have been sitting in ecstasy over the script and borders, a real joy to look at. They should bring anyone safe through any district of the eighteen different religious sects: one would only have to show them to melt the heart of a mussulman. I think Walpole will be useful, though rather discursive. I rather suspect he doesn't know very much about Assassins, but covers their country. I think the middle or so of the nineteenth century is the most amusing time for travel books – the world just accessible, and not too easy.

I have no duplicate snapshots, because the first lot has not arrived at all. We have never lost anything in the post here before, and I can only imagine that Macugnaga is too near the frontier for pictures. Our painter guest has just been seized by carabiniers and told he will have his tools confiscated if he paints outside the garden – except with special permit which takes a fortnight to get. I won't write all I think, as I don't want to end up in those little islands off Sicily – but . . .

Your loving
FREYA

ROBERT STARK
L'Arma
19 August 1929

Dearest Pips,

Much relieved to have news of you and no more violent happenings. I thought I would not cable, but ask you to cable me if by the time you get this you feel you would rather I came out this winter than next summer. I could

manage it either way you know, and I shall not settle my passage definitely
to Baghdad till the last week in September, and I do hope that if you think
it in any way better or nice for you, that you will cable me.

Your own

FREYA

Villa Freia

8 September 1929

ROBERT STARK

Dearest Pips,

Just heard about the Schneider Cup – and rather glad we have got it. The
papers here have been so horrid, what with Jews, and Snowden, that it will
be good for them to be beaten. I was listening to three young Italians at the
table next mine in Venice discussing what they will do with Palestine when
they get it, and felt so like butting in and saying that in that case the massacres won't be confined to Jews.

I have got my visa and found that I can get a berth on the 26th from
Trieste, and will wait till next week in case of news from you and then get it,
hoping you are all right.

Your own

FREYA

Villa Freia

12 September 1929

ROBERT STARK

Dearest Pips,

I had such a delightful dream the night before last. I thought that I had a
long long tramp to get to you, and when finally I arrived and found you
sitting at supper I strolled to the window and there to my surprise saw all
the coast of Menton below, with Villefranche and the Tête de Chien and all
in the distance. I was so pleased over this remarkable discovery, and the
thought that I could take a short cut and come up to you whenever I liked,
and I woke up with this delightful feeling and took quite a few seconds to
get my bearings again.

Your own

FREYA

Villa Freia

24 September 1929

ROBERT STARK

Dearest Pips,

It seems rather absurd that one can get to Baghdad for £20, and to Canada
for nothing less than £60. I think I could do Baghdad even cheaper, but have

been rather under the weather these two months and am going to take things easily and spend a fortnight at Brumana to recover from the sea (which always upsets me) and to be looked after by Miss Audi who is very good at that. I think all the domestic difficulties have really been too much this year and 'gone to my tummy', but I shall be fit again as soon as I get onto sour milk and no problems.

I have several introductions: the wife of King Faisal's Master of Ceremonies, the sister of the Minister in London, a Shi'ite Sheikh, and Mr. Philby who crossed from the Persian Gulf to the Red Sea and is the friend of the Wahabi King – and one or two more.

We had a lovely day yesterday going to Pordenone, taking the road along the Piave by Nervesa. The traces of war all gone, but the memory still there and a monument where the river was crossed in the final advance. I was in Pordenone and only remember it as a place where we got our first meal after two days in a frightful confusion of retreating troops. But yesterday we discovered a lovely winding street of old palaces with faded frescoes, and a palazzo municipale with two bronze men banging the clock bell; and a lovely Renaissance portal to the church. We had a wonderful sunset over the Piave coming home, sheets of red and yellow and a green sky under, and the hills clear like the teeth of a saw. I love that Friuli country, so fat and prosperous and contemplative. It must have been a sad blow to Austria when she lost those provinces.

We are putting up a stone table in the garden under the oleanders, in the hope of reconciling Herbert to meals out of doors in summer.

Must finish packing. I have looked out Gibbon for you as I thought it would be a good stand by for the winter. I don't know if you are as fond of him as I am. I have kept one vol. on the Crusades to read myself. Have also included my efforts in figure drawing.

Your own

FREYA

FLORA STARK SS Carnaro
29 September 1929

Darling B.,

I am looking at Mt. Helicon, rising up out of the Gulf of Corinth, topped with clouds and snow. The gulf is dark blue, slightly ruffled, and the long shapes of the hills red like rust or bracken, with shadows marking steep valleys or travelling clouds. All just as lovely as I remembered.

Three missionary ladies from Palestine are in my cabin, and lucky it was for me that they hit upon this boat or I should have beeen stranded quite alone among Germans and Zionist Jews (far the worst). I begin to wonder why the Arabs did so little to them. They are mostly from Central Europe, with sharp pinched faces and turn-up noses, and sit with their hats on at meals. Down below in the third class they sing their monotonous anthem, or dance in a circle three steps one way, one step back, with a grunting cry, evidently next cousin to the Arab dance. On the Friday night they had candles on their table, and altogether we feel submerged by the chosen people.

That dour old lady in the train who objected to my saddlebag being pushed at her like a battering ram turned out to be a charming woman, the mother of a Hungarian diplomat in Washington, and living in the country behind Trieste. She was interesting about things, and assured me that the Jewish massacre was financed by Italy. Anyway, from what these Palestine ladies say, there seems to be a great deal of work in this direction. I hope we keep the place long enough to make it independent of all the grabbers.

Love

FREYA

FLORA STARK

Brumana

5 October 1929

Darling B.,

I had an awful job getting off the boat. First, as we were landing off the little rowing boat, a wretched young Frenchman pushing by made me catch hold of the side, when another boat promptly came and crushed my finger which swelled up to twice its size in the twinkling of an eye: the young man was quite upset about it, but I didn't care about his feelings and kept my finger to myself in the most unsympathetic British way.

A native transport agency promise to take me and all the luggage to Baghdad for £9 'because they like me'. The English Company, the Nairn, charge £19 without baggage, and I can't think the difference can be worth £12. However I will tell you when I get there.

There is of course no doubt that first class is a more comfortable way of travelling. The *nice* young men travel first class it seems; we get nothing but curates and Jews. One of the nice ones got off at my hotel and came up to talk just before I left: he had beautiful eyelashes and a monocle and the manner of being bored with anything so trivial as life on this planet – but he turned out to be a soldier stationed at Mosul, was going all alone across the desert from Aleppo in his own car, and was quite learned in Arabic dialects: he hoped we might run across each other in Mesopotamia. This Grand Seigneur attitude to geography is truly Imperial.

I think I shall leave for Baghdad on the 25th. The desert journey sounds rather dreadfully fatiguing – so I shall be glad to get to a hotel where no one has to be spoken to amiably.

Your

FREYA

FLORA STARK   Brumana
                                                              7 October 1929

Dearest B.,

It is so lovely to be here; the very air and landscape seem just quivering with the joy of life, and I went to meeting this morning and was so delightfully greeted by everyone. Dr. Manasseh came yesterday and was much interested by my plan to ride to the source of the Adonis. I shall go and talk to Najm about an animal. Najm has gone up in the world, having inherited from his father and invested in a car, which he farms out and lives in idleness on the proceeds.

Miss Audi is devoting herself to try and get me fat before I get thin again in Baghdad, and her food is delicious. She has just lost her favourite cousin, so I came in the right moment to cheer her up a little in her lonely little house.

Your

FREYA

VENETIA BUDDICOM   Brumana
                                                              8 October 1929

Dearest Venetia,

It was like old times going to see Najm yesterday. I found his house in the middle of a crimson sunset on the other side of Brumana ridge, and three little girls playing about the doorstep. Najm himself was having a bath and soon appeared swathed in white and very cordial, and I had a great time hearing the news and all the complications that followed us. Najm had been back for some months trying to set up a shop in Suweida and saw all our friends – and *none* of them ever received a single photo. Isn't this too bad? I said I would write at once and ask you to send a new lot and I am meanwhile writing to Kanawàt and Resas to explain. Najm wrote to me twice, and of course I never received the letters.

I am going for a four days' trek across the hills to the source of the Stream of Adonis and then follow it down to the sea – will let you hear.

Dear love to you,

FREYA

Brumana
                                                    13 October 1929

Dearest B.,

I can't remember where I left off, or whether I told you I was taking Najm and a mule and going for four days up into the hills. Najm has turned gentleman now and refuses to look after mules, but came with me just out of friendship — an arrangement I cannot put up with for it means I never can get rid of him, and I do hate going round with an escort: Najm, and Majid the muleteer, with one of those plump flatnosed faces off the Phoenician tombs. He was quite nice, though arak and cards seemed his chief amusements. Then two mules and a donkey. I couldn't get a horse or a proper saddle, so just sat like a sack, and there are advantages in this method over these stony lands, for you can sit on either side or astride, or indeed anyhow, and get a rest. It was ten hours for three days with three hours' motor at the end, and I climbed Sannin (nearly 3,000 metres) in the interval — and not really the worse: in fact it was heavenly to get up into the high air, and among running water, and see little flowers, even though all the things we think of as nice harmless little plants seem to develop a thorn in this country.

I found Najm no good at all outside his own country, and became fortified in the conclusion that the only way of profitably travelling in the wilder lands is to settle in one place and get hold of someone who really *knows* the people you want to go among: Najm as a Druse among the Christians made me more of a stranger than I would have been all alone.

The first day we went up a valley I had partly explored last year — lovely through pine and fig trees all scented in the sun, up to the last of the tidy little red-roofed villages, then over a stony highland with the sea and the river — Dog River — and all its valleys spread below, till we got to the Khan Sannin. Two gentlemen in long overcoats and slippers welcomed us to a gramophone under the trees. We looked down to the sea, whose horizon seemed remarkably high as the sun dipped into it. Sannin is a terrific wall of a mountain, not rock, but all streaks of red stone and shale, and spread along like a great sleeping panther with long thin flanks. One climbs by going straight up — a dull grind, and not many flowers on the way — and then comes over the crest into a waste land of pits and hollows, and then up till Hermon and all the northern ranges are in sight beyond and below.

I rested in the afternoon — the climb had taken six hours. We started next morning over the shoulder of Sannin among stone sheets and tilled country, with a few peasants — because it is now the time for sowing: but it is very lonely up there. Luckily we met a man who told us to turn downward to look at what they call the Castle of Fakhra, or we should have missed it: imagine my joy when I found it to be an old Phoenician temple facing westward to the sea – and Beirut and the valleys – and leaning up against a labyrinth of those strange cleft rocks where an army might be invisible. I went in among them; you never saw anything so strange. There are thousands of narrow passages where the sunlight never reaches, and except by climbing up on to the open flat top of it, you would never get out of the labyrinth. I don't know what time the tower belongs to; it has arrow slits, and a little square pit in the middle which they call the Well of Blood, and narrow climbing steps mounting up round it in the passages.

I wasn't allowed to linger, as Najm *hates* ruins. We picked up the road again and went into what seemed the heart of desolation, a treeless land of shaly valleys full of thorns. The Nahr el Kelb here rushes out in two springs, the Spring of Milk and the Spring of Honey. I pictured green places with willows and grass, and was not prepared to find the first spring bursting out of this barrenness in a circle of grisly cliff spanned by a natural bridge of limestone.* There is something terrible and impressive in the place: an amphitheatre of sheer rock below and the arch of the bridge which seems to have been cut for the ancient gods to walk on.

We travelled some time in the barrenness, looking down on the Wadi Salih, the last tributary of the Nahr el Kelb, and as we turned a corner we saw a lovely sight: about 200 sheep and goats with their shepherds sitting camped about the Honey Spring which rushes from the ground in a real yellow mountain stream. It was lovely in that nakedness.

These shepherds are quite a different type from the flat-faced townspeople: they have fine profiles, burnt nearly black. I have an idea that the flat sort of faces always come from the sea board. They milked a sheep and brought me a foaming bowl and a copper bowl to drink from: we sat in a circle. Najm had brought a melon, which we cut and divided. I discovered a few sweets for the two little boys. The goats and sheep all made happy families, and the river rushed by out of the ground with all its voices.

We only rested half an hour, then went up a valley just as desolate though a stream ran through, and a few alders marked its course. It was beautiful, as all the bottom of the valley was terraced with young green corn, but the hills round were quite pitilessly grim. We found ourselves on the right side of the watershed, but with a weary way to go to Afka and had to creep all round the range of hills. Afka is the cave of Adonis, where people used to come in pilgrimage from the coast and hold strange rites in the groves around. We came suddenly round a corner upon it; the huge walls of the hills rounded into a bay, and the cave was opposite, a black hole in the immense wall: the place seemed to be shut in from every side. From where we stood the ground sloped down, red and covered with small cypress trees, down to the tip of the cave. Wild fig trees and bushes hung from the cliffs: the half moon was shining white in the sunset over us: there was a strange feeling of all the ancient secrets, a feeling of awe and fear. Below the cave, where the water flows and falls into a green pool, wild mint and maidenhair, and many fresh plants were growing: and it was brown water like a Devonshire stream. I drank in honour of Adonis and found it very light and sweet. I should have liked to stay and watch the moonlight creep down. There is a little village called Muneitra close above, and the Sheikh gave us lodging and a clean bed. All the evening I still felt the influence of the ancient religion, for there was the Sheikh's wife, with the profile that must have once belonged to the maidens of the temple – a quite perfect profile, so lovely, flawless, and cruel, that I was unable to take my eyes off it all the evening. One cannot dissect loveliness but I have never seen anything quite so perfect. It was not soulless, but it was not kind; the secret of it is lost to us, as the old worship is lost. It was wonderful to have that face to look at in the hills of Afka. The hair was plaited and loose over each ear, and the dingy European nondescript clothes seemed to make the wonderful face even more remote and secret to itself. We sat by the coffee hearth. The Sheikh got into his bed after slipping off his overcoat: the lady remained smoking her narghile. I slept on an embroidered pillow under a yellow quilt and the white cliffs of Adonis shining opposite in the moon.

Next day we had a ten hours' ride to reach the sea. Next year Afka will have a road and hotel. I was just in time.   Your

                                                              FREYA

* An army officer once wrote to me to suggest that these two beneficent streams might have been reported by the ancient spies of the Israelites, and the flowing of milk and honey became a symbol of the land.

FLORA STARK   Damascus
                                                  19 October 1929
Dearest B.,

I left Brumana quite sadly, all seeming so comfortable and familiar. A last affectionate visit all round, everyone so nice to me. I had dinner with Najm and his family – six charming children, running round barefoot to wait, and the pretty, nay *beautiful,* Druse women sitting round – and a very good dinner on the floor with my host, who was however a bit subdued, having rolled down a valley side with his car the day before. I was also a little troubled, because there were small white animals running round: afterwards I was told they were lice.

Mr. Edmunds came the last evening but one; it is only when I am going away that he gives himself a holiday and lets himself be really nice. We are very good friends.

At Beirut I took the train; we climbed up through the olives and vines, the engine hooting with joy at intervals, the country looking far more benevolent and mild than when I last saw it under snow. I wondered whether the fine edge of its loveliness would be wanting this second time, but no — it was the same unbelievable wonder: the far sweeping hills, the bare spaces, Hermon, and the villages in their poplar trees; the slow leaving of the West and red-roofed houses; the bare naked valley, and then the broad ranges of Anti-Lebanon; Zebdani in its orchards, every tree laden with apples of yellow quince, the poplars silver in the wind, the winding stream and thin air of these spaces, and the flat roofs and yellow mud walls. The yellow land has still the feeling of plenty over it, but a fierce sort of productiveness, quite different from ours. And then we plunged down between the walls of desert rock, and where I last travelled through the thin forest of blossoms there was now thick shade, woods along the stream, and glades and glades of plane and poplar and fruit trees. The country looks much more settled than when last I was here.

I got to Damascus; my Arabic now sufficient for porters and such, and pleasant to see the look of friendliness as soon as one speaks it.

I had barely got my things off when three black-veiled ladies were shown in, and turned out to be the two Azm sisters and a chaperone aunt — very pleasant, though their English and my Arabic have both deteriorated since last we saw each other. It was fun going round with the three ladies, the elder one strictly veiled; the two pretty girls only pulled their veil down when anyone began to stare. I think I shall adopt the convenient fashion. We came round into the pale gold sunset of Damascus, the electric illumination shining against it, the minarets very pearly and ethereal in that wonderful atmosphere. The twilight came down as we wandered through Suleiman's mosque with its lunettes of old blue tiles over the school doorways, and old graves among the flowers: the big square of splashing water full of light; the Moslems walking at the edge, and carrying their shoes to the mosque door: it was the evening prayer, we could not go in, but peered from the door at the row of figures rising and crouching again. It seemed incredible to be here again and find it all better than before. I feel I am in the real East again. I don't think I shall have time to call on the Missionaries.

Your

FREYA

Rihàne, nr. Damascus
                                                      22 October 1929

Darling B.,

I am sitting in a room furnished with rows of chairs in mother-of-pearl inlay, and an immense tall wardrobe of the same, which glitters at one in the morning when one wakes. It is a sort of country house with farm attached, at one corner of the village. We came in a ramshackle car; Mme Azm and the two girls and I had quantities of bundles. It was lovely to get away to life in the country, with the owners looking after their land and the wives attending to the household stores. Delicious things made of walnuts in grape preserve – the grapes boiled and mixed with flour into a paste and rolled round the walnuts. The aunt is quite young, about twenty-four I should say, immensely fat and rosy, with bobbed hair, and all sorts of evening dresses which she has been wearing for us. She lives here with her mother-in-law, an old lady with long nose and a sort of nondescript gown of white and blue stripes, who smokes most of the time. The harem consists of two rooms on either side of the *dar,* or raised loggia open on one side on to a delightful courtyard. On the other side are the kitchen and dining-room, with two maids with checked cotton veils over their heads and pink frilled trousers, running round. We can get out into the stables, but are careful to call out before doing so and ask if there is a man about. I am getting to feel quite ashamed of my unveiled condition, and turn my back with the rest when we pass a peasant on the road. The girls and the young wife are inclined to be careless about these matters, but the uncle, Najib Effendi, keeps them up to the mark. To come home and find six women and two maids all waiting to be pleasant must be a delightful feeling and is I am sure responsible for that sort of assured and reposeful dignity which the Moslem has. From the feminine standpoint, the life is easy enough too: I think our Western strenuousness and sense of responsibility would be very hard on them at first. There is a sort of privacy with no privacy, for all the women wander about in all the rooms, so that even if one wanted to read or study it would be very difficult.

We had lunch at a long table with yellow oilcloth, and dishes of food from which everyone helped themselves – a few extra spoons and forks put for my benefit. After lunch our host went off to the male part of the house, and we sat on the floor of the mother-of-pearl room playing dice with six cowrie shells and a round embroidered cloth across which you move pawns: a simple game. About four we walked out and looked at the fields for sowing, came back in the twilight with the goats and sheep, and went in turn to have a hot bath.

We had another very delicious meal in the evening, and then sat out on cushions, the starlight over the walls of the court and a lamp in a glass lantern lighting us up. I discovered that I could play chess with the uncle. We then had the lute out, and the plump lady in her white evening gown played, while the uncle got his pipe out and accompanied her. Then Amatellatif's bed and mine were spread on the floor, and we all retired.

This is now my fourth day, and I feel quite accustomed to the harem, though not inclined for a lifetime of it. There is a deadly boredom about it. The way of passing time is not really more monotonous than the way most of the girls at Dronero, say, spend their time; and the talk – clothes, gossip, relatives, food – is exactly the same. The only difference is one of possibilities – someone very strongminded *can* get out of the rut at Dronero; here, I don't see how they could.

Yesterday we talked to one of the herd-boys, a Beduin lad hired from his tribe to look after the village goats. They asked what he carried in his bundle. 'Bread,' said he, 'will you eat?' He earns 19l. [4/-] a month, and yet his offer to share was perfectly genuine and his manners those of an equal.

We had another afternoon with the gramophone, and another walk in the evening, and a long talk with Amatellatif about herself and things in general. It is all very like Italy only rather more so. She has a cousin who wants to marry her, but she won't and is allowed to say no; on the other hand, a man she would have liked has been refused by her brother. She is such a pretty, elegant girl, and her sister, too, and they seem to be very happy in their seclusion.

They are all amiable to me though we talk little, my Arabic being really very inadequate. In the evenings and afternoons the Effendi spreads his carpet in the *dar* and intones the Koran in a beautiful voice: the two older ladies, their heads swathed in white, spread their carpets behind him and pray in silence holding their two hands palm upwards for the blessing from heaven. I would like to watch and listen, instead of having to go on playing dice close beside them with the young people who seem never to pray at all.

You would be surprised to see me now, as I am writing with the eternal gramophone and the ladies sewing, and my eyes are – according to them – much beautified with a long black streak underneath them. Soon I shall go and have a bath. It is all wonderfully clean and nice in its own way. It is only the communal life I find difficult.

Tomorrow we return to Damascus, and I must get all ready to leave at six the next morning.

Your own
FREYA

Damascus Palace Hotel
24 October 1929

Dearest B.,

Just a line to say all is lined up for my departure at six tomorrow morning.
And I have five introductions (native) for Baghdad. I had a lovely day in
Damascus – it is the most fascinating of cities. I now realise under what
a strain I enjoyed it when I was here, every noise and jolt a pain to me:
now the jostle and dust and tumult is just part of the fun. I strolled through
the *Suqs*, called on my dark friends and found only the lady and children at
home: another lady, her neck wrapped in white with a black veil – the
picture of St. Theresa – came in: she was commissioned to find a wife for
the son of the Vizier of Haiderabad who is travelling for pleasure in Syria.

Then back to the El Azms. The Moslem family took me to its bosom, and
I am going away laden with walnuts and raisins, and a little mother-of-pearl
casket to keep kohl in for my eyes, and was kissed all round, and given
heaps of letters.

Your own

FREYA

VIVA JEYES   The Zia Hotel, Baghdad
26 October 1929

My dearest Viva,

I got here yesterday. I was rather glad to arrive, though the native company did its best and gave me a good car and driver; we covered the ground
in nine hours the first day and twelve the second with a really excellent
chauffeur who made the rough places as smooth as the nature of them would
allow. It is a wonderful experience – and better in a way in the open car
with all the vagaries of native casualness than in the respectable seclusion
of Nairn. The English ladies who were to travel with me had turned into
a Turkish family from Aleppo whose male members keep a rather low-down
eating house here; and a Levantine gentleman, polite but slippery. We never
stopped for lunch, but went on and on from eight in the morning till night
over the immense empty spaces. Camels, hundreds or thousands, countless
anyway, were at the fringe of the greener country – but then there was
nothing, no life but a few birds, no green but some faint patch in the worm-
wood or the rushes, the red and yellow earth lying in almost invisible ridges,
hour after hour with no life but the white sheets of the mirage slipping
away before us, like lakes and islands in the distance. Here indeed the
sun like a strong man runs his race, and *nothing* is hidden from the light
thereof. The convoy, scattered at great distances over the waste, rushed

along with spirals of sand behind it. In the evening in the starlight we came
to Rutba, a light shining far out over its windowless wall – four towers, and a
gate, and a tribal policeman with the wild Arab face and star on his forehead,
with his long red cloak and the gun in his hand, standing at the gate which is
always kept closed. It is very like the sort of place the Jinn used to produce
when the lamp was rubbed, I am sure. And then you dine on salmon
mayonnaise and custard and jelly and read the sort of notices on the walls
that might belong to a golf club-house in the country, and the British
officials are all talking shop or shooting or such and look so nice after the
French in Syria. What a different atmosphere it is – quite indescribable.
Meanwhile the poor Aleppo ladies and such eat whatever happens to be
inside their disreputable bundles and sleep in heaps inside the cars in the
courtyard. I could not insist on spending the night in my comfortable little
room when they wished to be off, but there was a vagueness about the time
of starting which got me out of bed first at ten, then at twelve, and finally at
one. The gate was opened: 'Peace be upon you,' said the soldiers. In no time
the light of Rutba was swallowed up, and nothing human left but a faint
gleam from our consort ahead, which soon lost itself also. The desert is very
immense when one is alone in it at night. The old moon was on one side
and Orion, swinging over half the heavens it seemed, was on the other,
climbing before our eyes in the cold clean air. At eight we reached Ramadi
and customs, and in another three hours, at 2 p.m., we saw the Tigris and
clattered over the long bridge of boats to Baghdad.

FREYA

VENETIA BUDDICOM   The Zia Hotel, Baghdad
                                                         October 1929
Dearest Venetia,
    It is very remarkable – here I am in Baghdad. I sometimes wonder how
it comes about. It is a long flat city in a flat land, and all you see as you
come from the west is a fringe of palms and a mosque. The bridge of
boats is not nearly as beautiful as it sounds, and there is a faintly English
flavour of the 'High Street' about the one tarred road which runs down
the length of the town. But the *people* are there; and I shall be very happy
I do believe. That is after all the real interest: the people here are of all
fascinating sorts – the beautiful ones being Kurds. Never have I seen more
fine-looking men, so agile and strong with legs bare to the thigh and red
turbans, and long hair under, and a wild aquiline handsomeness that is
quite intoxicating and I only wish I could paint it.
    The Christian ladies appear to go about in the lovely silk wraps which

208

have vanished from Damascus, and the Moslems wear their *'abeias* in a clumsy way over the top of their head with a black veil. I got here very tired and did nothing yesterday but write to a man who is recommended by my friend in Damascus. I hope he may come to help me to a room and am waiting to see before going visiting among British and being told not to.

This morning however I did stroll among the narrow little ways and grated wooden windows, the mysterious blank walls. I came in a little quiet corner to a little garden with an open door, and old Sheikhs in turbans sitting round a crowd of small children with books – it was a pretty sight. Just opposite I noticed an Arabic script saying, 'This house is empty and for sale.' It is only a blank wall, but I have taken the name and am going to look into the matter and see if I might not settle in it till the place is sold. Five gentlemen in tarbooshes were very pleased to help me with the address, which I could have managed in time for myself.

I am now here with only £10 till November 15th, but feel optimistic enough for anything.

Your

FREYA

FLORA STARK   The Zia Hotel, Baghdad
                                                    28 October 1929

Darling B.,

Mr. Munìr Wakìl has just turned up – the Bahaist* friend of my black tanner friend in Damascus – and has come up to the scratch beautifully so far, except that I was rather overcome by finding him a lovely tall young man with meeting eyebrows and full lips and a most amiable expression, dressed European and with the sort of Highland onesided headdress which the government officials here wear. He is in the irrigation. He is going to find a room; and if not soon, then he will ask me to come and be a fifth among his four sisters. And he will come *every* day at three to show me Baghdad. What am I to do if all my native introductions prove as over-powering, and the day with only twenty-four hours? Meanwhile I find I live here in luxury, bath, tea, and all included, for 15/- a day: it is very pleasant to be comfortable for a bit, but am wondering if my ends really will meet.

I went round to the museum this morning. The Ur collection is amazing – the sheer beauty of the gold work so remarkable, and very wonderful to find the filigree jewelry, the mosaic, and inlaid ivory of the Italians, here in Mesopotamia nearly 6,000 years ago. These old Sumerians appear to be the people who brought its civilisation to Egypt. But where they in their turn came from is yet unknown.

Today I discovered the markets, all vaulted brick arches, with lots more light than Damascus, and even more fascinating from the varied types. There seem to be two distinct Iraqi types, one full round face, with thickish underlip, one long very narrow face with pleasant quick eyes and rather high heads. Then there are the magnificent Kurds, and the Christians, Assyrians, Jews, Greeks, Turks, Persians, and who knows what, beside the real Arabs from the desert outside. The Christian women wear the lovely silk wraps (like my white and silver one) – all beautiful colours, a joy to watch as they go about the streets among the black veils of the Moslems.

It is very pleasant to be in a free country again. What a difference it makes, and why, is hard to say, but one feels it everywhere. And the people may not like foreigners, but there is none of that sense of fear: they behave as if they know they will be fairly treated – it is the same sort of pleasant feeling a dog gives when he comes up to you instead of crouching his head when you move your hand, which is what you always feel in Syria.

The Shi'as are fanatic here and one cannot enter their mosques. I should like to get into touch with them, but it is a toss-up as one cannot very well combine Shi'a and Sunni and I don't know which my fate is to be.

Love from

FREYA

* Religious sect founded in Persia in the nineteenth century.

FLORA STARK   Baghdad
                                                                  30 October 1929
Dearest B.,
    I went yesterday to Mrs. Drower's* and came back sadly disappointed and much perplexed at finding no letters from Asolo. It was dreadfully disappointing.

Mrs. Drower was very pleasant. She is kind and sensitive and cheerful. We had just had tea when Mr. and Mrs. [Leonard] Woolley walked in. Mrs. Woolley is remarkably fascinating, with something strange and possibly cruel about her: but quite irresistible I should imagine. It was quite sad to leave the pleasant house, all so beautifully clean, and comfy chairs and books.

Today I have had tea with my Bahai friend – a fascinating way through the poorer quarters, across the old bridge of boats, one thread of mixed humanities, the yellow city in long lines of warm brick behind: through the unfashionable markets, dirty and crowded with every colour and smell, and then through little back streets into a small court with the brick house built round, and the mother and grandmother, and relays of sisters to receive me. They were very pleasant, and my Arabic got along – and I was able to consume one large glass of pomegranate juice, tea, and biscuit, and two candied apples – very good.

I left them and went to Mrs. Drower's as it is her Arab at home day. She speaks Arabic fluently – I do envy her. I miss all sentences that are over about ten words.

Your
FREYA

* Wife of legal adviser to Iraq Govt.

ROBERT STARK
Baghdad
2 November 1929

Dearest Pips,

I thought I had got a house yesterday – three rooms, a roof and a cellar, newly whitewashed and painted blue round the windows and window bars: and a handsome varnished door with Venetian gothic arch and brass knobs. The roof is surrounded with corrugated iron rather askew for privacy, with holes cut in it so that one can look out without being seen. The stairs are steeper than anything that doesn't belong to mountaineering, and I don't remember any glass in the windows now I come to think of it – but there is a lovely tree to look at, sprouting from a mosque courtyard. The rent of all this is something above 1/- a day, but the hitch is that they want to let it for a year, and I cannot go to more than six months. So my friend Munir Wakil the Bahai says to the people that I don't want it anyway and we wait developments. The whole neighbourhood took a friendly interest, and produced the latchkey, which is over a foot long. The place is near the big new straight street, and very convenient – more so than the other possibility which is across the old bridge of boats in the poorer suburb and far away from everything. But it is now in the hands of Allah and my Bahai, who promises to have me settled by the end of the week.

On Monday I go to stay a few days with Mrs. Drower, and so see the leading side of Baghdad. She is very charming, and so kind and interested in the people and knows a lot about them, though she did not know or believe that anyone could get a lodging for 1/- a day or near it. But I think the nicest way to know people is *not* to be important or wealthy and so come upon their genuine kindness: if you have a position here, it is always that which counts, and many tales are told of the way the native turns from you if anything goes wrong; but I find that they are as kind as can be to me who have nothing to profit them by.
Your own
FREYA

Baghdad

                                                                      3 November 1929

Darling B.,

I've got my house! I've had to take it for a year, but an obliging friend of
Munir's is going to write a paper promising to take it off my hands for ten
per cent less than I pay whenever I want to get rid of it. How to pay is now
the problem, and I have written to Barclays to tell them I shall overdraw. Do
please see that that cheque from Mario comes the quickest way, for I shall be
desperate if I don't get it by the end of the month : I can just last till then,
by overdrawing for the rent. It's almost too like the *Arabian Nights* to be
penniless in Baghdad.

I missed the opening of Parliament because I was laid up yesterday, and
am still groggy on rice and milk, and very cross with a cold and this internal
upset. I quite see why the old Babylonian religion thought of legions of
demons in the encompassing atmosphere : one just breathes them up as
one goes out, and it seems that now till the rains come is the worst time. It
was 89.6 in the shade at 8 a.m. yesterday – just comfortable for me.

                                                                      Your

                                                                      FREYA

HERBERT YOUNG   Baghdad

                                                                      8 November 1929

Dearest Herbert,

I must write to you this time, and especially as my news is all so satisfactory : my cold gone or nearly; my house actually rented; and a kind unknown lady has just offered to lend me a horse to ride on. Every morning I
go to school and learn Arabic in a class with twenty-six little naughty girls
who all rush to lend me their books, pencils, seats, paper, and advice and
listen with awe when I read very slow and correct sentences out of the third
Arabic reader.

Mrs. Drower is kindness itself, and introduces me all round both to native
and English, so that I feel I shall soon know the whole of Baghdad. In her
early days here she used to speak Arabic well and Gertrude Bell used to
damp her efforts with snubs. It seems that her Arabic was nothing very
wonderful, just as Lawrence's, and Kitchener's and all these celebrated
people – rather a comfort to the despairing student. They made a little go a
long way.

As soon as I get settled, I am going to look out for a Mullah to tackle the
Koran and start work seriously.

    Lots of love.   Your

                                                                      FREYA

Baghdad
                                                  10 November 1929

Dearest Car,

Just think what I have done today. I have been threading little blue lapis lazuli beads from Ur on a pink thread for the museum. Mrs. Drower brought them home in a cardboard box, all mixed up with bits of bones of ladies who attended the queen's funeral and were then knocked on the head. They are nearly four thousand years old, and just like what you find in Venice now, except for the value of the stone they are made of, and it is marvellous to think what instrument was small enough to pierce those tiny holes.

                                                              Your
                                                              FREYA

ROBERT STARK   11/186 Amara Quarter, Baghdad
                                                  14 November 1929

Dearest Pips,

I have just got into my house. A lady at dinner last night asked me if it is 'fit for an Englishwoman to live in', and I'm sure I don't know, but it looks quite nice once you climb through my dank little well and up the incredible steepness of the stairs (of which only the narrowness keeps you from falling down headlong every time, so that you are like Pickwick's cab horse, supported by the shafts). I have also got an Armenian maid coming tomorrow and a nice boy in the meanwhile.

A tragedy has just taken everyone by surprise: the Prime Minister, who seemed quite happy when sitting next Mrs. Drower at dinner on Tuesday, came home from the club on Wednesday night and shot himself dead through the heart. He was the most if not only honest man in the cabinet, and comparatively a friend to the British. He wrote a letter to his son, a boy of nineteen now studying engineering in Birmingham, and went out on to a veranda over the river, and shot himself, his wife holding his arm and begging him to shoot her instead, and his daughter looking on. It was just that these filthy politics were too much for him and he was so badgered by every party that he could stand it no longer. Mrs. Drower and I watched the funeral as it passed our window: there was a huge crowd, very silent, but no hostility visible.

I am just reflecting what an awful place one of these flat-roofed towns must be in times of massacres. There is no way of defending your house, for anyone can walk over from the next roof and find himself at once and with no barrier in the heart of your house. I have put a pot of paint just in anyone's way coming down from the roof to my bedroom, and if a cat comes along and overturns it in the middle of the night I shall get a most awful fright for nothing.

Your own

FREYA

FLORA STARK   11/186 Amara Quarter
                                                         14 November 1929

Dearest B.,

I don't think my house is really fit for social functions: my new Armenian maid said it was dear at 330 rupees a year. I have moved in today and painted a green bookcase, and the Bahai came and put the curtains up and procured me food from the restaurant in one of those little contraptions which consist of one dish on top of the other in a sort of pyramid. Tomorrow I hope to get fairly straight. My joy at present is concentrated in my two pet animals, modelled in steel from Isfahan: one is a wild sheep, the other an ibex: they are very lovely, and Mrs. Drower has baptised them Aku and Maku, which means 'there is' and 'there is not', and sounds very like them.

Ever so much love dear B.   Your

FREYA

OLIVIA BARKER   c/o Mrs. Drower, Baghdad
                                                         18 November 1929

Dearest Olivia,

I thought this was going to be quite a nice slum and as full of human interest as the narrow street will hold. However in a moment of weakness, a sore throat and a smell and the advice of all my friends combined, I went to the poor little man who has the impossible task of keeping Baghdad healthy, and asked him if the dead ancestor or whatever it is might be removed. He came along amiably and as soon as he saw the house began earnestly begging me to leave it, and has found me a room over the river. A nice American woman* has offered me a room also, and I am now hovering between the two. Otherwise Baghdad is all I asked for. I happened on the nicest of the English and I have got my lessons all fixed up, except Koran study. They are not thrilling in themselves, but I have come to the conclusion that it is the only method by which one can really get at this people. If you had seen the two grim old Shi'a Sheikhs this morning and the absolute transformation, the look of tenderness, the only word that describes it, when my friend told them I had come on purpose to study the Koran.

I have been looking into Assassins and find Persian is essential. Who knows? One life is an absurdly small allowance, and Canada every eighteen months or so an added complication; so that instead of the moral repose that I ought to get in Europe if I ever want to work, it is just one rush and fatigue. Papa's things just as hopeless as ever; he *won't* have a partner, and can't and wouldn't wish to leave. And now he writes so happily that I cannot wish for anything else. After all I do think that to be busy with the work you enjoy is as great a happiness as one can wish for. Mama and Papa both have that in a measure which very few people manage to get.

I am being interrupted all the time by my Armenian maid. I cannot let her sit in the smell downstairs and so she is doing embroidery beside me and suffering from my silence. It is such fun to have this funny little place all to myself. I have spent £15 on furniture, stoves, and 1s. 6d. a day for rent, and am quite heartbroken at leaving.

Your

FREYA

* Mrs. Kerr, head of the girls' school.

VENETIA BUDDICOM

Baghdad

24 November 1929

Dearest Venetia,

The greengrocer who lives opposite in a little open booth sold me his black and white headcloth to cover my tea table when I gave a party, and came the other day to say that a wealthy Moslem was anxious to give me lessons on Arabic and to read English with me – all for love: at least I hope not that but anyway not for money. He was described as middle-aged with a family, which turns out to be thirty-five, pleasant plump and grizzled. He doesn't seem to care much about the English, but sits for two hours chatting Arabic and going through the newspaper with me, and has now suggested a visit to one of the Shammar chiefs up the Tigris. I don't think it is really essential, but it seemed to me it would look better to ask for a chaperone, but I must say that the presence of even the most understanding and charming official person seems to cast a shadow.

I am not to be here long, in this house I mean. All the ghosts of all its inhabitants arise and smell during the night till I can hardly breathe and I am looking for something less poisonous; though otherwise I do enjoy being in this disreputable quarter. One day it is a fortune teller coming up, you pass your hand on a mirror and then she looks and sees what is not, with a plausible air: yesterday a small street fight and the night before a death with rows of black hooded women crouching in the dim courtyard and shrieking their barbarous grief. The street is not more than two yards across. All the refuse is thrown there and collected on donkeys early in the morning so that the atmosphere is slowly degenerating through the day. The trouble is with the houses however, every family living over its own cistern where the accumulated filth of ages oozes up through the brick and makes for the parchment faces and sunken eyes and, I am sure, the jaundiced fanaticism which distinguish the townspeople here. In the night you hear sharp whistles at intervals, and that is the police – but whether the whistle is meant to startle the householder or the thief I haven't yet fathomed. Anyway a smart Iraqi in uniform came with a big book and got nearly a rupee out of me for the nightly protection.

I had a ride yesterday south to the Dyàla river, a good hour along the top of a dyke called the *bund* which gives a view of the yellow hard desert earth and shallow hills. The river would be nothing special elsewhere, but here its still sheet of water and grey-green trees (willow I believe) were like a sudden revelation of loveliness, and we came back by a wood through the government experimental farms, well watered and with trees planted on the roadside and shooting up, and smelling sweet like England.

Your

FREYA

FLORA STARK   Baghdad
                                                    25 November 1929

Darling B.,

Your letter and, to tell the truth, the two enclosed cheques came as manna in the desert yesterday. I found them at Mrs. Drower's when I went to get her advice before plunging into the next housekeeping adventure. I had seen a dear little house with Mrs. Kerr in the morning in a clean and respectable part of the Moslem quarter – really a dear little house for £20 for six months. I would have settled on this if I had not seen the room on the river, and yesterday Mrs. Drower gave me tea and we went across, and when she saw the lovely view, and big court with shrubs growing in it and a view of palm trees behind, and nice wide balcony over the Tigris she said I could not do better and that the distance wouldn't really matter. So I have taken it from Wednesday and do hope to be really settled by the end of the week.

I went from school to Dr. Raghib's family and took the two ladies to look at the museum: their only comment on the treasures of Ur was that they should have been dusted more carefully. They have lived two years just opposite the museum and never knew of its existence. Their idea of pleasure is to drive in an open car round the suburban roads of Alwiyah and 'look at the English', a sort of substitute for a zoo. I was taken, and found it quite amusing to watch the curious spectacle of my compatriots, playing golf, etc., from this new angle.

It is rather nice to meet these friendly genuine Moslem elements again, with no thought of politics among them – which seems to be the disease of Iraq: and it seems that the feeling is not really so friendly at all. What the people really want is not very clear, for the demand for independence is just made by a few politicians who know that they are asking for what has already been agreed upon. I think it is much more a sort of psychological problem – a feeling of superiority which is I believe quite real but which we do not trouble to hide, nor notice that it is a barrier. My Bahai and his family are doing all things for me for nothing, and the teacher brought by the greengrocer is teaching me for nothing: if I were a proper Britisher I should not allow this. I should insist on paying, they would charge too much, and neither would like each other. As it is I shall have to find really nice presents for them, and they will have the two pleasures of being kind and getting a present, and there will be a pleasant relationship.

My teacher will follow me across the river. He is a funny little fat man and sits on his own stomach in an upright manner and tries to be polite while I read the rude things about the English in the paper. He doesn't believe the Koran himself but is pleased that I should like it. He has been among the Beduin and at Stamboul, and is a very fair type of the modern civilised Arab.

Your

FREYA

ROBERT STARK   Baghdad

27 November 1929

Dearest Pips,

It has just dawned on me that this will be a Christmas letter – my loving wishes. I wish I could fly over and spend it with you.

I am lunching at this hotel, having taken refuge from the dust storm which is whirling ouside – as I have no house of my own today. I have abandoned my own. All the neighbourhood told me I was wrong to leave them: I feel rather poor-spirited myself.

I get a ride out into the desert twice a week and get the good air into my nostrils. The ground is lovely of course because one can go where one likes, but very hard now and with troublesome shallow holes. They play polo and as soon as the first rain has laid the dust I am going to look at a match. But I find that my time is getting desperately full and my teacher always stays two hours instead of one and often more, and spends the time telling me of the delinquencies of the English. My Arabic is not good enough to argue but I hope to get my own back in the spring.

My new room has a balcony and four big windows on the river and its only drawback may be cold and the distance. The nearest way is by boat across to this (eastern) side and then along the ugly new street which is tarred and runs right through Baghdad and is pseudo-European. My school is off it at the far end among the little narrow ways: every day I turn off at the blue and yellow tiled bate of Haidar Khaneh mosque and go up past half a dozen Beduin women crouching over baskets of their flat bread, past a group of Kurd porters with red striped cotton turbans and thick felt waistcoats, by a sweetshop and a mattress carder's and a corner where an old one-eyed man sits in the dust with a tray of dusty pink and white poisons for innocent children, through a district of private houses with studded doors and latticed balconies almost meeting overhead, till I reach the school. It is quite an ordeal to read aloud in class etc., but very good for the Arabic, and I know really more of the grammar than most of the children, though less of the spoken language.

It seems that even the British here have picturesque imaginations and have been asking whether I am a spy or a Bahai. It is beyond anyone to think that one can do Arabic for *pleasure* it seems.

Your loving

FREYA

VIVA JEYES   Baghdad
                                                          [end] November 1929

Dear Viva,

My new house belongs to Michael the Shoemaker from Mosul and his wife and two dear little boys, and my room has five big windows on the river and a wide balcony in front and the sun after just peeping in of a morning goes round and shines in at the opposite window for an hour or two before setting. Not all the panes are quite entire, but Mrs. Longrigg the wife of the financial adviser has sent me four lovely heavy woollen rugs which I have hung up today. The Longriggs and Sturges live just a few houses further up so that I am now not only healthily but even respectably situated. I only hope this may not discourage the Arabs. Communications are supposed to be easy. The first day we went down to the riverside and shouted out to the boats which are supposed to act as buses: 'Oh father of the boats hear us," but the father of the motor wasn't taking any notice and I had to run along the river bank and cross by the Maud bridge of boats. Down the river bank southwards are flat mud hovels where the peasants live: a little pale maid in her dark blue gown and with her slim little figure and silent barefoot walk comes every morning with a bottle of milk. She has a gold circle with turquoise and little gold dice hanging from it sticking in the nostril and her name is Jamila.

On Tuesday I had tea with a Syrian girl educated at Columbia University, and now teaching here, and then met one of the local editors, and an Armenian who is translating Lawrence (and doesn't think very highly of him). These were all particularly anti-English. It seems a dreadful pity. My hostess said to me rather pathetically, 'We should so much like to be allowed to love the English, if they did not always make us feel they were snubbing us.' On the other hand not more than about two people in a thousand can find any interest in *really* mixing with the natives. So what is the way out? It is all a wonderful drama, and I love to be watching it, but it is a heartbreaking job to those who have given their best years to it and see it not only unrecognised but with every prospect of being annulled very soon.

Your loving
FREYA

FLORA STARK   Baghdad
                                                     6 December 1929

Dearest B.,

Feeling *very* homesick. I sent you a telegram the other day for my fancy dress, for Mrs. Drower tells me I shall be going to a dance at New Year, but I do not know: at present I am feeling uncomfortable, as all the people I meet (except dear Mrs. Drower and Mrs. Caparn) are rather suspicious of me and have been asking whether I am a spy. I fear it will be very hard to keep in favour with both Arab and British, and the tragedy is that we seem to have brought a whiff of our own snobbishness among the Iraqis: I find that those I come upon independently are much nicer and more genuine than those I know through British introductions.

I found out that L[ionel] Smith[23] had wandered into my slum and left a note, and so I went to the Education Office and finally saw him – such a charming person, refreshingly unofficial to look at. He has lent me a pile of books, and led me down by the old bridge along the river's edge a new walk home, and talked about walking tours, and is inviting me to dine next week.

Today was a blustering rainy day and my teacher, packed very tight in a raincoat which swathed him without a crease (except a few horizontal ones), came for me at two, and we launched out into the choppy muddy expanse of the Tigris with great difficulty, the stairs being coated down the bank with very slippery mud which began to suck you in slowly as you stood on the jumping off place. I got on board before it closed over my ankles, and we had a fine spin down the river and no real wetting though the teacher assured his family that 'we took refuge with God from the strength of the water'. Last week he told me that in summer all Iraqis who wear European clothes 'take refuge with God from the discomfort of their socks' – a piteous thought.

The brother's house is a pleasant one-storeyed place with a courtyard full of oleander and orange trees, and a long brick reception room painted green, with mats on the walls and floor and the chairs arranged as if to be sold by auction tomorrow. Three men were sitting in decorous silence smoking, and I was put on the sofa beside the most honoured one of them and had to try and talk in my awful Arabic which seems to get no better. We sat for a long time, and then had coffee, and then tea with lots of cakes, and the two Arab-dressed gentlemen became very amiable with their pleasant easy manners. I asked to see the ladies, but this was discouraged till the very end, and then the motor bus was waiting and I couldn't stay. The ladies were busy with the tea preparations, so could not be expected to see me, so the mu'allim explained: but it seems rather dull for them, and not at all so pleasant as among the Druses.

Your

FREYA

HERBERT YOUNG

Baghdad
9 December 1929

Dearest Herbert,

A very happy Christmas to you.

I have had a week-end at Alwiyah, being thoroughly British, with a dinner party of ten people (which terrifies me) and general luxury. Came back yesterday and called on a Bahai lady of Turkish origin with a completely globular small husband who complained to me that his wife insists on trying discipline on their one little girl. The little girl has chicken pox, and we were being received in her nursery: I arrived early, and having just held the little darling's hand, heard the news with a slight shock: the next American lady who arrived – it was an 'at home' – got half across the floor and made a painful scene before she realised (and said) that the harm was done. There was a pause in which the room divided mentally into East and West and each thought things about the other: a young Moslem and I then tried to lighten the atmosphere by enumerating the Arabic names of all the diseases we knew, and then lots of people arrived: the German consul who edits

Persian plays, the British officer who has married a Turkish lady with an appearance as picturesque as (they say) her past: the pretty American with a rich bored-looking Syrian husband; one or two serious young Moslems, looking so much more dignified than anyone else, and so on.

Last night I got home after dark. You can't imagine how lovely to be rowed across the dim waters of the Tigris, with the outline of palms against the sky and the few lights of the houses on the banks.

My room is beautifully warm now with the stove burning paraffin recklessly.

Love from
FREYA

FLORA STARK Baghdad
10 December 1929

Darling B.,

The river looks like a dream at nights – the stars bright above it, and the reflection of lights in the water. The brown banks winding away in a gentle curve and a boat or two gliding along. The square rafts with shallow edges, with oars made of long rough poles and a few planks nailed across at one end, are as ancient as the old Babylonian carvings and more so.

Today as I walked down the fashionable side of the river a strange man walked up to me and said 'Are you Miss Stark?' He was the postman, with letters for me. A wonderful place it is for knowing other people and their businesses. The ramifications of the East must ever baffle us who have so much less time for sitting and talking and watching and listening.

Your
FREYA

ROBERT STARK Baghdad
10 December 1929

Darling Pips,

I have been to a Jewish wedding. A huge house, full of people as it would hold – mostly Moslem ladies in black who come uninvited to look at the bride, who was sitting in white and silver, with a diamond ring over her white kid gloves and a bouquet sent by King Faisal on a table beside her. A few old ladies wore the little band of blue satin embroidered with pearls on their head and one had the proper gold sort of turret arrangement in the middle of it, but it was mostly fashionable Parisian. We came late, and did not see the actual ceremony, when the bride and groom drink out of the same cup and then dash it to bits on the ground (which seems a tempestuous opening for family life).

I had a visit yesterday from an elegant young man – the king's chamberlain, a friend of my Damascus friends. He has been to New York and Columbia University, and thinks the Syrians are happier than the Americans as a whole. I wonder whether we shall ever give the East anything quite equivalent to the leisure we are trying to deprive them of.

I am going to give a dinner party to two Arab ladies and Mrs. Drower. I feel rather nervous and hope it may be a success. Husbands will be allowed in after: I could not face the problem of feeding them.

Your own

FREYA

VENETIA BUDDICOM Baghdad

10 December 1929

Dearest Venetia,

This afternoon, in a clear blue sky with a few shining white clouds floating about in it, I was watching the nine aeroplanes which brought the new High Commissioner; three of them headed the flight and turning separate ways came slowly down in great circular sweeps to the palm groves, while the escorting six flew away. No one is too hopeful, for the difficulties are beyond any High Commissioner, but they are specially hard for anyone with no experience except Indian.

While the arrival was taking place Mrs. Drower and I went to a big Jewish wedding in a house outside the town (north-west), on the loveliest reach of the river I have seen, where it bends into a broad sheet of smooth brown water with brown boats and the waving palm gardens and the four minarets of Kadhimain and the blue dome where Abu Hanifa is buried, shining up among the tree tops. One never gets accustomed to the sudden alternation of beauty and squalor, kindness and cruelty, every contrast jostling about in this chaos of a world.

My room on the Tigris looks very nice now: a square curtained place like the Kaaba hides my dressing arrangements, I have my camp-bed and have bought a rug, covers, cushions, a chair, table, lamp and stove. Kind people have lent sofa and curtains and I have bought four ornamental candlesticks and two gazelles (metal) and feel that I live in elegant and refined surroundings and I pay 4s. 6d. a day to be fed and bathed and generally looked after by my landlady. She is a pretty woman and looks really lovely when I can ever see her tidily dressed. I vary in the most inconstant way between liking the friendliness and charm of the people and being exasperated by their hopelessness, and the same with the British – they are such splendid people and doing such magnificent work, then just our insular stupid way of hurting everyone's vanities makes us hated all round and one's feelings just torn all ways. This is a very poor letter, but I wanted to be in time for Christmas and am *so* sleepy.

Your loving
FREYA

PENELOPE KER   Baghdad
12 December 1929

Dearest Pen,

This morning I went to Ctesiphon – a cold clear desert day, with the sun bright over a yellow earth and the low far cliffs and little tiny knolls and creases of the earth all caught up into a blue sky by the mirage. And we had to make a great detour to reach the arch and saw it like a huge temple with minarets in the distance, its façade end-on looking like columns – getting bigger and bigger and more lovely as we drew near till we could come close enough to see it in all its majestic desolation. There is just one façade and the great arch of the central hall left. I climbed up behind an Arab going like a cat barefoot: thought for a minute I was going to feel giddy, but that humiliation was spared, and it was very like good rock-climbing. And, below, all the flat land lay from Hillah south-west to Karrada north, fields and desert and the shining curve of the river half hidden: the little mud village, its dome and palm gardens and untidy neglected graves, and Seleucia the old dead city across the stream looking also like a new graveyard, for Americans are digging there.

I am trying to think of a Xmas treat for my class at school – rather difficult as they average from twenty-five to nine years old.

Your
FREYA

FLORA STARK   Baghdad
15 December 1929

Darling B.,

I went in to return Lionel Smith's books yesterday, and had an amusing talk with him: he had been informed that I meant to go and live alone among the tribes, and had advised the consular man here to look me up and deal with me and dissuade me. I told him that I thought this sort of fabrication the limit; he defended himself by saying that I cannot deny that I am 'eccentric', which of course I did most emphatically deny – and then he told me the awful nuisance that helpless females who have got into difficulties have been to the government people. It is a horrid feeling to have all the virtuous sitting round waiting for something to go wrong and then say 'This is what comes of it.' I only hope nothing goes wrong.

The idea that one can be a genuine imperialist and yet believe in a newer vision of the methods of Empire seems inconceivable. I told Lionel Smith that it seems to me that we have been popular wherever we went until our women came out: then the social barriers are up, the vanity of these people is hurt, and the harm is done. And he told me that here it is the women and not the men who keep the natives out of the club (three-quarters of the men would be in favour of electing the Iraqis, only their wives won't let them).

FLORA STARK   Baghdad
                                                      17 December 1929

Darling B.,

What a blessing that Paradise isn't run by our Civil Service, or so few of us would get in. It seems that I have put my foot in it most *dreadfully* by accepting the mu'allim's invitation for the Beduin Sheikh. I am surrounded by a kind of frost, and Mrs. Drower tells me that all the men disapprove of me. It makes me feel like a kind of pariah from my own kind, and awfully disgusted, because after all I really have done nothing and, beyond wishing to talk as much Arabic as I can, and regretting that we can't be less superior and more polite, I am not even pro-native, certainly as much of an imperialist as any of the people here. But Mrs. Sturges told me today that one *can't* be friends with the natives and British both; and so what is to be done? It seems to me an almost unbelievable idiocy, and I shall have to put up with being out of it all and getting on steadily with my grammar, and I suppose it is good for one's character. Mrs. Kerr gave out at the last moment and told me that Lionel Smith didn't want her to go with me; so I should have had to go alone, if dear Mrs. Drower hadn't come nobly up to the scratch: she hasn't yet told Teddy that she is coming. It is only for one night, with a tame Sheikh who is a friend of most of the people here – so this fuss is too ridiculous. The Sheikh came today to call, looking so nice with his flowing 'abba and fine head, so infinitely better and more dignified than these degenerate townsfolk who have lost their own virtues and not taken ours. And it was a joy to listen to the good Arabic of the tents. We are to go on Friday, and the Sheikh Habib has gone on to see that the falcons are being starved so that they may be ready to hunt for us. It will be great fun, and we will pay the Devil when we come home. I have written a note to Lionel Smith asking if he is really responsible and whether it is I or the Beduin who are bad for Mrs.

Kerr (in a polite way). I reminded him that even a dog is allowed one bite before being suppressed: and I really haven't yet had my bite.

Mrs. Sturges would have loved to come and hunt with the Sheikh, but Mr. S. said he thought 'it would be cold for her' with the tones of an iceberg. She now wants to come and study in school with me, but I bet that will be squashed before the first lesson even starts. The truth is that the people here don't want any English in the land except themselves: they feel responsible, and yet can't actually order you about if you are an independent traveller. In fact it really *is* that attitude of *A Passage to India,* though I would never have believed it before, and it does make one rather sad.

Your own

FREYA

CAR KER Baghdad

22 December 1929

Darling Car,

Just feeling a wee bit depressed with Xmas coming on, your letter and all the indiscretions are so lovely and make me feel so near it all and as if I were having a chat with you over the fire, instead of sitting on the edge of the Tigris with a paraffin stove. I am really very comfortably settled and beginning to find the days busier than I can manage. Today, Sunday, very pleasant, for I went and lunched with L. Smith in his nice house and lovely garden, and drank a large mug of beer, in spite of which I was able to go out and catch locusts on the hockey ground. He is very nice to me and charming in himself, and likes me I hope, though I don't really know; but I have a pleasant feeling that he is a little part of Napier and W. P., Glasgow, and the really good things and it is nice to find the link here in intervals of Arab.

Mrs. Drower and I have just returned from a visit to Sheikh Habib el Hazeran of the 'Azza; so handsome with his big sheepskin coat and Arab headdress and charming manners. He is a relation of my teacher's, who brought him to call one day and we arranged the expedition to get a day's hawking after gazelle and bustard and duck. The Sheikh went on to see that his falcons were starved in readiness for the expedition and we followed next day amid the general disapproval of the Husbands of Baghdad. By 8.30 a.m. a very ramshackle old car drew up with our 'Mu'allim' and a rather tattered driver with a wall eye; and a talkative useless gentleman with a smile. We all packed in, our bedding and knapsacks around us; and were off in a thick white mist which lay in swathes along the desert earth. We went on expecting it to lift; at 11.30 we got to our last village – mud walls with little gates in them and old clumsy bolts of wood, and palm woods as glades be-

225

hind. The thick mist was creeping down through the spiky branches, but even so the glades with their undergrowth of green shrubs looked very beautiful. We got to our first really muddy bit here.

We found a car embedded in the desert and two members of the Kurdish parliament very anxious not to be left alone with the Beduin who were coming to their rescue (we heard they were rescued that evening). Meanwhile we had to be very careful. Our talkative man got out and examined each soft bit as we came to it and then turned and beckoned with his finger as if our car were a rather shy baby. We nearly stuck twice: but the third time we *did* stick. The driver tried moving the soft mud from in front of the wheels and we all tugged, while the talkative one went to find streamlets to wash the mud off his hands. Mrs. Drower has learnt the patience of the East and says nothing, but I did get goaded into telling him that we could all have a wash on arrival.

The mist had cleared, showing distant black tents and the strata lines of the Hamrin hills – and we came to cultivation. We got out of the worst mud, and a fine-looking Beduin came sent by the Sheikh to meet us. At four we reached his village, its mud houses on a tiny swelling knoll, with a little new garden beginning to grow in front of the Sheikh's house and the tribesmen gathered round his coffee hearth on the ground. The Hamrin hills lay a three hours' ride away, pink and blue in the sunset, and Tell Balsyam, some collection of old buried cities, near by, still producing ancient square bricks for the Sheikh's building. We saw seven gazelles, speeding away white in the sunlight as we came along; and in one of the old bricks, some remote gazelle ancestor had left a footprint when the clay was soft thousands of years ago. We saw bits of old pottery, blue and earth-coloured and red, strewed at intervals on the desert ground.

We went round to look at the village – and saw the girl grinding corn between two stones, sitting in the dark: and then we came back and sat in the Sheikh's guest room by a blazing fire of sesame stalks, with the Beduin round the edges of the room. Mahmud the servant got his *rebaba,* played with the fingers and a bow on one string, and they showed us the four different modes of their music. And then we were mysteriously asked into our bedroom before dinner, and found whiskey, brandy, crême de menthe, and wine ranged on our dressing table, and felt unequal to live up to our European reputation in this respect.

We had a wonderful dinner, really good – pilau, and a stew made with figs and meat and raisins and grain – and the good bitter coffee. And afterwards we called on the Sheikh's wife, the most lovely creature you can imagine. I believe there were other wives, but they were not presented: only an Armenian slave whom the Sheikh had bought from the Beduin who had seized her when a child: he had married her, and she looked well and happy. They were charming people altogether, and very like the pleasant mountain people one may lodge with in the Alps.

Next day seemed very threatening: too dark for hunting and we feared if it rained we might be stuck there over Xmas. Our car was the last to come up: the government had stopped all that came after because of the mud. So we returned, by a better way, along the banks of the Khalis canal, a winding road running by the water through desolate country – abandoned deep ditches, and villages slowly falling back in ruins into their ancient lands, and brown stretches of hard earth and thorns. Hope to go back there next spring.

Your

FREYA

VIVA JEYES

Baghdad
25 December 1929

My darling Viva,

I was to have gone off to dine tonight, but the lady has a cold, and really I am pleased to have my Xmas Day alone with my own thoughts, and to let them wander over to you and Scotland, Canada, Italy, half the world where my various selves are scattered. A wonderful world in its variety, so dingy and splendid, and lovable and mean. And I do think that the art is to love it always, whether we are happy in it or not, don't you? These rather heavy platitudes are the result of pondering your little motto and wondering at Euripides' choice of the three best things. For surely riches are not among them and strength can be done without, as you poor darling must have also discovered – unpleasant discovery it is; and happiness can be done without. But love does remain. If I had been Euripides I think I should have said best of all is the power of loving. I have been reading Boethius, most charming and pleasant, and must be infected by the *Consolation of Philosophy*.

I think one of the most remarkable virtues of the East is its extraordinarily good temper. Things go wrong, the dinner is late, the new servant leaves in the middle of the morning, the children are crying – my landlady never has a cross word even near her lips. Of course it has the disadvantage that there is no internal force caused by attrition to bring the dinner a little more up to time, and it was one and a half hours late today, but still the polite temper is practically universal. My landlords are rather charming people. I went through the little simple Xmas rite with them last night before being rowed across to dine at the Drowers. They had hung lanterns in the court-

227

yard, and prepared a pile of thorn bushes, and when I went down we all held lighted candles and Joseph, who is ten, read the story of the Nativity from the gospel: then we lit the pile, and the flame went up clear and straight towards the palms and the stars, and looking at their handsome faces as they stood chanting the Syrian hymns, I thought of the first sacrifices, Abel and Abraham, and the old faith coming down through all the forms and ages. When the fire sank we all leaped over it three times with a wish, and then I went down the steep steps to the muddy Tigris bank and rowed across its smooth darkness to the lights on the other side.

I got up heriocally at four this morning and went with Jamila (my land-lady) to her Syrian Christian church. It was two hours, and I fell fast asleep half way through, but was glad I went. A few more years and the pretty silk *izars* they wrap round their heads and bodies will have vanished for good: but this morning in the lighted church they looked like a bright flower bed, and rustled like a field of barley whenever some ritual caused a movement. The Bishop, in cream and gold with scarlet lining, gold shoes and crimson stockings, and crimson gloves with the stigmata embroidered on them, with a long beard and tall mitre, was trying to light the fire in the middle of the church. Here too it caught and flamed straight up among the circle of bright silk and the rather drab-looking male congregation.

Your

FREYA

DOROTHY WALLER

Baghdad
25 December 1929

Darling Dot,

I am settled in a tidy room on the river with a nice Syriac Christian land-lady. She *will* go to the balcony and shout '*Min?*' (who?) to any afternoon caller, nor can I get her to keep her stockings anywhere except round her ankles. This is rather hard on the wives of Advisers to the Ministries if they come to call but they are bearing up rather nicely, and I get rides and danc-ing and dinners at intervals, with harem entertainments in between. A most amusing harem evening on Monday with two Moslem ladies from Damascus who took me to a Turkish house in one of those little dark streets full of unexpected drain holes and overhanging balconies. A servant under a turban and dilapidated ulster was ready to show us upstairs into a large beautiful garden court full of green plants, and then into a long room lined with carpets (which make it very stuffy) with six ladies round a brazier. Such charming faces: especially the older women. Very like the rather stodgy provincial noblesse of France or Italy. We sit in rather heavy silence at first, gradually begin to talk of interesting subjects like comparative tiresomeness of husbands or the trial of having a second wife in the house. One grumpy lady got out and left after a while, and the woman next me said that she was her own husband's first wife. 'Some men are never content: they must have seven or eight.' 'How shocking,' say I, 'it is surely very wrong to have more than four.' My nice feeling on the subject was obviously approved of. The younger generation was dressed in fashionable Parisian style (a little indiscriminate) and played the piano to the latest jazz: the older ladies had the decent Moslem black and hennaed plaits under the black double handkerchiefs.

While we sat sipping tea in little Persian glasses and telling ribald tales, the black servant woman crouched by the door, smoking cigarettes and joining now and then in the talk, and it all seemed very remote in spite of the shingled heads and the piano.

Your

FREYA

FLORA STARK   Baghdad
                                                              27 December 1929

Darling B.,

I went and called on the Cookes today and found only Mrs. C., he having gone with L. Smith and the High Commissioner to Babylon for the day. She had a lovely fire and sat in a high-necked red knitted dress telling me in a dreary voice anecdotes of Gertrude Bell. G. Bell was a great friend of theirs, and of L. Smith's, and one gets quite a different picture from that drawn by the people she did *not* like. She was quite elderly of course when she died, but even that year would go striding across the fields with L. Smith, Mr. Cooke in the middle distance, and Mrs. C. trying hopelessly to keep up far behind. And the last day of all she bathed in the river and came home feeling too tired to sleep on the roof, and so had her bed made downstairs and died there in the night.

Mrs. C. also tells me that L. Smith is like Gertrude in not liking many people, and in showing which he does and which he doesn't. I do hope he won't show me the latter. I am feeling rather in want of a little human kindness just now or rather someone who is *not* kind but likes me.

I saw two pilgrim boats going upstream today to Kadhimain: flat barges packed from bow to stern with dark figures and three huge banners, two black and one green, flapping in the wind, upstream: and from the packed decks came the monotonous chant of the Shi'a, fierce and repeated over and over with no variation: I could not catch the words.

Your

FREYA

ROBERT STARK   Baghdad
1 January 1930

Dearest Pips,

Here is to wish you a good New Year: I thought of you as it came in at the windows last night, me dressed as an Italian peasant, in a fancy dress ball at Alwiyah club: all the Baghdad British were there and it would have surprised you to see how many there were. I got quite a lot of dancing and enjoyed it, but really more enjoyed the day before when I was taken off by Mr. and Mrs. Cooke and Mr. Smith (who is my friend and the adviser to the Education Ministry) to sit in Saïd Mustapha's garden of cabbages. Saïd Mustapha is the cabbage king: 'father of cabbages' it goes here. He has acres of them, surrounded and interspersed with palm trees, and irrigated by two oil pumps from the Tigris; and they looked very beautiful, blue and green like a sea with waves, as we sat on a divan among them and had a tin table and white cloth with all sorts of tea things before us.

I have just found out that the Baghdad Christians believe in an evil spirit called 'deu' which kills people: obviously the old Arian word 'god' turned into 'devil'. I believe the gods of the conquered are usually turned into the demons of the conquerors, but it is an interesting old survival.

You will I hope be properly thrilled to hear that I start *Persian* lessons next week: so as to get enough Persian before I leave to get up into the country of the old Assassins and try to see if any legends of them remain.

Your own

FREYA

FLORA STARK   Baghdad
5 January 1930

Darling B.,

I had a pleasant ride yesterday by the north of Baghdad, the Middle Gate (which is the only one of the old gates still left) a melancholy round bastion and bit of wall in the midst of an untidy depression filled with tombs and railway shuntings, and children and buffaloes where the suburbs and the Assyrian refugee camps begin. You get a good view of Baghdad as you

230

approach: the Ghilani Mosque, with its blue dome and minarets and palm trees before it.

 ˙ I lunched with L. Smith today and looked at his photos, beautiful pictures of the Kurdish and Bakhtiari hills – he goes up trekking and loves it. Capt. Holt came in to tea and we walked home, and he has asked me to ride on Tuesday if nothing intervenes. He is responsible for my starting Persian, and we have got out maps and find the old home of the Assassins not really inaccessible, but very high so that late spring will be the time.

Did I tell you about the Csarevitch? It seems that a poor young refugee got here across the Russian border through Persia – and announced himself to be the Csarevitch: no one could make out if the story was true or not – but they have now tried a medical test to see if the peculiar disease which prevented any scratch etc. to close up and heal, affected this young man: and apparently the test is in favour of his really being the Csarevitch. They are writing for news to know what to do with him, and meanwhile he is amusing himself with the rather less respectable Russians here. And *voilà* all the gossip.

I had some dancing at the club, feeling very middle-aged among all the nice-looking girls who seem to get there from goodness knows where. What was more exciting was my Persian lesson. The old teacher was a judge it seems, though he looks far more like a Buddhist beggar carved in ivory: and he came with an ancient ulster filled with pockets out of which he drew all the most worthless curios for which he asked large preposterous sums. Poor man, his children have typhoid and the woman won't send them to hospital as that would be a pollution. He is going to come three times a week for sixty rupees a month, which is rather ruinous.

Tomorrow is the 'feast of the baptism', Jamila says. They put a bowl of holy water before the altar, and dip the cross in, and leave it at the chancel rail and anyone can come and dip a cup in and drink, and get their wish or healing. And after tomorrow is St. John the Baptist's feast.

Mrs. Young [the wife of the Vice High Commissioner] is taking four Arabic lessons a week from my Mistress Sabiha, who now nearly falls on my neck as she believes me responsible. The other ladies have one lesson a week all together, but I imagine that will not last very long.

Your
FREYA

231

Baghdad
6 January 1930

My dearest Venetia,

Thank you my dear for thinking of my Xmas with all your troubles, and with so much insight into my weakness for unlawful extravagance. I shall be able to indulge in a silk dressing *'abeia*, and not feel that I am doing anything criminal. I am rather hard up just now having just invested in a Persian master, who is teaching me Persian in Arabic, which is good for both. Persian seems very easy by comparison, but if it goes on doing so is of course to be seen. The object is to go up to the ancient (now vanished) castle of the Assassins in one of the valleys between Kazvin and the Black Sea. The Oriental Secretary to the H.C. [Capt. Vyvyan Holt], who is a really first-rate young man, full of understanding, is going to procure a lorry to take me cheaply to the foothills, and then (in about three or four months) my Persian is supposed to carry me on. It is really heart-breaking that you are not to be in all this. But if all goes well (and given that I can manage it, for I really don't quite know how to do the finance), I think this will be a preliminary visit, and some day soon we must go and perhaps settle awhile in a village there or in the Kurdish hills in Rowenduz, which is a hill town between two gorges and all the ranges of the Turkish border.

My dear, you can't imagine what a place this is for taking an interest in other people's affairs, nor what a mutual shock my first contact with proper conventional civil service society has caused. No one else (respectable) appears ever to have settled in a shoemaker's home on the banks of the Tigris, nor has anyone succeeded in living in Baghdad on two rupees a day. One lady has asked me if I am not 'lowering the prestige of British womanhood' by sitting in school among the Iraqi girls. Today on my way there I had to be carried across a puddle on the back of a Kurdish porter, which I am sure would have shocked the ladies of the Alwiyah suburb into fits. For a time, except for one or two people who were really very nice all through, I felt rather like an outcast; the men nearly all disapproved and looked on uneasily if their wives were nice to me – apparently expecting something explosive to happen every second. The East must have rather a distorting effect on people's perspectives. I feel that there was something to be said for the poor bull in the china shop, whose most innocent and natural movements all seemed to cause a smash.

I had a pleasant morning listening to an old story-teller woman, a Christian Assyrian, on Mrs. Drower's terrace. The story was a jumble: Androcles and the Lion, Jinns and princesses, the young. woman dressed as a man who wins people's money at chess, the sort of medley of the *Arabian Nights*, procured by centuries of stories handed on by word of mouth: and the old woman with a charming puckered old face and one very bright eye, and the other blind, got so excited over her adventures, seized our coats to impress the climaxes on to us, and was altogether the best part of the performance. She also told us how one can make oneself bullet-proof by boiling a hoopoe at night by the Bab Wustani or the Talisman Gate of Baghdad: you must never turn round though the Jinns come and pluck at your clothes, but when the breast bone of the hoopoe has boiled so long that it floats to the surface, you take it and tie it on your arm, and you are bullet-proof while you wear it.

Today the Tigris is like a small sea, the waves all going upstream and the east wind and rain beating like hurricanes – turning the palm trees nearly inside out.

I can't tell you how often I wish for you out here. How pleasant it would be to sit here together in my quite warm room with the Tigris flapping its waves below, and maps and plans to make and life in general to talk about. The more I see of people, how set they are apt to get, and dead to all the moving things and the meaning of things, the more I feel how good it is to have one's friends near to talk to.

My dearest love always.   Your
                                                                    FREYA

FLORA STARK   Baghdad
                                                          9 January 1930
Dearest B.,
   Such a lovely day today. After the downpour, the north wind blows and is drying things up as fast as it can. New Street is decent and dry: the others are still a sort of sea of chocolate soup in various stages of thickness. I spent this morning (it being the feast of the Iraq liberation from Turkey and no school) in calling on Mrs. Kerr (who was out) and then found my way through the streets of mud, keeping on the outside edge and realising what it meant in old days to 'take the wall' of anyone; and went to Mrs. Drower's for lunch. Two ladies joined, and we were all off for Kadhimain, which is only about four miles off and one of the Shi'a holy cities, where the Imam Musa is buried. It is a lovely way out of Baghdad running past the King's palace through palm groves which now have already a bright green flooring of plants and grass: and above the metallic shimmering palm leaves appears first the Blue Dome of Muaddham and one blue minaret, then, when we leave that and cross the river, the long sun-baked walls and drab bazaar

opening of the holy city itself, and its double gilt dome and four golden minarets shining surprisingly over the dingy colour of the rest.

Sayid Ja'far, the 'Mayor', was our host, a descendant of the Prophet with his green turban and very red nose not derived from the drinking of water, and an amiable twinkle and benevolent face. We went round the mosque: first a look at (I think) the north door from the roof of a bath opposite; one can see the lovely gold domes and minarets at close quarters, and the tiles of the great archway like a garden of flowers, chiefly rose and blue with delicate flower borders and a band of writing in white on blue majolica. A crowd going in and out, touching the heavy brass chain which hangs across the door at the height of a man's shoulder and which is so holy to touch that the metal in the middle parts of it has got bright with touches. They had no objection even to our cameras, but when my foot nearly touched the sacred threshold the policeman drew me back in the most alarmed manner. The inner building appears through the doorway, more high arches, with stalactite work of mirrors that glitter towards you in the middle of a wide flagged court.

What one misses here is that the beautiful things are so rarely in beautiful settings: it is almost impossible to feel *satisfied,* as one does in Italy: always there is a jarring or sordid or cruel touch somewhere. And yet it is indescribably fascinating.

You would like the seven gates of the sanctuary: two are really lovely – a façade of delicate rose and blue tiles, flowers, landscapes, garlands in small delicate Persian workmanship. And the crowd is more picturesque than Baghdad – fierce Persian faces of pilgrims, and flowing robes of the Mullahs and people who live by the shrine. In Kadhimain they still think a Christian touch pollutes them and I believe Sayid Ja'far's family, whom we called on after tea, were none too pleased to shake hands.

We wandered a little in the bazaar, and I bought most attractive painted wooden combs – the kind that were first no doubt invented by the Sumerians.

Your

FREYA

ROBERT STARK

Baghdad

10 January 1930

Darling Pips,

Such a good adventure to tell you this week, and I am sitting up to do so, having just come home from it safe and sound. I have been inside the Kadhimain Mosque, which is so holy that Christians are not allowed even to touch the threshold, and would in fact be killed if found inside. But I wore a black veil over my face and a black *'abba* over my head, covering me all up, and black shoes that looked as un-English as I could find – and so dressed up went from here with two native Syrian Christians, also got up. We did the dressing in their house and sent the servants to get a taxi so that the driver shouldn't know, and then we sped along the four miles to Kadhimain about 7 p.m. with a row of dim lamps either side the road all the way to the holy city. Our friends there are a Shi'a doctor's family, and we couldn't find the house: we got into the bazaar and had to make ourselves conspicuous by asking. The bazaar is a Rembrantesque sort of place at night, full of shadows. We found the house at last and then all sallied forth, the doctor leading, a servant and lantern ahead to light up the various sloughs and drains of the road, the brother Kerim behind, and we in true female Eastern fashion trailing at intervals as best we could. I was very anxious not to let the wretched veil slip off my head.

We got through a dark gate into the enormous quadrangle of the mosque, like a great piazza, with groups here and there, and a few lamps lighting the mosaic portico, and the gold and mirrored lunettes of the sanctuary in the middle. The stars, very bright, overhead; and one had a great feeling of space. No Western note here. It was a weird feeling to know that really one's life depended on not being recognised; and still weirder to see people looking straight at one and to remind oneself that they couldn't possibly see through the black veil. We went up to the door of the sanctuary – our host exchanging greetings with various Sayids in flowing robes and green or white turbans. At the gate we took off our shoes and a man with a stick poked it into the toe and lifted the impure object to one side. The marble was very cold to stand on. 'You are people of the house,' said a misguided Mullah to our host, and took us into the shrine himself with the proper prayers: he stood at the front great gate and prayed in the beautiful half singing voice to which they are trained, an invocation to Muhammad and Ali, and then – with 'God is great' – we stepped back into a mirrored place: then through another great curtain into the holy of holies, the tomb of the two Imams. It didn't seem very large, and the whole centre is filled by the two tombs whose carved wood can be seen dimly through the glass, and the iron grating, and then the enormous silver grill with bands of silver texts perpendicular around it, all polished by the hands of the faithful who press round, pressing their hands and bodies against it and kissing it. The atmosphere of the place was extraordinary. Such intensity of passion. A woman sobbing beside me, kissing the silver grating again and again; people crouching on the ground with their heads against it; old Sheiks immovable

235

there, with their hands upturned, their faces rapt, their eyelids lowered, lost to all sensation. And the strongest impression was that of these passionate hands, pressing their way round the four sides of the great square tomb – Kerim murmured to me not to move off but to go round also, which I did, my hand along the thick bars but not kissing, being a Presbyterian. When we reached the third side, we stopped, and our Mullah again chanted a prayer. Muhammad, Ali, Musa the holy Imam : I did not catch it all, but the sound was extraordinarily moving. On the fourth side, an old Mullah was offering candles for the obtaining of all one's desires : very like Italy really, except for the intensity of the whole thing and the fact of course that these people would not hesitate a minute to do you in.

I am just home now at ten and wondering whether this is going to get me into trouble when it gets known. I believe one or two Englishwomen have been in before, but not many, and I know the official attitude will not be very cordial.

They have been having great bother in the south lately. Our people have now got hold of the Wahabi rebels : * Ibn Saud very cleverly pushed them up till we had the bother of having to accept their surrender, with the consequent dirty job of dealing with them. It is rather a problem : if one hands them back to Ibn Saud to whom they belong, he will kill them and that seems cold blooded though I believe they deserve it.

Do write soon. I think Baghdad will find me for another three months anyway.

Your own

* Revolt of the Mutair tribe. FREYA

FLORA STARK Baghdad
12 January 1930

Darling B.,

I don't know what has happened to my Mu'allim : he has stopped coming. He paid a call with Sheikh Habib dressed in a lovely new silk gown with long sleeves falling over his hands, and perfumed : and I sent chocolates to his wife : and that is all I know of them. As a matter of fact, now with my Persian and schooling I have as much as I can do to keep up.

I had a lovely ride on Friday. Just as I was contemplating going to pay some long overdue calls, who should walk in but Capt. Holt, with his horses waiting round the corner. He took me out by Zobeida's tomb across the brown country where the young wheat – or barley – is showing already a new vivid green, and the Beduin flocks are crowded with lambs. It was glorious cantering along : and we came to two tiny ditches which I jumped, and then over the mound of the Abbasside city with its potsherds scattered round it, and so home.

Saturday I spent at Mrs. Caparn's; riding, and then a big dinner party with some very pleasant people who knew all about me it seems. It is quite good for one to have to lead this sort of life in the full critical view of a whole community – but I think one should have that training when one is young and not come out as a debutante in the thirties.

Your

FREYA

HERBERT YOUNG

Baghdad

16 January 1930

My dearest Herbert,

I have just been to a most interesting lecture on Kish, watching the slides of the Deluge and the graves of the people who were buried before that, and the marks of their chariot-wheels studded with copper nails on the tyres: of course neither tyre nor wheel exists, only the copper nails and the place in the earth where the rest should be, but the clever archaeologist can supply more difficult objects than these out of his inventiveness. A little clay model of a chariot has been found (any date between 2,500 and 3,500 B.C.) with two animals beside the driving pole and a team of five in front, of which one seems distinctly to be an elephant.

Tonight is the night of 'Qadr' for the Shi'as (last night was that of the Sunnis): during it, God apportions the year's fortunes to all and sundry, and the shrines are full of people praying for a good lot. May yours be of the best! The little boys are celebrating it by dancing about in the moonlight of the river bank and letting off petards which are disturbing to the nerves in this country where shooting is such a common art. A Jew was shot in the bazaar the other day for asking to have his bill paid: he wasn't killed, but no doubt he will give longer credit next time.

Your

FREYA

ROBERT STARK

Baghdad

20 January 1930

Dearest Pips,

I have had a good ride today with Capt. Holt, after a week more or less indoors, with wind rain and mud; it was lovely to feel a pony under one and the wind blowing the palms about in the distance and the ground drying up nicely so that we could canter. Capt. Holt is alas going to leave in the spring: he is going to spend his time studying Russian in Moscow. At present it is possible he may be going to the conference between King Faisal and Ibn Saud down in the south: at first just a dozen or so were to go, with H.C. and one A.D.C. – and to sleep in the aeroplanes: then King Faisal increased the number to fifty; now he has announced that 450 is a necessary bodyguard for his dignity.

On Saturday they had the unveiling of the memorial to Miss Bell. I did not go, but had eight Moslem ladies to tea – rather overpowering, but pleasant, they were mostly officers' wives, and one of them told me how her father, when serving with the Turkish Army against the Muntafiq tribe south of Baghdad, got taken prisoner after wounding the Sheikh. They told him that they would see how the Sheikh did, and if he died they must kill him, and after three days the Sheikh died and the officer was killed.

You would like the Sumerian fork I saw the other day – a really lovely object – two-pronged with some winged animal on the handle. I am going to indulge myself and spend £3 on an Assyrian cylinder seal.

Your
FREYA

FLORA STARK   Baghdad
                                                            24 January 1930
Darling B.,

I have lost trace of dates of letters and yours are late this week because of the mud in the desert. Everything is damp and dirty and it is still raining off and on, and the streets unspeakable, and the returning in the dark to my house seems wonderful to everyone, though it is ever so much easier than the old path down to L'Arma. But the hotel-keeper's son on our side of the river has been found murdered away by the Dyala: the hotel clerk, whose job he had been given, took him away in a motor and strangled him and then put both his eyes out, because it is supposed that the picture of the murderer shows in the pupils if you are strangled. It's a horrid story, and the Chaldeans, among whom the tragedy occurred, are much upset at the discredit.

I went this afternoon to see the charming Ghilani family, the hereditary keepers of the old mosque whose turquoise dome is just opposite their house. I was taken to the lady's sister-in-law, an ugly but attractive old woman who is given over to devotion and sits on a mattress in one corner of a room which one does not profane. If one goes in, the whole place has to be spring-

238

cleaned: I did not gather and was just going in when horrified exclamations stopped me and I stood on the little mat at the threshold and talked to the old lady. Your own

FREYA

PENELOPE KER Baghdad
25 January 1930

My darling Pen,

This morning I had a rather sad experience. I was taken to call on Queen 'Ali, the wife of the deposed King of Hejaz. She is kept in a big house lower down on the river, and the house and its yard, with a rear exit to visit her in-laws at King Faisal's palace, is all the range of these poor ladies' lives. We banged on the door, and at last a little black boy with a red gown and turban came running along, opened the door and let us into a yard . A big board, like a scoring board for cricket, was just about six feet inside the door, so that even when open no one could look into the courtyard. If the house caught fire, all those females inside would be burned. A beautiful white saluki came bounding down the steps to meet us. But the house was old and squalid, with its earthen filter for water in one corner and the painted porticoes of light blue wooden pillars picked out with yellow. Upstairs, we went into a long room all upholstered with embossed yellow velvet and purple curtains and large enlargements of royal photos on the walls – Faisal, and Hussein, 'Ali, and his son the young Emir who is learning to play tennis in a British school in Alexandria while his mother lives this life of ten centuries ago here. A lady-in-waiting with untidy hair and shabby old flannel coat entertained us, till Her Majesty came in, in a little green ready-made house dress, very simple, with bobbed hair and the most unhappy eyes you ever saw. She is still quite young and had been used to a pleasanter life in Constantinople (where she belongs) and even in Mecca: people hate to visit her for she hardly speaks or even answers, but sits in her yellow chair on the opposite side of the room with her fierce unhappy eyes and rather pale plain little face, saying 'ay' to all efforts that are made to entertain her. Today she was more talkative than usual, and at times looked quite pretty and gentle when she smiled. The black slaves came in with very heavy steps because they had been made to put on high-heeled shoes, and gave us coffee out of black and gold cups, and we then came away feeling saddened in the lovely sunshine. A man outside, who sat in the mud skewering a huge fish to roast over a fire on the ground, was a much happier sight. Your

FREYA

Darling B.,

Last night Mrs. Caparn took Mrs. Harvey and me to see the Queen.*
It was after dinner because of Ramadhan, and I wore my Asolo dress.
We went up by a police sentry through miles of what might have been
hospital corridors with very inferior rugs spread along and, instead of the
Nubian slaves, little girls in high heels and knitted jumpers and an apron
tied over them, who took our coats off. Then we went into a big room,
rather bare walls, and crimson furniture – quite dignified in its bareness;
and the little figure of the Queen, with an ermine wrap and gilt shoes,
standing up very straight and with a charming smile in front of her crimson
throne, was really queen-like. We managed our curtseys nicely and then
sat at some distance, and as Her Majesty didn't help at all but merely turned
with her beaming smile and brilliant black beautiful kohl-brimmed eyes
whenever you spoke, it was rather difficult to plunge into chit chat. Mrs.
Caparn can get along in Arabic but I was supposed to do the talking, and
got through somehow. The two princesses presently came in, slim, rather
plain, with their mother's big eyes, and something very young and pathetic
about them. They both talk English but were happier talking Arabic I
thought. A white fluffy cat sat under the throne and the white ermine. The
Queen's face was ugly and charming – a huge mouth and hennaed hair
which she has bobbed, but the only things noticeable are the vivid eyes so
brimming with life that it seems a miracle she should say nothing.

Presently the little girls in aprons came along with coffee; and then in
ten minutes or so with tea; and then in another ten minutes or so, with huge
slabs of cake; and then Mrs. Caparn said we must be going – which
seemed the wrong way round when sitting round a throne: and we got
up and curtsied again, and got all down the length of the room without
turning our backs. The princesses just outside the door told us that dozens of
Arab ladies were being kept waiting till our audience was over. I rather
wished they had been let in before we left.

I had a beautiful ride in the morning – two and a half hours through the
rich garden country by the river where the Tigris makes a huge loop and
looks almost northern with its low scrubby banks and blue distance:
some ancient silhouette of river vessel on the still water, fishermen,
bare to the thigh, pulling their nets, and inland, glade after glade of tall
palms with the corn stunningly green beneath, and orange trees full of fruit,
or the bare fig boughs, or peach orchards with the tip of the boughs just
reddening for the spring.

Such a horrid sight as I came by the bridge the other day: a dead body washed up by the side.

Ever so much love dear B.

Your
FREYA

* Wife of King Faisal.

MRS. GRANVILLE   Baghdad
11 February 1930

My darling Fairy Godmother,

It is now Ramadhan, and till this moon has got round and disappeared again, the people fast, the shops are closed till the sunset gun has gone off and the people eat their first meal. Then the streets wake up: fruitsellers, coffee shops, the sellers of sticky sugar sweets peculiar to this time drive a brisk trade, and all Moslem Baghdad starts being sociable till 3 a.m. when the next meal is eaten. I have been visiting several Moslem ladies, going out about seven through little tortuous streets lit at long intervals, with a soldier here and there keeping guard, and a dim crowd in turbans and *'abbas* going to and fro. We walk along, a little group all hooded and veiled in black (except me) with a lantern carried before us: find some door under an overhanging balcony (all the doors are open now), and from some upper room you hear the lute being played just as the Arabian Caliph used to hear it. You go into the courtyard which is the centre of all Baghdad houses and usually rather smelly, up steps, the brickwork all brightly painted green or yellow, into the reception room which is usually very gaudily printed velvet, and there a circle of ladies sits with the chair backs all straight round the walls, and usually the sofa at the end of the room vacant as no one likes to sit in the place of honour. Gradually the conversation livens up. The ladies, in all sorts of odd clothes from full evening dress to striped cardigans and jumpers, gossip: the coffee and the tea pot are brought round and after sitting an hour or so we move on to the next house. There is no room for wheeled things in those narrow streets, so that the crowd gives one rather the impression of some fantastic distorted Venetian effect. And above the dark line of houses now and then you come upon the mosques, their dark blue domes lit up faintly by the ring of lights which shine round the minarets.

My landlady is fasting for three days. She says it is the Nineveh fast first started by the people of Nineveh when the Lord rebuked them and it has

241

been kept ever since. So she says, and I should not wonder in this ancient land.

We had a dust storm yesterday, and everything was coated: one eats, breathes and moves in it.

Your
FREYA

OLIVIA BARKER
Baghdad
13 February 1930

Dearest Olivia,

There is a ferment of anti-British feeling and I have had the usual Moderate's fate of falling between two stools: the Nationalists would have welcomed me kindly, but one doesn't feel it possible to be too intimate when it might work against one's own people: on the other hand my innocent excursions among all sorts of queer and interesting sets have made me go down as a Bolshie or worse among the good people who tell me with virtuous airs that looking after husbands and children takes up all their time. I have some rather peculiar friends as a matter of fact. One of them has just been asked to leave the country for illicit dealings in morphia and I spent yesterday afternoon with his wife and newborn baby, mother, mother-in-law and father-in-law, the accusation in five sheets of typewritten Arabic being read out to me. It was a curious document, eleven childish charges with the morphine one sandwiched in the middle, frequent interruptions and Allah to witness that the doctor is the most innocent man in the world, and the doctor himself, with a little rat-face quite untrustworthy, explaining that his worst enemy is going to be on the bench to judge him. Very like the Italian attitude only more so, and no saving artistic sense, so that nothing ugly or shocking seems to give any feeling of repulsion. On the other hand there is far more of a religious feeling and this is really the strength of these people.

Yesterday I went over one of the few old things in Baghdad, the old palace of the Abbassids which is shut away in the wide enclosure of the citadel and now littered with rubbish, but its beautiful brickwork is still a joy to look on and the carved brick decoration of the gate and great hall. It is all Persian work, cut in sharp deep chiselling out of the yellow brick, with patterns of leaves and hieroglyphs and arranged, where the vaults spring from the walls, in a series of overhanging niches and jutting corners that gives a charming sense of lightness. The rooms must have been immensely high, like deep wells with a small hole in the middle of the roof for the light to come in by, and a few small windows with sills, so high that there was no looking in or out.

Everything is old here when you come to look beneath the surface. I was shown a girl's bracelet, pearls and gold, made on the *exact* pattern of what is dug out of the Babylonian tombs. And all my native Christian friends these three days have been keeping the 'fast of Nineveh', to expiate that city's ancient sins.

I feel that, after three months, I am only at the very beginning of things and there would be a thousand interesting explorations to make.

Your loving
FREYA

ROBERT STARK   Baghdad
                                           14 February 1930
Darling Pips,

We went to a rather attractive place last Saturday, not more than forty minutes' car ride from Baghdad and with cultivation close by, but actually in the desert with the black flocks and tents about in the distance among grass just sprouting, invisibly to all but Iraqi sheep. It is Akher Kùf, a corner of an old Ziggurat built up like a Dartmoor tor with ridges of three feet or so of solid raw brick like the earth around, and layers of reeds, still doing their work, and appearing with rough edges just like the crystal ridges that run along the granite of the Tors. It is a shapeless block, very tall on a sloping mound once built up to support the temple; and is the home of wolves and hyenas and such who live in its crannies and scatter the whole surface of the mound with bones. You see it between the shallow undulations of the desert earth as if at the end of a 'vista', and very impressive. Far away Baghdad palm trees and the golden dome and four minarets of Kadhimain: and the good desert air, inexpressibly light and unlike any other. I can't get out without longing for the free spaces.

After next week I shall devote myself to a little sightseeing – go down to Ur and possibly somewhere north, though it is almost impossible to move without the fuss of police all round.

Your
FREYA

Darling B.,

I have been trying during these days to pull together the strings of impressions collected during my three months here. It has been a mixed time in many ways; particularly so because I had nothing to prepare me for the difficulties of it. I have only been liked apologetically as it were, and people who began by being nice gave it up in despair, which has been dreadfully painful. I have been feeling how incompetent I am to live in company at all and sometimes felt it was hardly worth it. When you once start with a wrong impression, *all* you do or say is fitted into it and interpreted in its light: I have also realised that the real difficulty is not the eccentricity of my being here but the fact that I do seem to be a foreigner and a stranger: the people who have ever lived abroad 'placed' me at once and have been charming all through: and now as a matter of fact lots of people are beginning to be really nice to me. There have been some advantages too with it all: the passion of hurt vanity and hatred which our unconscious exclusions rouse among these other people have become comprehensible to me. But with it all and in spite of having been put out about it, I don't feel that resentment towards the British attitude which so many people seem to have who come up against them from 'outside'. In fact I like them all. They live on a moral island and it is bound to have certain disadvantages, but I think the balance of advantages is greater on the whole, and especially for a people like ours who are bound to live in minorities. It is like the Roman church – no mercy for heretics but a strong unity in itself. The conformity is one of form more than anything else: if you had brought me up in a proper English way, I would have known that so long as one says and does like everyone else (and that is so impossible to guess!) one can think what one likes.

What I do feel however is that this habit of conformity loses most of its advantages when you come to the few people who have the actual framing of policies in their hands: they *ought* to have all the creative virtues which are not encouraged in the official – just as the material which makes the best rudders is not what is most suitable for the inside of the steersman's head. And one does feel a rather terrible want of a steersman here just now.

In spite of not being ready for it by any means, I believe Iraq will have its independence – if only nominal; the current that way is too general all over the East; and we help it by educating more and more people in this direction so that we pull them back with one hand and push them on with the other. We might at most delay the matter for a generation or two at great cost – and on the condition of making things more difficult when they come to a head.

The plea that Iraq is unfit to govern itself seems to me rather feeble: one might say that of dozens of countries in Europe. The real argument is that we cannot risk a bad government in Iraq, interfering with several vital interests of ours: oil, and the Indian route and such: if we could keep these safe, it seems to me that the Iraqis might enjoy their bad governing if they wish without doing us any harm.

If some really great man could gather the whole question together and lift it from the field of politics (which have become anathema) to that of commerce: Iraq to be run through Persian oil or some such as a business concern and the local government left to itself in all that did not immediately regard us, I don't see why the matter should not be feasible. It would mean shifting the whole emphasis of the Empire from politics to finance: and we have always had a prejudice against amalgamating the two. But it is what the strong nations are doing more and more.

And I feel that all our future lies in these few years. *Before* these natives are independent, our own alternative policy must be ready and working.

I believe a great man would do it. Would shape a really new conception of Empire for our generation, a principle with life in it. Wouldn't one gladly give a lifetime to find such a one?

Your

FREYA

FLORA STARK   Baghdad
                                                                4 March 1930
Darling B.,

I have been bad in writing these days, but I had one boil on my nose and then one inside each ear; they are the amenities of Baghdad spring. The one on my nose went away in time for the Bachelors' Ball and I really enjoyed that. I sat out two dances and danced one with Major Young, and got his views on Baghdad – evidently a *cri du coeur*. He says that all these little British societies abroad are 'quite unspeakable' and the worst is that they can't even choose the people they like to know inside them but have to go by seniority. I told him that I was in their black books, and we settled to talk of pleasant topics like Bach with the fellow-feeling of being equally disapproved of.

My dinner at the A.V.M.'s was very amusing; Lady Brooke-Popham told us about the meeting of the kings: Faisal making a very poor show beside the King of Nejd, physique, personality and everything; and finally, after they had been once alone together, Ibn Saud begged that it might never happen again, as Faisal instantly begins to whine about his lost kingdom, which of course is not tactful under the circumstances. So a Britisher had to remain to keep things on a conversational level.

Your

FREYA

FLORA STARK

Baghdad
4 March 1930

Darling B.,

I went to the theatre to hear Fatima Rushti in *Salambo*. The love-making is too obvious for our Western taste, but the tragic part was very fine – and the singing too with the long drawn-out accent of the consonants. We were down in the stalls, and the only women there, and quite nicely behaved to – except that the fleas were numerous.

Today I have had all my Bahai friends to tea. Next week I have to pack and already begin to feel it is all at an end – not a wasted winter and full of things I shall like to think of later, though it has been rather a severe schooling.

Love to you dear B.

Your

FREYA

VENETIA BUDDICOM

Baghdad
6 March 1930

Dearest Venetia,

It seems that my doctor friends (whose wife was introduced to me by the El Azms in Damascus) are being sent out of the country as fast as possible for illicit dealings in morphia. I went today and found a circle of lamenting females, and the ladies cold towards me for not having the Englishman on the bench reverse judgement in their favour. What can one explain in such a case? I am sorry for the little bride with her new baby – so genuinely devoted to her awful little ferret of a husband whom I always thought of as rather on the shady side of things. My other friend, the handsome Sheikh who comes to call in a yellow silk gown with ruffled sleeves and hands dyed with henna, apparently spends his spare time in robbing the helpless wayfarer and annoying the authorities: no wonder the virtuous look on me with glassy eyes. As a matter of fact the ladies would like to like me, it is the men who are all so very upset about it.

Your

FREYA

My dearest Viva,

We left at 6.30 on a lovely spring day with the Eastern chill in it – which cuts you in two like a knife so that we wrapped our heads in woollies and padded our fronts with pillows and were quite glad when about two hours across the flat half-deserted fields brought us to the Hindiyah barrage. We went out into desert after Hindiyah with gardens on our left – palms and a thin veil of blossom below them: then into gardens, glades and glades of palm and narrow reaches of water: magpies and kingfishers: traffic of donkeys chiefly: and suddenly a few ramshackle houses, and this is Kerbela.

Mecca and Medina are of course the holiest of all, but for the Shi'a Moslems (and they cover half Iraq, all Persia, and much of Central Asia and India) Kadhimain, Kerbela, and Nejf are almost the more sacred. Along the stretches of desert as we went it was strangely touching to see here and there some gaunt figures of the Persian pilgrims, walking months on end, over that unending blistering freezing flat land: sitting two together by the roadside, or walking with a woman and child plodding behind, or lying stretched flat on their faces on the sand with the little yellow desert flowers and purple irises springing up around. Nejf is right out in the desert and springs like a vision on their weary sight – a town inside a buttressed wall with its golden dome and minarets of the promised city. But Kerbela is hidden in its palm groves, you come in through mean and dirty suburbs, and then gradually through streets porticoed in a miserable way by crazy palm-stem pillars, by cafés full of dingy seats and pale malarial faces, in to the centre where the *suqs* run in a shadowy circle round the mosque where the body of Hussein lies. There is not a European in Kerbela, or in Nejf either, but the police welcomed us politely and Mr. Cooke knew Sayid Abu l'Hussein who wears a green turban and is respected. We expected to be followed about by looks of black hatred, but as a matter of fact many of the people seemed friendly enough, and a coffee-keeper allowed me to pollute one of his seats by standing on it to photograph the great door and two black flags which show the way in to the Mosque of 'Abbas.

Near Kerbela was the place of the battle where they fought all day, a little band with no hope and against great odds, and suffering from thirst, and were killed one by one. A relative of Sayid Abu l' Hussein, also in green turban and with an unhealthy untrustworthy face, took us up on to a roof and we looked down into the court of the mosque and its brilliant mosaics of Persian tiles, on to the groups of Indians, Turkomans, Arabs, sauntering in their own sanctuary there. Some wealthy Indian prince gave money for the gilding of the dome and minarets, and most of it is done – all except half a minaret for which the money seems to have wandered by the way into some no doubt holy pocket.

In all the shops of Kerbela you see booths, where small grey tablets rather like soap are sold: these are pieces of the sacred earth which only a true believer can buy: he puts his forehead on it when he prays. I said to Mr. Cooke that I supposed we could not possibly get hold of one. He said nothing about it, but after, when we were out in the desert, produced one for each of us from his pocket: but how they came there I don't know.

We were shown the very friendly side of it all: walked from gate to gate of the two mosques – taking care not to go near the threshold but being allowed to snapshot freely; then taken to a charming court with flowerbeds and an arbour and water in the middle with goldfish, and there we sat while various personalities in black turbans (learned men) or green (descendants of the Prophet) came and talked, till two huge trays of sticky pastry, cream, honey, bread, oranges, leban were carried to the upper room and we sat down and tucked in as hard as we could.

You go straight into the open desert from Kerbela, skirting the palms far away on your left, and with a clear horizon on every other side – it used to take two days, and there are three old khans, deserted now, which once used to swarm with pilgrims; a few Bedu, and the police, are all the inhabitants, but the yellow walls and round buttresses, and the arched gateways, still look very fine in the landscape. Then, as I said, Nejf comes to you like a vision – black walls, gold dome, and its graves strewn around it the colour of desert sand, with here and there the blue glazed domes of richer graves. Coffins come rattling along in Ford cars to be buried here from many distant lands. If you die of the plague or anything contagious, you have to travel 'dry' – that is to say you are buried for six months first and then dug up and brought here. For £50 you can be buried in the sacred enclosure itself: there is a limited number of graves available, and it never diminishes. The people who are not buried dry are of course rather unsanitary travellers, but less so now that the motor gets the journey over more quickly. Right across the bit of desert between Nejf and Kufa you can see a funny little tram on wheels being drawn by horses; that is the Nejf water supply, and you can buy a fat skinful of water for half an anna. The desert air is all in and out of Nejf's narrow streets. The people are freer and healthier and have the good walk of the desert people, but even more fanatical than Kerbela, for Ali is buried in Nejf and it is the holiest place of all; and though we went with the sons of the Killidar, they themselves kept us as far as they could from the door of the mosque, and pressed in between us so that they might prevent

248

the pollution. There is a beautiful great door to the Nejf mosque, done far more simply than most with coloured glazed medallions in good plain brick-work and the golden gateways of the sanctuary itself showing behind across the court. I should like to stay in Nejf for a month or so. Mr. Cooke says it would be perfectly feasible as the Killidar's guest, but of course the government people here would make a fuss. Mr. Cooke quite sensibly thinks it is a mistake to try to make these places safe by never letting people go there, the best way is to make them safe by getting as much traffic through them as they possibly can. As far as exploiting the tourist side of Iraq goes, we compare very poorly with the French in Syria. I do think that the average Englishman is naturally antagonistic to ideas as such: he sniffs and sniffs at them like a pony at a bog, while everyone else has long been getting to the other side.

We left the pilgrim's city and went again across the desert to the cultivated land and Kufa on its edge – a tiny little town with a huge empty khan and half dead little *suq* and the great mosque buttressed like a fortress. It had all the charm of a place that has once been flourishing and then died suddenly without any dingy transformation in the process, and here again the clean desert air was like freedom after the stuffy narrow ways of the inland towns. Ali was murdered in Kufa, as he was praying in this very mosque. His body, at his request, was loaded on a camel and was to be buried where the camel kneeled down; and so as it wandered out browsing into the desert, and rested on the little rise, the city of Nejf was born. That is the legend.

I must really finish this letter and hurry you past Ezekiel's tomb at Kifl. He is bunched together with five 'friends of the Prophet' who are kept in a back room as it were, with a few polished stones which take away whatever pain they are rubbed against. Ezekiel belongs to the Jews, and one can see at once the more artistic race by the decoration, and the beauty of the rugs. An old Jew went round with us, blue-eyed with heavy lids – quite different type and I don't like it much. His young helpers were all Moslem however, and all the faiths come to visit Ezekiel, and the hands printed in henna on the walls are all Moslem. This also is a little half-dead village, with small dingy *suq* among fields and palms, and lives by its tomb and pilgrims: a little court, and minaret of Abbassid-worked brick crumbling and tottering – the holes loud and busy with pigeons, and a stork on the very top. Outside the village is a little colony of weavers, their bodies half buried in the ground which is thus brought to a convenient height for managing the shuttle. We hurried north and in the last sunlight saw what is left of the Tower of Babel on its mound, a very impressive hill built by the hand of man. Then to sleep in the rest house at Babylon.   Your

FREYA

Baghdad
8 March 1930

Dearest Venetia,

Just back after a glorious tour. I am going to begin at the end and tell you about Babylon and Kish, for I shall not have time for more and that is what you would have enjoyed most – especially as Mr. Cooke made us see it all as it once was and stole a brick of Nebuchadnezzar for me into the bargain (so good for my luggage). We saw Birs Nimrud, which was once Borsippa, and the Tower of Babel, in the evening with the last of the sun behind it – an impressive mound like the Pyramid with its bit of solid brick tower on the summit. There is a mystery for the whole top is covered with great blocks of brick coagulated by fire: Mr. Cooke's theory is that the weight and friction of the brick tower above them must have melted them as the whole thing came crashing down. Anyway there they are, a mystery, and symbol of the old legend. The river has long left the land, and it is now desert or desert-like fields, rising into mounds where the dead cities are strewn. We got to Babylon at nightfall and settled in the German rest house, to a supper of Bovril and sandwiches and an entertainment after from the small village boys who sang and danced: 'Oh Father of the railway, curses upon you who carry my love so swiftly away': or 'Her beauty shines as far as Basra and Baghdad and Damascus and turns the Moslems into unbelievers'.

Our first day was cloudless blue and sun, but next morning the clouds came up in great bands over the desert and suited that old melancholy land though we grew anxious: the last archaeological visitor having been imprisoned for five days by weather. We walked for nearly three hours over the mounds and pits of Babylon. Nebuchadnezzar was really *worse* than Herbert Olivier and when one sees the scale of his buildings one can quite understand the decay of the empire after – it must have completely exhausted his own resources and his subjects' patience, for he built three times, always widening the circuit of his palace quarter, and raising the level of the town bodily, burying all he had built before, including the beautiful Ishtar gate with its carved animals. The city rose on great solid walls eighty feet thick in one place, fifty-seven in another. The sacred way, flagged with great blocks, with a parapet of more blocks and two rows of glazed lion figures to line it, ran alongside one of the walls, through the Ishtar gate to the King's palace and the temple of Ishtar at one corner. The great hall of Belshazzar is approached through two courts, where the offices and officials' houses were, and the hanging gardens on the left near the Sacred Way and the river. We did not linger here, for the weather grew darker and darker. We hastened across the obliterated river bed to the Parthian city opposite, which was inhabited down to the thirteenth century: then back again to a Greek theatre; in the distance the pile of debris where Alexander brought Marduk's Ziggurat bricks to build a second Tower of Babel: and the flat sort of small hill where his friend Hephaestion was buried: the charred pieces of wood were still found there. Then – greatly daring – we decided to risk Kish after all, chiefly because Mrs. Cooke was to meet us there. We went across open desert, *strewn* with dead cities like dunes in the sand on ridges of old canals – all dead: we passed camels and saw them trying to jump the ditch, a ridiculous clumsy sight: one collapsed, and its load of two small infants came rolling down in perfect silence and with great composure over its tail while it lay helpless astride the ridge.

At Kish, a little low mud house with a small square of barley and ornamental jar on a pedestal before it, enclosed on three sides by the building: there is nothing else visible, and here the mission lives, Mr. Watelin and Mr. Martel – two charming Frenchmen. What a relief to be with people so interested in ideas that they do not take you for an unnatural phenomenon whenever you express one. They assured me that with one exception I am the only woman in Baghdad with a soul of any sort. Whatever it is, I know it is unique here and a most inconvenient commodity: but it was charming to sit and talk French and be liked and have a delicious lunch with one's *tumbler* refilled with champagne at intervals: and our hosts asking when they could see us again. And Kish is older than Ur I believe: anyway the streak of earth which represents the deluge is quite a good way up and all sorts of pottery found below it. After the deluge a new layer, different sorts of pots, are found. But the exciting thing is that these earliest pots were beautiful, painted and decorated in an age long before the discovery of metals. The ages come up gradually layer by layer – from the flints to a lovelier terracotta relief of Ishtar than I have seen anywhere except among Greek things. We got an ancient pot each and came home rejoicing, trying to roll ourselves round the treasures so as to preserve them from the bumps of the road. Kish is really more impressive than Babylon to the naked eye, for its temple walls still stand with their broken surfaces to catch the light and shade, like the newest skyscrapers in New York. It was another of Nebuchadnezzar's palaces and never finished: and next year it is going to be blown to bits with dynamite so that we saw it at its last. Next year I hope you will be out here to see the next.

Now darling V., do send a *post card*, because I am *always* wondering about you. Really very unhappy about you, for it is too long to be ill. We will have a good time together again some day. Your

FREYA

Baghdad
                                                      13 March 1930
Darling B.,

As I went down into the 'bellum' to go out to dinner last night, I put my
foot and gilt slipper bang into the mud, and was much annoyed with the
boatman, who had shown me the wrong place. 'But your head is safe,' said
he, and of course that is a disarming way of putting a damage to one's shoe.
He told me as he rowed me up that a purse and five rupees had that day
fallen through a hole in his pocket and been lost: 'This is destiny,' says he:
'it is the power of Allah' – and I didn't like to say that a stitch in time was
what was needed to make the power work differently.

                                                          Your
                                                        FREYA

Mosul
                                                      15 March 1930
Darling B.,

It is good to be up here at last. Mrs. Drower and I came by train to Baiji:
a night in the train and wake up with early sun shining on a flat green
country with a ridge of low hills, Jebel Hamrin, on our right. Car waiting.
Breakfast in the train, made by Mubarak, Mrs. D.'s good Bahrein Arab,
with the effect of his red kefiah and the immense woollen fluffy 'agal he
always wears like a crown, rather spoilt by a very bulky burberry. We had
six hours by car, most of it delightful over the short desert grass – red tulips
or anemones here and there, and wild mignonette and marigolds growing
over the ruins of Asshur. This is still a wonderful ghost of a fortified city:
no habitation is there now except the empty rest house of German diggers
before the war; but one can still feel it under the blanket of all those ages –
a fine place for a young nation to grow up in, the hills in small shallow
ridges behind it and the rich lands and river before, and many further ranges
visible far off in the north and east. Here the Assyrian power grew and
spread and gradually left its old home. We scrambled over it and then sped
along, and sat to lunch in the sun and wind with endless dipping horizons
of various green around us, and camels and tents, grazing homes of the
Beduin everywhere in the distance. Then we came to stone in the landscape
– the first after the stoneless southern plain: arched doorways, milestones,
stone ridges: sloping roofs here and there with storks building on every one
of them. Hills on the horizon, and here and there lonely round mounds
where cities are probably buried.

Mosul itself is full of charm though dirty: not the *sodden* sort of dirtiness of Baghdad however. The bazaars are full of colour: good costumes – Kurds in baggy trousers and padded waistcoats round their middles: Tiaris, with small sort of pagoda felt hats and shrewd mountaineers' faces: Christians, with bright colours, and baggier trousers than the Kurds. These towns all rise 'on stepping stones of their dead selves'. Across the old bridge, which begins on wooden boats studded with great nails and looking very Viking-like, and goes on, when it reaches the bank, in a series of stone arches; and has women washing on stones like Italy: across that, is Nineveh, with a little clustered town built on its mound so that no one can dig it up.

Your

FREYA

Mosul

17 March 1930

Dearest Car,

Now I am up in Mosul and spring just beginning with a tang of the north in it: no palms here but peach blossom, and pear trees just bursting into fat little bunches, and rolling shallow green hills like downs, with strips of ploughed land: and far away, the Kurdistan snows and the Turkish ranges. And the streets and bazaars are cobbled with stones like a proper northern town, and have every sort of mountaineer and plainsman swaggering about in them.

I spent a lovely peaceful morning yesterday in what was once Nineveh – a low very wide saucer of downs and wheatland, with a shallow wave hiding it like a rim where the old ramparts lie buried. There is nothing much to see, only this consciousness of great peace over what was once so tumultuous. The mound where the palace must have been, still standing high like the old hulk of a ship with a slow stream meandering round it: and over against it, the other mound of Judah which cannot be dug into as the Moslems have a very holy mosque on it. I wandered over it and they all became very friendly, and we discussed carpets of which a special red kind are woven here. They are Moslems and showed me one Persian rug where the Shi'a Persians had woven the name of 'Omar so that he might be trodden underfoot: and these people had hung it carefully on one of the walls out of danger.

[continued] 20 March 1930

Mrs. Drower and I are now well out in the desert, a marvellous grassy world – and we are staying with the chief Sheikh of the Shammar. We have a big tent to ourselves with white mattresses and purple cushions spread in

253

it, and all the tents of the Sheikh's family and slaves spread around, with horses, donkeys, camels, and small foals and children all out enjoying the short delicious season. I can't tell you what a scene of peace and loveliness it is: the women sit out with their tents open on the sunny or shady side according to the time of day, and show us their old barbaric jewels and magic beads. Some bring children, or cure serpent bites, or if they touch a man's cloak, will make him instantly love you: and one, which was offered me as a present yesterday, is to be rolled on the carpet and any woman you happen to dislike is brushed out of existence on the instant; this is called the 'carpet stone'.

Many of these Shammar come from far away south and have a good deal of negro mixture. We are guests and they are charming to us: one has a wonderful feeling of safety and protection within the limits of the tribe: the fierce thick furry dogs roam about the outskirts ready to attack wolves or strangers. In the midle of our camp there is a little grassy rise: one can look out thence to the Kurdish snows, and the Sinjar hills and French border, with other mounds rising as if from a green sea – and the grass full of flowers.

Your loving

FREYA

MRS. KER   From the Shammar tents N.W. of Mosul

20 March 1930

My dear Mrs. Ker,

I have just taken photographs of a noble gentleman of the Devil Worshippers or Yezidis. He was a guest in the great tent of the Shammar Sheikh with whom we are staying, and came to join us round the dish of rice and meat which is placed on a mat of red and yellow gazelle skins in front of the Sheikh and his friends. The great tent is a wonderful sight in the evening – lit dimly by two or three lanterns, with the embers of charcoal at one end where the black coffee-slave crouches among his huge beaded coffee pots: the guests and tribesmen are ranged down the three sides, half invisible among the shadows, and the Sheikh himself is looking most magnificent, just like one of the Assyrian conquerors with his hooked nose and short black beard, and long eyes, and standing immensely tall and broad with his sheepskin coat about him as he receives us. He tells us that he has 70,000 tribesmen, scattered between Urfa and Kut all down the west bank of the Tigris: in the old days before Ibn Saud broke their power, they went right down into Nejd and their tribe entertained Doughty and G. Bell at Hail and sent their orders across the breadth of Arabia. The Devil Worshipper was a magnificent being, travelling on horseback with five attendants from Sinjar in the north. They wear their hair in locks over the shoulders and a high peaked cap of felt with the turban and tassels wound round it, and white clothes – and must be some very old race with long faces, quite a different type from all around.

Mrs. Drower and I went up to their chief sanctuary – Sheikh Adi in a little mountain valley full of trees, fig, oak, all sorts; and birds, and water running over stones – a pleasant sound : all the ground covered with flowers and flowering shrubs. It was lovely up among these stony grey hills; and to come upon the two white fluted towers of their sanctuary in the peaceful valley. By the side of the door, as you go through two little paved courtyards, you see the black carving of a serpent which the devout Yezidis kiss when they go in. Blue should not be worn, nor any word be spoken beginning with the 'Sh' which is the first letter of Shaitan; nor can one find any lettuce or radishes in all the valley, for the legend is that Satan tried to hide under the leaves of these plants and they refused to shelter him. The inside of his temple is a gloomy place, with oil dripping from two square shallow lamps with a tiny wick floating about in them, and no ornament except a few Arabic inscriptions and three draped sarcophagi of their saint and two followers. We stepped along very carefully by the light of a candle, taking care not to put our feet on any threshold but leaving a rupee on the outer one as we went out. The water is lovely as one comes from this land of slow muddy streams : a clear stream runs into the temple itself, into a cistern, and is said to come from Zemzun, the well of Mecca : and outside there are two more stone cisterns where the Yezidis are baptised, and where a lot of fat spotted newts lie in peaceful contemplation of their own holiness. I believe Layard described the valley during its autumn festival when it was filled with lights and pilgrims : now it is becoming known and will soon be spoilt; but the road is still bad enough to keep it fairly secluded. Here we are for five days in a little camp of about twenty tents, and beginning to feel at home and very happy among them all. The whole desert is green; short soft turf spread like a pale blue sea with periwinkles and anemones – blue and white. Red ones are just beginning and a black arum lily which looks very wicked : and tiny iris – and all our camp is full of bleatings from the lambs and kids; foals and tiny white donkeys frisking about. In the north-east are the Kurdish ranges, long white ridges. It is too good to see hills again.

My love to you all.

FREYA

Shammar tents near Mosul
                                       21 March 1930

Dearest Pips,

I am writing from the guest tent of the big Shammar Sheikh of north
Iraq, and Mrs. Drower, who has brought me, is writing down stories about
Jinns which his slaves are telling her, squatting round in a circle. You would
so love it here – the lovely free life of the tents, and pleasant family feeling
of the tribe. I feel I should like to belong to a tribe – something so big and
comfortable, if you do come to grief, you do it together: and there is none
of the horrid petty bickering feeling of the towns.

I had three wonderful days in Mosul before coming on here and can't tell
you about all of them they were so gloriously crowded. One of the nicest
days was among the old Christian villages: I was all alone and went about
with most of the population, looking at the very primitive churches which
had to be opened with huge keys: one had only a woman left as guardian,
and after refusing to get into my car as if it had been a devil she opened the
outer door, then lost heart altogether and fled out from the village to her
husband for protection.

I began this day at Nimrud, where nothing is left but the great grassy
mound, the lovely view over the rolling green country (like Dartmoor in the
distance) and a few winged monsters half buried in the ground. But there is
something extraordinarily poignant in this solitude of the old Assyrian
cities: just a Beduin and his flock, and an old bit of brick with the wedge-
like writing I picked up in the ploughed land as I got out of the car. All the
Beduin here wear Assyrian seals among the bead strings they keep for talis-
mans: against snake or scorpion bites, for milk or children, to make their
husbands love them or to kill their enemies, or one to shut up anyone who
contradicts you. This magic is an awful nuisance to the collector as it sends
up the value of beads, and I had to renounce a lovely agate seal, which I
believe was quite early, for five rupees (being rather low financially).

Just heard a nice Arabic proverb: 'If you spit against the wind, it will
blow into your face.'

I had a good day wandering round Mosul; there are old churches and
mosques one goes down to below the level of the ground. Here and at Mar
Behnam, I saw the chain and collar by which madmen are tied near the
altar and left for three days till the collar is supposed to fall apart and leave
them cured. Lots come and are cured, so I was told.

The big mosque is a wonderful old place. The old Mullah told me that
Mosul is the only town Saladin failed to take. The people thought they could
not hold out against him and sent the Queen's daughter to beg him to spare

the town: but he said 'Mosul cannot be given for a woman's prayer' and sent her back: which so annoyed the Mosul people that they pulled themselves together and kept Saladin at bay.

Your own

FREYA

FLORA STARK Shammar camp Tell Ijlan off the Nisibin road
23 March 1930

Dearest B.,

This is the last evening here: tomorrow back to Mosul – and it seems too sad to leave the lovely life in the open air: our tent is very nearly open air too, and cool at nights, and a mysterious dew on all our belongings in the morning which seems to prove that dew must rise from below.

Monday

We came away this morning – the desert too lovely to leave, all foaming with white flowers: all the old ruts, and the traces of old camping places, marked with flowers – and the land swelling and sinking, like English downs.

We left very cordially and were a success I believe. A good long talk last night; heard about the wolf – more legends: how you hush your baby, by saying 'In the name of Allah, in the name of the wolf' (*Bismillah b'-ism ed-dib*) and he won't cry – and Sheikh 'Ajil explained that the wolf is to be the last creature left alive on earth before the Day of Judgement.

Your own

FREYA

ROBERT STARK Baghdad
31 March 1930

Darling Pips,

How I wish I could send you a little of this gloriousness: the nights just pleasantly cool with all the windows open, the days dazzling and not too hot; and everywhere, from every court and garden, the scent of orange blossom. Certainly from November to April, with the exception of the few dust storm days, Baghdad is the perfect climate.

Today I showed Mr. Cooke my flints and obsidian and shards of pottery found on our own 'tells' north of Mosul – and both he and the head of the museum here say it is a most interesting collection: all the painted shards, and the stone implements are pre-Deluge, long before Noah. It seems almost incredible that one should go picking them up casually out of the grass.

I leave for Persia on the 10th. I have got my route mapped out for me by

Mr. Watelin, the French archaeologist of Kish, who is one of the few people who have ever been near Alamut. He says it is a most peaceful population – no danger of any kind except mosquitoes, for which one takes a net. So my next will be from Hamadan.

Your own
FREYA

FLORA STARK   Baghdad
                                                                    9 April 1930

Darling B.,

Capt. Holt tells me that Ibn Saud has married, or anyway seized upon, the daughter-in-law of his enemy whose husband was killed in battle: the old Moslem custom – pre-Moslem indeed – going on just as savagely as ever in this enlightened age. They say that these tribal Sheikhs have now discovered that the motor is a most useful instrument for raiding purposes.

I am now going to finish off the packing and clear out of the house and get through the parting with the family, which will be a sad affair: Jamila wandering round just like a dog when packing is going on.

Next letter, *inshallah*, from Persia.

Your own
FREYA

VIVA JEYES   Baghdad
                                                                   10 April 1930

My dearest Viva,

I am incapacitated for the time with a broken muscle. It was a foolish accident, due to the susceptible temperament of my pony, two or three mares being about while I was standing him near the polo ground and watching the play; he suddenly reared, pirouetted round and had me off all among the Iraqi policemen. However the doctor says I can travel if I tie myself round with a bandage.

I am sad at saying goodbyes here. I feel I have good friends, and they all think kindly of me and far more of my capacities than I ever thought or imagined. And I believe my chance will come, and a good one in its time, and, if I can have the time to give to it, I may do really good work yet. Everyone *now* says 'what a waste' if I don't come back – such a different note to six months ago – and even Capt. Holt, who is Oriental Secretary and does the work Gertrude Bell used to do, and tells me that I am quite mad, takes it as a matter of course that I am to reappear among his archives

258

where all the troublesome characters are docketed. I was most deeply touched when I left my lodging – so much affection, and really disinterested affection, for I could hardly get the people to accept their rent or the little milk girl to take a present.

Your own

FREYA

ROBERT STARK

Hôtel de France, Hamadan

17 April 1930

Dearest Pips,

   Your note came just as I was leaving Baghdad, and I must begin by answering as to your selling out. It isn't a thing I would like to advise about, as it is just entirely depending on your own feelings about it. You know that Asolo and L'Arma are both ready waiting, and that it would be *lovely* to have you a bit nearer at hand – especially as I don't see any prospect for a long time of being able to manage the financial part of the voyage out to you more than once in two years. That seems a long time apart. On the other hand you must think whether you would mind leaving all your surroundings and settling back into the life in Italy. I am sure I *can't* make any suggestion – except to recommend as strongly as I can that you don't worry over anything except just your own feeling in the matter. We shall have enough to live on *anyway* if you come along, so that this need not enter into the matter at all. And if I can go on a few years with my languages here, I think I shall be able to get a really good position and make everything comfortable financially too, enough to do nice things like trips to Rhodes or Rome when we want to. The thing is to think out the two sorts of life and think of *yourself*, dearest Pips. Of course I would rather have you in Asolo, because I should see you more – but not if you are not to be happy there. Otherwise it is very easy. We will furnish the house next door, so that we can be independent if Herbert finds us too much, and you and he can collaborate in the cultivation of bulbs: I may bring you all sorts of rare kinds from the wilds of Persia. But I don't want to influence you either way. I shall try to be out by end of August. I have had to change some War Loan and it has upset the year's budget, so that I won't have enough balance to come out before – but I shall hope to be there for the apple picking, and of course it would be like a dream to fetch you away before the winter and not have that constant ache of knowing you out there in the cold weather. And if you managed to sell for anything that gave you an income, we would go to Rhodes for the spring and enjoy ourselves. But if not, I will just come out as often as I can. I do want you to feel that you are doing what you

259

like. What an awful pity I am not a man, to be of some use in working there with you.

Now I must tell you about Persia, though I have not yet begun examining more than this hotel garden, as I am rather sorry for myself with a strained side-muscle I got when my pony reared and threw me down by the polo ground. It is nothing serious, but was very excruciating over the bumps of the road, and will take a fortnight to get right again. I had moved to the hotel in Baghdad and was doing no good and spending too much, so I just came on, *coûte que coûte,* and shared a car with the matron of the hospital and a young daughter of the bank manager just out of school. We got off at 5.45; Baghdad looking comparatively clean and empty, except for lorry-loads of pilgrims: they travel in sort of cages with wire-netting sides on which the water skins and jars are hung, so that the view from inside is completely hidden. It is dull and flat as far as the frontier, except for the long, red bare backbone of the Hamrin range, which I believe does not own a tree. And the flowers seemed over; but we had a crowd of green sunbirds flashing round us on the way, sitting in rows on the telegraph wires, and catching the sun like jewels. At Khaniqin the railway rest house provides breakfast – in a lugubriously neat room, enough to take the Oriental flavour out of anything.

It is an awful business to pass an Oriental frontier, as it means drinking tea with every official, who is probably hurt if you don't. We spent an hour, mostly drinking tea, but partly spreading our things out on the road. We are supposed to be very unpopular here just now, and English doesn't carry any-where: it is all Persian or French. I find I can only just get about with monosyllables, and lose the replies completely, but I hope to start with a teacher tomorrow – two hours a day for 1s. 1d. The hotel pension is two tomans – about 6s. 3d. a day – and it is a lovely old Persian house in a walled garden full of blossoming trees, with a tank and geranium plots round it in the middle, the little channels of water running over stone troughs. The bedrooms are in a long row on the first floor with a wide bricked veranda before it – and the dining- and sitting-room in a little pavilion all by itself. Outside the walls are thickets of poplar trees just coming into leaf, and the snow ridges behind – 13,000 feet is the high peak – and we are 6,000 here, and nearly dead with cold after 93 degrees and a dust storm in Baghdad.

We got into a wonderful, wild, waste country as soon as we were in Persia: tumbled seas of mountains, with pale green valleys, very shallow, and blue and red ridges, and no sign of humanity except the white road and a police post here and there: little mud villages, very miserable – and then a mud town on a rise, Qasr Shirin, with old walls and ruins on a hill nearby, but sunk into the earth. It all felt untidy and poor, and ugly bits of modern car life all about, and the unspeakable Persian hat like a Cook's tourist agent's who has long forgotten to shave. But in some subtle way there was a pleasant sense of freedom after the efficient machinery of Iraq, and I feel there is something to be said for these people who prefer to be poor and keep us out of their way.

You can't imagine the loneliness: you feel, as you go from plateau to plateau, with more rocky ridges, with immense vistas and no human house in sight, that you have climbed into some moon landscape, only with a clear light and thin veil of growing things flung over it, and pure thin air. And then we turned by a little village with a bridge – Sari-i-Pul – into the valley that runs to the Paitak Pass: and there it was the real mountain again, as it might have been Simplon or Gothard when the road was still used. Long strings of immense covered carts with a carpet spread high above the horses: and the strong Kurds or Lurs or anyway hill people: their faces obviously belonging to our family, only wild because of the strange felt hats and black locks sticking out on either side. After the pass, you come down into a lovely open valley – Karind – where the women from Iraq were camped out during 1920: and a lovely place for tents too, with a thin veil of blossom and poplar leaves over the village against the rocky valley sides.

We got to Kermanshah late at night and spent next day there in pouring rain. I was really as tired as could be, as each bump gave me a twist. Next day however was lovely – the ranges round Kermanshah shining in snow – and again we went through seven hours of the great tablelands: sometimes with a slow river, sometimes with just rolling downs for infinite miles; once through a great plain where the road breaks off for Isfahan and a lonely mountain with a flat top made me think of Soracte as you see it from the Viterbo road. We climbed up and up to the Asadabad Pass into the snow: six weeks ago our driver and fifty other cars had to spend eleven days blocked in the little low hut at the top. The people here in Hamadan sometimes get right cut off from the world, no cars, aeroplanes, nothing.

I must catch this mail. Dear love, dear old Pips. I shall be anxious to hear what you decide.

Your own

FREYA

Hamadan
                                                    19 April 1930
Darling B.,

I feel so glad to be up here and able to do some work, though not feeling very energetic: I seem to have been wasting my last two months. Only I do feel my time has not been wasted: I have been learning the queernesses of my compatriots, which are just as strange as those of the natives.

Here there are not many British, and the houses we have called on, the Consul (Summerhayes) and some oil people called Williams, are charming. It is a simpler life altogether, more walking in the country and less entertaining, and not so much dashing around with motor cars. The little cabs are far more gorgeous than in Baghdad, with bright velvet flowered seats and the arms of Persia stamped on the woodwork, and on Fridays they all go heaving over the cobbles crammed with unshaven Persians whom they deposit in rows on carpets by the river or here and there on boulders and tombstones, where they sit apparently in silent enjoyment. Some smoke enormous pipes with thick stems. The ladies, very highly painted, have far less pretence of covering their faces than in Iraq. They all look much more European: a rather degenerate Mediterranean race in the towns, and good hill types in the country.

I am feeling rather sorry for myself what with chill and my side, but the weather is warmer and it will be lovely now. Miss Iles, the matron, is quite good fun: she has been out eighteen years and tells me the accumulated gossip. I noticed when we came what an inexperienced traveller I am: there were two bedrooms, and I had not looked into them, but asked her to choose: well, she hesitated, but finally chose the big and comfortable one leaving me to a horrid little room (which I have changed). I would never have had the determination to do this.

Lionel Smith came and had tea before I left. I can't tell you how sorry I was to say goodbye to him. As for Capt. Holt, I didn't see him again and have just sent him a message to say how sad I was to be found less amusing than a Russian verb: and I don't know whether he is coming to stay with us or not. If he does do so, do you think it would put the lid on if we travelled home together? It would be 'all the pleasure and none of the pains' of the honeymoon with someone to look after tickets and all that; and I am quite middle-aged and safe: so what do you think? He suggested it himself, but of course he may get alarmed afterwards, which is what I believe happens. It is only dear L.S. who goes on always pleasantly friendly and the same.   Your own

                                                        FREYA

Hôtel de France, Hamadan
20 April 1930

Dearest Pen,

This is being written in a garden with little streams running through it, and a square tank in the middle, and blossoming trees all round; and I am really more surprised at being here than I can tell you – surprised at its being I myself, if you know the feeling. We are 6,000 feet up, and the snowy ridge behind, half hidden by the poplar trees, goes up to a gentle peak of 13,000. Hamadan, with a tumbling stream and low untidy little mudbrick houses slopes down into the plain, very shallow, and brown as yet; and the Kurdish hills are on the farther edge, blue and distant. There are wild tulips, yellow, and white and very dark purple violets in the hills, and wild daffodils and hyacinths and Crown Imperial, but I can't go to look for them because I fell off a horse in Baghdad, and strained a muscle; hoping to be well next week however, and then I shall walk and walk and rejoice in the feeling of turf and a hillside under my feet again.

It was wonderful coming up from Baghdad. I was not sorry to leave, as the dust storms were just beginning and I had left my own nice room and spent three days on a sofa in the hotel feeling *degraded* into a tourist.

I wish you could see my Persian teacher. He looks just like the circus clown with a hennaed beard added – and badly put on too, for it sticks right out; and his absurd frock coat and peaked cap, which is the modern polite costume in Persia, give him the most low-down musical comedy appearance you can imagine. We had some difficulty in fixing a time. I suggested the morning, and he said 'Would 5.30 suit you?' He promises that I shall be able to speak in a month's time and I am going to work at it as hard as I can: at present I can just ask my way and get things from the servants, that is all.

We are going out today to look at Esther's tomb. Avicenna also was buried here, and old Assyrian seals and things are found in the ground. I never get over the fascination of the *age* of all these lands – back and back, and we never come to the beginning, but find still older traces of old and tired civilisations. The earliest bits of pottery, which they find among the flint instruments long before metals were known, are decorated so beautifully that they must have ages of practice behind them. Of course there must be marvellous buried treasures in this country, only it is very hard to get permission to dig here.

There is no one in this hotel except passing motorists; yesterday it was the ex-Shah of Afghanistan and his family, only as it merely looked like an ordinary fat man sitting in the garden, I did not look at him with any attention.

Your
FREYA

Hamadan
23 April 1930

Dearest Car,

It is wonderful to be writing from Persia. I wake up with that feeling every morning, and then feel how very like one's own country it is – not so much Scotland as North Italy – if one looks beyond the poplars to the snowy ridges: but if one looks out over the naked plain and the far bare ranges, it is just Persia, some high land in the centre of the world, getting near the very central table-land where all history began.

The tomb of Esther is here: a neglected dome in one corner of an untidy square where a few Persians slouch about in their absurd long frock coats and peaked caps, looking like people in a mid-Victorian farce. The tomb has a large stone door like those of the Jebel Druse, with a hole where the rabbi's arm goes through. We had an appointment with the rabbi at five o'clock and were waiting for him on the steps of the tomb when a Venerable Being with a Beard came up and took our proffered hands in both of his, pressing them gently between his grey cotton gloves: we were deeply impressed, till the real rabbi came, with a longer and broader beard and we found the other to be merely a Dervish of no importance. Inside the little vaulted room are the two carved wooden coffins, all swathed in damasks and brocades: Esther and Mordecai, side by side – and in a little room close by, a beautiful case with the rolls of the old Testament written on parchment in lovely lettering. And every Friday night the Jews of Hamadan (there are 5,000) gather here, and the book of Esther is read out to them. They seem to be on friendly terms now with the Moslems, but it is only quite recently. In fact as far as one can see everything is beautifully peaceful, and all the population intent only on picnics and motor cars, or little drives over the cobbly streets in a small 'fiacre' vividly upholstered with crimson velvets and flowers, and a hand for luck stamped in henna on the horse's back if it happens to be a white one.

Lionel Smith persuaded me to come up here with the matron of the hospital in Baghdad – and this has made me be welcomed as a respectable member of society by the British of Hamadan, though it was about twice as expensive as my own ideas of native travelling. Anyway it could not be pleasanter: the hotel garden has hoopoes and blackbirds and blossom of every kind, and the most amusing lot of nondescript passers-by, as Hamadan is a necessary stopping-place on the road. Very few English, and it is rather a pleasant feeling to be in a country which is living its own life, however it may be mismanaging it.

My Persian is getting on: I can get about the bazaars and shops. I have an old scamp of a teacher with a beard dyed in henna and a twinkle in his eye which doesn't quite disappear even when he tells me that he has twice seen the Hidden Imam. He got rather annoyed with me for asking for details of his costume and appearance – which appear to have been ordinary coat and trousers. Anyway he is an excellent teacher and comes two hours a day and promises to make me ready for talk with the Assassins by the middle of next month.

Your
FREYA

FLORA STARK
Hamadan
26 April 1930

Darling B.,

I had a most interesting evening last night, being taken to dine with the Governor, a nervous thin elderly man, with the nose and quick movements of a bird – and most charming manners. We sat for over an hour in a long room, hideously carpeted, with cakes and the little glasses of pale tea beside us, and I found I could follow the Persian and join in in a feeble way, quite enough to enjoy the conversation. We presently went in to a charming dinner table, over which pansies and almond blossoms had been scattered, with a tall sort of Crown Imperial, which grows wild here, standing in the middle. The dinner was excellent: mayonnaise chicken, soup, chicken, then pilau with some bitter vegetable (most delicious), cutlets, and stewed fruit; the best cherries, preserved in sugar and brought from Lake Urmiah, that I have ever tasted: and most delicious spiced wine. (I am feeling rather ill today.) We talked about hunting, food, politics: the sort of talk one would have with any country gentleman in a quiet district. What was so pleasant was to feel that here were no axes to grind, no one thinking what was to come of the interview: it really is good to be in a country that is managing its own affairs and where we can just travel about on our own merits. Everyone speaks wonders of the Shah, and the immense changes he has made: the safety of the country, and its general prosperity. He has a good head, and his little son looks very like him in the photographs. A large sum is being devoted to Hamadan, for a new boulevard and a reservoir of water: in these towns the old costumes and picturesqueness have so far gone that one does not regret the innovations: they had better get them over and done with. I don't know what it may be like in the hills.

Your

FREYA

VENETIA BUDDICOM   Hamadan
                                                         30 April 1930

My dearest Venetia,

I can't remember how long ago I wrote, or where I left off. Had I reached Hamadan? It is a poor little mud and brick town of low houses and cobbled streets with a brawling stream tumbling downhill through the length of it, and little bridges across that remind one of willow-pattern plates: but it has a glorious setting – the Elvand range behind, still white with snow, and the plain and the Kurdish hills away across it. I have settled down into it and to a quiet life of Persian grammar. I have rather a treasure of an old Shi'a teacher in a turban: he has spent forty years teaching American missionaries, and now that he has found that I like old Moslem traditions better than the missionary piety, his Shi'a fanaticism is coming to the top and he spends two hours a day interspersing texts from the Koran with all sorts of odd bits of superstition and tradition. How the wives of Hamadan poison their husbands with wolf-fat; and the 121,000 prophets that have tried to improve the world since it began; and the wickedness of the present generation.

My Baghdad friends gave me letters to the Bahais here, and they have been taking me to prayer meetings and such excitements – I was looking at their two schools this morning. It is rather touching and pathetic to see them doing it all on their own, with very scanty means. The Mission here has nothing to do with these people – and this just shows how silly these missionaries are: the Bahai teaching is so near the Christian in its results, and they are the only really tolerant sect in the East.

I can't make out whether this new Persian regime is really doing very well or very badly. The British business people here are very down on it. They are playing about with the currency and lowering the price of bread arbitrarily and so on, so that all business with the outside world seems at a standstill. The people on the other hand seem really enthusiastic, and there is perfect safety and a real look of national feeling. From just a casual traveller's point of view it is much better to see the work being done, even badly, in this natural and wholehearted way than with all the friction of

266

Iraq. It makes one realise more than ever that people *prefer* their own muddles to other people's efficiency. They are getting Westernised, but in a happy-go-lucky way of their own – playing football and bribing the police, the old and new all jumbled side by side. I, by the way, am busy making friends with the Chief of Police, who is the most amiable plump-looking scamp who evidently takes life easily and now lives in this hotel while his wife is in Teheran. Such an odd mixture comes through here. The distance between towns is so great, and nothing in between, that everyone has to stop in these places. Dutch diplomats, the consul from Iraq, Russians with peculiar manners, all sorts of weird commercial people with a few weirder ladies, young Englishmen with their luggage piled behind them on a Ford lorry – and every shade of Persian and Arab on its way to and fro.

Your own loving

FREYA

STEFANA DROWER

Hamadan

3 May 1930

My dear Mrs. Drower,

Thanks ever so much for sending on my mother's cheque: they are always like manna in the desert, and I was wondering how, having got into Persia, I could ever afford to get out of it again. I have just bought *emerald beads* (so they swear they are) for fifteen tomans: and was wondering how to pay my hotel. I know you will sympathise.

I leave for Kazvin on the 15th – and no one seems to know how one is to find a guide: but I am, as you know, an optimist, and my old Mullah says he will introduce me to the *'Ulema* of Kazvin. It is all such fun, and the British here are very charming, with Mr. Summerhayes the Consul a perfect model of non-interference.

I had such a pleasant day yesterday, walking up among the orchards: a little peasant woman joined me and we jogged along together till we came to her vineyard: and there we sat down and made a fire and took a forked stick to use as a pair of tongs to pick out the embers for the samovar, and made tea and stirred it with a little branch pulled off the almond tree, and talked about life in Hamadan and how her husband, who is a policeman, gets fourteen tomans a month and his clothes and a horse – which doesn't seem enormous pay. It was all so nicely removed from the disgusting politics which lie like a blight on the towns.

FREYA STARK

FLORA STARK   Hamadan
                                                              4 May 1930
Darling B.,

I had lunch with missionaries today and then they took me to drive out, a lovely road with the snow mountains and their poplar fringe on one side, the wide rolling plains and hills on the other. We came to a little stony river and a bridge and turned aside down a poplar avenue to an old baroque house, all peeling stucco, looking down its terrace and across the walled garden to the trees and hills. Once a lovely place: the Corinthian pillars and garlanded balconies and windows show what it must have been. Opium, or civilisation drawing them to Teheran, has probably accounted for the land-lord's absence. There are lots of such lovely places round about. Outside was a great square 'piazza' which used to be the stables: over a hundred horses could feed at once, for all round the outside are little niches where the feed could be put into small troughs, all in mud brick.

We got home and went to church, and had a terrible sermon on Prayer and the Radio – the Lord being compared to the Receiving Station.

Yesterday I called on the mother of my Bahai friend. He is a terrible modern young man with a butterfly tie but she has a most beautiful old gentle face, with her lace pinned under the chin as the fashion here is and her cotton *chadur** draping her whole figure from the head. About eighteen ladies came to see me, and we sat and ate sweets, and salad dipped in a strange bitter seasoning: quite nice – only I was wondering all the time whether my typhoid inoculation would be really effective. I can't follow anything like a general conversation yet and could only look at the faces, always interesting enough.

                                                                   Your
                                                                  FREYA

* Semi-circular garment worn to cover head and whole figure.

FLORA STARK   Hamadan
                                                              5 May 1930
Darling B.,

I had a lovely ride this morning, among orchards and poplars and a grey-leaved [willow] tree with crinkly bark they call *sangid* which bends over the lanes like a canopy: and there were long stemmed kingcups by little running streams. All the peasants out, calling to their oxen as they turned at the end of the furrow: and the snow melting off the slopes of Elvand in the sun. Everyone in Persia who wants to irrigate his fields builds a little mud dam across the road and lets a stream run through. One river made use of the road as a natural bed for about 150 yards. We finally reached a large mud village, and after getting into a deep pool in the main street, with the water well over the footboards, we were told we couldn't go on beyond. We sat under trees for lunch while two donkeys were brought to take us on.

This evening I had my Bahai garage owner to call. He tells one sentimental platitudes about the sorrows of his life. He married a wife whom he had not seen, ten years old, and sent her for four years to school: and she is not his ideal, so he says. 'Few wives are,' says I consolingly – 'and hardly any husbands.'

Your own
FREYA

FLORA STARK Hamadan
6 May 1930

Darling B.,

Don't know why but I am so very depressed this evening – feeling so old, and as if my whole life were wasted and now it were too late to do anything with it: such an uphill work, with so much less health and strength and power than most and already half way through and nothing done. And as if what I *do* do were not worth doing: no one seems to think it is, but just wonder at me and are sorry for me if they are nice, and disapprove if they are not. To be just middle-aged with no particular charm or beauty and no position is a dreary business. In fact I feel as if I had been going uphill all the time to nowhere in particular, and – like poor Venetia – most dreadfully lonely, envying all these women with their nice clean husbands whose tradition is their tradition, and their nice flaxen children who will carry it on in the same simple and steady way. And though it *is* my tradition too, no one thinks it is, because of a silly difference of form and speech and fashion – so that I feel as if I *had* no people of my own. If only I could eventually find some work that would make me feel settled and interested. I hope it may be: but no one seems to want women very much – and I don't quite know that I am fit for anything but philanthropy, and that would not really thrill me. Well, I think it must be because no one any longer makes love to me except when they are drunk.

I went yesterday to call on the Governor's wife and two daughters. It was quite pleasant: their manners very agreeable, and our Persian just enough to be able to talk about pilgrimages, curios, and silver work: they had some really lovely specimens of the Isfahan work which is so hideous when not very good. We sat round the walls and sipped little glasses of tea and had about half a dozen silver dishes of biscuits, cake, sweets, preserved cherries, all placed within reach. It is rude to go away before one has had two glasses of tea. Then you say 'Will you command our excuse. We have given so much trouble,' and go.

I had a lovely ride today, through the orchard country to bare red hills full of thorny plants with yellow flowers with red centres: some poppies and little crimson vetches. And we followed the road to a col and looked across to more bare hills with a white track showing, which leads to Luristan, and where the motor cannot go.

I have collected a lot of stories from my Mirza – and am very sorry to have to leave him. Once again I was right and the experts who have been years out here, wrong: they told me the Koran was *no* use now for getting into touch with people. If I had not known the Koran and been able to talk to the old man from his own standpoint, he would never have started all these tales. The Koran has been their one source of inspiration for centuries: it is their background – and however Europeanised they may be, one is sure to get nearer to them *really* if one comes at them from behind as it were, through the things they knew as children, or that their parents and nurses knew, than if one comes through the medium of a new civilisation which means something quite different to them than it means to us. When I take the old Mullah's standpoint, I know where I am and what to expect: when I take a European standpoint with a 'civilised' Oriental, I can never know where I am, for I have no means of judging what 'European' means to him: it is certainly not what it means to us.

I feel that I really may end by doing something; only it is not a thing that can be hurried. But in three years' time I could know enough Persian, Turkish, Kurdish, and Arabic to get about, and I believe I would be the only English woman in the Near East to do so: and then something amusing is bound to turn up. As it is, another six months here will give me Persian: it is most comforting to find how easy these languages are after Arabic. It is merely a matter of learning the words. If only I had a better memory it would be such a blessing.

Dearest love to you both.

Your

FREYA

Hamadan
                                                    7 May 1930

Darling B.,

Being already completely bankrupt and unable to pay my hotel bill, I felt no hesitation in buying a string of ancient lapis lazuli beads of all odd shapes and sizes dug up from the ground. I can get any amount of cornelian necklaces for about 3/- each if you want them. There seems to be no other jewellery worth having here: the people are poor, and do not deck their women as the Beduin do.

I called on the Bahai schoolmistress, so pretty with her pale green *chadur* wrapped round her as she came to the door to say goodbye to me. A very European room, and a Negro slave from Baluchistan who had been born in the house and refused to leave when all the slaves were freed. We had some delicious sugar sweets with rose sherbet inside them. My hostess told me that even 'important men' are not always able to eat them with decorum, as the sherbet oozes out as soon as you bite.

                                                    Your own
                                                    FREYA

VENETIA BUDDICOM   Hamadan
                                                    9 May 1930

My darling Venetia,

Mama has just written with news of you and really not good. I can't tell you how unhappy I am about it, for I did hope to hear that you were getting on now.

I miss you more than I can say these days and think of you so much that sometimes it almost seems as if you were with me. My trek will be very lonely. I go to Kazvin on Monday and make NE. for the Caspian which I should hit at Khurramabad: but I don't know if I shall reach it: you will see there is a large uninhabited patch to cross over very rough passes. If I get to Alamut (this side the pass) my main object is gained and I may come back the same way. The main trouble I expect will be swollen streams as there has been lots of rain and snow and it is still early in the year. Also, my dear, I am going most absurdly unprovided with money owing to a hitch in the getting it in time: I shall have only about £2 to start with from Kazvin when I pay up here: the only comfort is that there will be the less to rob.

I can get along in Persian now, though *very* badly: but enough to read the newspaper headlines and pass the time of day with the peasants. I took a long walk today (five hours) up the valley which ends in the gentle white cone of Elvand. Up there the blossom was still out: I walked through woods of baby apricot trees: you could see *nothing* but blossom, and every breeze shook it down like a heavy shower. Nothing more lovely could be imagined: the trees were just a few feet taller than I, so that I was on a level with that sea of white flowers: the grass very green below it, and studded with little grape hyacinths. The whole valley was one green wood of trees of every kind and a white torrent foaming through: and I walked on till the trees got sparse, beyond the last village: then only willows, and the little thin blades of corn, and sheep grazing in the thorny patches, with boys in wide blue cotton trousers and the little black felt cap like a bowler with no brim, and bold brown faces. I sat down with a woman and two little girls and had lunch – some mess of a sort of bean they grow here and very good. The two little girls were called Balkis and Tuti, and had bright hennaed hair, and were a disappointment to their mother owing to their unfortunate sex. None of the men you meet here on the road say good day to so inferior an object as a woman, but they all speak politely to my sais if he rides behind me.

I have been riding a good deal, and it is very lovely in the orchards and along these winding streams. But the truth is, I am very lonely and feel worn out with the strain of being considered a phenomenon all this time. It is restful here: the few British nice and simple and sympathetic.

The Persian, only so far as I have seen him, I don't like nearly as much as the Arab. The Arab really is *free* in himself: here it is feudalism at its worst – the miserable villager downtrodden and ready to take kicks from his land-lord, who grinds him down without mercy. The Arab woman may live hardly, but the poorest have gold and silver trinkets to wear, and feel at home in the tent of the Sheikh: here there is hardly a jewel – the people are miserably poor – though they look healthy and much better than the towns-folk. I believe nearly everyone smokes opium: They say fortunes are wasted on it all the time, and there are poppy fields all round about.

There are so many birds here. In fact all the landscape is just like the Persian embroideries and pictures: absurdly big birds perched about (hoopoes for instance) and intricate patterns of branches and flowers where all the different fruit trees grow together.

Your loving
FREYA

Gd. Hotel (so called), Kazvin
                                                    13 May 1930

Dearest Pips,

The adventure is starting: it is all being set going and now promises well:
a Bahai letter I have is to a doctor who owns several of the villages en route.
I have already separated myself from civilisation by leaving all my respectable clothes behind and am here with only my tent, bed, and saddle-bags full
of woollies and things. The tragedy is that my boots rub: I am going to get
some of the native things with cotton tops and soles made of linen in close
layers put on perpendicularly, and then cut to the required thickness and
kept together by camel's hide. If I can, I will bring you out a pair: I'm sure
you would like them.

I got a seat in a native car for four tomans yesterday: 12/- for 216 kilometres isn't bad is it? It took us eight and a half hours over great plains
bordered with bare hills, and then another great plain – till one thought it
would go on for ever and ever. In all this distance there is not a single town,
and not many villages: just the road, and perhaps twenty to thirty cars and
lorries in the course of the day. One or two strings of carts on their squat
wheels and bodies like the Ark, with the driver sitting on bright carpets high
up above the horses. The whole desert was full of flowers.

At 12.30 we reached a big village and stopped for lunch. I pooled mine
with the family behind: someone provided a carpet and we sat in the shade
of baby poplars. The men bought hardboiled eggs from an old peasant
squatting there with a basket and it was very pleasant. Two beautifully
groomed Englishmen in a lovely car whizzed past, but luckily did not think
of looking at our native group, far less imagine a British female there, so I
was spared the look of pained surprise. The family is travelling back to
Resht with an elderly mother, who still wore the old-fashioned costume –
enormous black bloomers sewn into black stockings of the same stuff and
gathered into voluminous gathers at the ankle. Once inside them you must
feel as if you were in a sort of cage.

There was a charming little orphan girl, a brother's daughter, and she was
being taken to be brought up as a wife for the eldest son, now at school and
eight years old. The little girl was called Fatima, and seven years old, and we
made friends though I couldn't understand her talk, and we fed the hens
who came inquiring round us. I did my best for Fatima by telling the people
that we considered that if girls were married before fifteen all their children
would die – and they told me that they would keep her at school and not
marry her yet for a 'long time'. I always keep my Persian grammar handy,

273

so I now fill in the 'waits' by learning new words and can bear the uncertainties of travel with much more philosophy. We got here at 6.30 after a long run across a dull plain: the roads all very good: and my Alamut range getting more imposing at the back of Kazvin as we drew near: it was misty and faint, but fine shoulders of hills, with no visible peaks. As we came near the trees (one doesn't *see* these towns till long after the green in which they hide themselves is visible) I couldn't make out the patches of bright yellow blossom in the hedges – till I passed close by and saw that it was the yellow Persian rose.

A horrid new street leads all down the length of Kazvin: a doctor has been given carte blanche by the Shah and has laid out the whole place in boulevards and electric lights: the roads are cut quite ruthlessly (the Shah told him he could cut the Royal Hand off if it happened to be in the way) and no compensation is given: and the Persians are all fearfully pleased. Perhaps one would be if one were a Persian: there seems nothing for it but to be European and so the sooner they do it the better from their own point of view: but it doesn't make it attractive for travelling.

Your own

FREYA

VENETIA BUDDICOM Kazvin

14 May 1930

Dearest V.,

There is an agreeable atmosphere here of native provincial life, very like a small Italian or French town. The hotel owner is an old Parsee turned Bahai with a shrewd face and a twinkle, and not above a glass of whisky with his guests – the remains of the Fire worship no doubt. His son is still a devotee of the ancient Persian history which belongs to the Parsees. Then there are a few Russians who spend all day here talking and talking so that you would think they were trying to imitate their own novels.

I wandered all over the bazaars this morning in that labyrinth of faded splendours, which the business of Kazvin today can hardly fill, and watched the little pale-faced boys knotting their carpets with incredible speed. One could pick up heaps of treasures if one had money and time: all Persia is crazy for modernity and selling its old stuff, and there it all is, treasures here and there among the rubbish: but one ought to know a great deal. I hardened my heart however, as I am so broke that I have to borrow off a kind Armenian here and shall be on the verge of bankruptcy till I get back and trust to Providence that some money may have turned up.

My Bahai letter introduced me to a delightful elderly doctor who owns a village and a brother on my route. These religious ramifications are marvellous: if you pick up one thread and really get hold of it, you can follow it from Morocco to Central Asia and goodness knows how much farther, and always find friends. What a pleasant feeling it is to be all ready, with the road before and civilisation already in your thoughts behind you. How sorry I feel for people tied by their silly motor cars to the long white roads that leave the huge plains of Persia and all its ranges undiscovered on either side.

My poor Armenian friend is trying to stop a man who has stolen £100 off him from getting across the border: he has been for three days trying to persuade the local justice to send a telegram to Teheran – and has only now succeeded: so that probably the thief will be safe by now. For anything except serious business the people are charming. But I have come to the conclusion that to put off doing troublesome things is really a much more serious fault than it looks: I think it means a fundamental lack of will-power – for you will notice that *no* nation which has this defect will ever get on: it means that it hasn't got the backbone to make itself do something it doesn't like, and of course there is no hope for it. I certainly like the Arab best so far as I have seen.

Love dear Venetia from

FREYA

FLORA STARK Kazvin
14 May 1930

Darling B.,

The Persians, even the police, think nothing could be more natural and commendable than that one should travel from London to visit the castle of Hassan-i-Sabah, and look upon me as a sort of religious pilgrim with great respect. The muleteer says he is going to be 'like a mother' to me.

Ashnistan
15 May 1930

A lovely oasis of trees and vines just where the ground begins to swell up into the hills. We have been travelling four hours. We have not met a single wheeled thing today, and after leaving Kazvin suburbs, have only seen one man 'travelling'. A lovely feeling of friendly loneliness and silence in the great plain and its ring of browny-green hills. We can now only see the outer bastion of the Assassin country, but when we were further off a shining white peak appeared behind it, the snow with a surface as if it had been

275

ironed, which it gets after having been melting in the sun. Behind this glorious peak, and inconspicuous, is the little point which is really the highest of all Elburz. The extraordinary thing is not that the Assassins should have been hard to dislodge, but that they should ever have gone up into these hills.

When I came down to the loading I was surprised to see four mules: and the muleteer's gay old mother and a little boy with a sharp little peaked face which I have now discovered is due to dysentery: I have been trying to tell them not to give him bread and hard eggs, but they go on stuffing him while agreeing with me in a sad voice, and when I part with my biscuits he only treats them as an *addition*.

The desert was full of flowers: I wish I had a book for them. I put the muleteer out by walking for an hour, feeling very cool and fit under my sunshade, while he was like a stream in the sun and evidently finding it hard exercise: I begged him to ride, but he was too polite and so had to put up with the discomfort. The two who actually lead the mules are fine wild looking fellows; Elias is from Alamut itself and no doubt a descendant of the original Assassins which he looks like in a handsome way. He is beautifully made, and looks nice in loose jacket and trousers of every patch and shade of blue and the black felt hat which has not yet been ousted from the villages and comes in useful to dip water up with when you are thirsty.

It was lovely to come in from the desert through what might have been a park of ancient mulberries: I have never seen them look lovely in *shape* before: willows, walnuts, planes, poplars, alders too – and the whole place loud with the cawing of rooks so that one might have felt it was England.

Your own

FREYA

FLORA STARK Chala

16 May 1930

Darling B.,

This steep hillside of wheat and grass and enormous walnut trees looking out across the Shahrud valley below Chala village. I am so lucky: I have a guide who really wants to do what I like: I mentioned a wish not to eat in the stuffy but friendly village room and he immediately took my quilt and the mule-cloth of grey felt with a black pattern stamped on it – and brought the lot out here; and though he will sit close behind to guard my sleep and his little boy is drinking tea with awful noises, I really have nothing to complain of.

We reached Dastgird – in a little fold of the first foothills – at five last night, and went to a very nice clean room in the village and soon had all the children and quite a lot of females looking in at the door. I seem to be the first European woman along this route. The intelligentsia of Dastgird decided that I had read about a buried treasure and was coming to dig it up – especially when I went into the mosque, a neglected little whitewashed room with an inner room where the grave is of Ia'qub the son of the Imam Muhammed who is buried at Kadhimain. The hand of 'Abbas was there on a silvered stand, and a few old candlesticks, and faded green covering.

When we got back, before it got dark, I saw to my bed in the courtyard, and put it up and the mosquito net over: being the first Englishwoman I had a free hand and could make any precedent I chose. There is a good deal of fanaticism – but it melts away as one sits with the people: the women begged my guide not to drink out of the same glass as I, and the old 'fellah' at Ashnistan refused my chicken – but changed his mind after.

We had a glorious pilau for supper – with my raisins, and ladlefuls of liquid fat poured over, and a bowl of leban which here they call mast. Then I went on setting precedents by getting some water heated and turning everyone out of the room in which I washed and then crept under my net in the yard. It was pleasant to go to sleep with the stars through my net and the crunching of the mules in the yard. Then the three muleteers came and settled beside me on the ground, with the saddle-bags in a heap in the middle: one hasn't got that feeling of absolute safety as far as one's property goes that one has as a guest of the Beduin: and in fact my hostess' first question was where I kept my money. They are very poor; and one pays for one's lodging: but they were healthy and cheerful people and extraordinarily European in type, with straight nose or slightly curved, quite different from the real Oriental sort of curve: and when they roll the sleeves up off their hands which are nearly black in the sun, their arms are as white as ours.

I didn't sleep well, partly because Isma'il (who annoys me by always inventing the name of anything I ask for) had spilt the paraffin of the canteen over my sleeping sack and I couldn't get away from the smell. The moon was large and bright and seemed to be in the same place right above me whenever I woke up. She was still up there when 'Aziz came and asked if I would like to go, and I went into the room and dressed with the gradually awakening interest of the pairs of eyes from the bundles which represented the children of the family on the floor. I don't think any peasant's house in

277

Italy as poor as this and possessing so few things would be cleaner – and they had nice things: the copper basin, turned over, had a scalloped edge and carved pattern: the earthenware water jars have a lovely shape which belongs to Kazvin – and the rough carpets have pleasant colours.

We left at 5.30 with many blessings. I made a mistake by giving chocolate to the children, and the mothers, suddenly very suspicious, forbade them to eat it, so that I found the youngest dissolved in tears on its bed. Even my raisins they would not eat. In fact I really feel now as if the whole modern world were non-existent: one can still get away from it, if you can get out of reach of the motor car.

Today we have been climbing up the pass – about three and a half hours over green shoulders where the green is all thorns or flowers: you never saw such a variety, even in the Alps. I walked for a good bit: and this and my craze for flowers and snapshots make me a joke to my party. Some day I must make a list of the reasons for which I have been thought mad and by whom: it would make such an amusing medley. Anyway it is almost as hard to persuade the Assassins that I come to their country for pleasure, as it was to persuade the British Civil Service.

The Chala pass is about 10,000 feet. Near the top we fell in with a big caravan of friends – from Alamut and the neighbourhood: they were all friendly when I was explained to them – and when one came on top and the glorious valley lay down below, intersected by long ridges rising up to it in snow and as if a white drapery were thrown over the seat of Soliman's chair and only the arms left black and sharp against the sky: and when we looked across from where the Shahrud showed a bit of gleaming bend, up to the Assassins country (or down, rather, for we were so high) and across to the Syalan pass which is still blocked, and the farther pass of Salambar where we are going, and the snowy range; and the whole great valley lay there like an inaccessible country from the rest of the world, the people were all pleased at my enthusiasm. And then we came down with this glorious view always changing before us, till we came past water, to some big cedars and Chala village, and here under the walnuts by a little twinkling stream.

It is lovely to be among beautiful trees again. Tall planes and poplars here and the great walnuts and yesterday the lovely mulberry trees of Ashnistan. And nice to come to the little patches of ploughed land tilled up on the hillside at impossible angles – and hear as one comes down, from far below and across, the men shouting to their oxen at the plough. There is nothing fierce here: the wild ridge of the hills makes it an inaccessible but not a hostile country: one feels as if it were still a place of its own, living its own life of the hills, the women too walking about unveiled with good sturdy legs and pink faces.

I have to give medical advice – which usually is to tell them to go to the hospital in Kazvin. There is no doctor in all this enormous district.

Your own

FREYA

FLORA STARK   By Shahrak in the Alamut Valley
                                17 May 1930

Darling B.,

It seems very strange to be really here, and such a scene for legends. Imagine a long valley cut off on every side by high passes or barren hills : at the head, out of sight, Elburz and the Tahti-i-Suleiman : at the outlet, where the Alamut stream runs into the Shahrud, they meet in two rushing muddy floods at the foot of a narrow gulley between sheer stratified cliffs tossed up at a steep angle.

We got off at 5.30 this morning and I walked down (poor 'Aziz feeling he must do likewise) revelling in the flowers : it was wonderful, going down steeply to the narrow cleft of the streams where a small flat piece of ground allows of grain and plane trees; and wild English roses with sweet briar-scented leaves were in bloom. Then at 8.30 we looked up the Alamut valley with a stream winding in many ribbons down its flat bottom, and a row of bare red treeless hills, absolutely barren, all along the northern side. The whole place gives one the feeling that, walking down into it, you are in a closed place shut off from all the world. It must have been practically impregnable (I believe it was only taken by treachery). We are now going to turn left from the main valley and see Alamut castle itself, and sleep at Shutur Khan on the riverside. A lot of crows with brilliant white waistcoats of a kind I haven't seen before are standing looking at us in a row just like the village children. It is hard to realise that here I am the first English, possibly the first European woman who has ever come this way. It is still a little community : a good type too, with nice straight features : busy with their fields and knowing very little outside their own valley. There used to be a post, but 'the two postmen died and so it stopped'.

I have had a disappointment : Elias the muleteer was a real image of the Assassin descendant, with his wild locks coming out under his cap and brilliant eyes and thick eyebrows : I was waiting to get a good mountain background for him – and last night the wretched man came to supper all

279

spick and span with his three weeks' beard shaved off and all his locks cut away, and shaved in front to the top of his head which gives such an intellectual look to the Persian peasant.

Your own

FREYA

FLORA STARK
Zavarak
19 May 1930

Dearest B.,

I haven't been able to write and such a lot to tell. We got to Shutur Khan, where the Doctor's brother lives, in the afternoon the day before yesterday, and found he had gone off for the day. However they showed us into a room with nice carpets, and in time the laird arrived, a man with a nice face of a gentleman rather rusted over by the country. We sat on the veranda outside, looking from our little valley into the big valley running below. At the head of the valley, where a black mountain closes it, the great rock of the Assassins' castle is plainly visible though two hours' mule ride off.

We slept the night, and presently – before supper – had a visit from the one police officer whom here we simply call 'The Government'. 'Are you going to take tea with The Government?' The Government was rather a nice little Persian with an enormous district all to himself: 15,000 souls who all quarrel, he says, and says his hair is going grey. He was exercised over me, only I am now an expert with hostile police. However the little man was much too polite to make it really obvious that he suspected when I obviously took it for granted that he didn't, and kept telling him how charming the police in Kazvin and Hamadan are. I couldn't find out anything about the Assassins, but we started next morning, leaving the sunk bed of the stream and coming out on a wide grassy platform tilted southward. The castle rock is always in sight and as you come near you see what a magnificent position it was: romantic isn't the word. It holds the whole enormous fortified valley, overlooking it from one end to the other over the lower ranges, across the tilted pasture-desert to the snowy range of Elburz and his brother peaks.

The Syalan pass leads down to it, and the only other outlet except the bottle-neck we came through leads down the valley below it, so that an enemy would have to climb uphill through weary open spaces before even reaching within range of the castle.

When we reached Qasir Khan, we found ourselves expected. Someone comes nearly every year – and one woman and an old Assassin with aquiline nose and hennaed little pointed beard knew all about it and appeared with a samovar and two helpmates with spades. Then we went up a desolate stony valley tilted up the hillside with the great rock on our right. It is a huge mass, with the hillside hollowed out behind, and when you get to the neck at the back of the cliff, you look down the other tilted valley on the other side of the rock and see Elburz gleaming across with slabs of grey rock in the foreground. We zigzagged up to the rock and saw what was left: a bit of buttress and wall and tunnel cut through the skeleton of rock which runs along the length of the whole thing – evidently just a completion of the natural defences. There are two rooms cut in the rock below, but inaccessible: at least they all begged me not to go, and to say the truth I funked it, not having very reliable footwear and a fearful drop if one slipped. But I do not regret the cowardice, for I believe there is a tank down there where seven black dogs breathing fire sit and guard the treasure. Anyway, looking down you see a few vines which grow from this water, and they say they give black grapes different from any others that are known in the country. We had lunch and made tea with the samovar in the tunnel with the whole of the Assassin valley below and the rocky hill behind. We reached Shutur Khan in the afternoon and found The Government waiting with the laird in a little room with one chair and table and two carpets on which we sat down and talked.

Then I had really a great stroke of luck. A rather unprepossessing unshaven gentleman came in to call, with the Pahlevi hat which looks very wrong here, and after salaam and all half rising, and all sitting down, and then all rising again to the newcomer and making little murmured polite inquiries, and settling down again to collect ourselves again after the disturbance, we began to talk about the castle. The new arrival had seen us yesterday at Badasht: Badasht, he says, is corrupted from Baghdasht which means a desert garden: and where there is a great stone in the river bed just below this place he says that there is an old building high up on the cliffs above: that there are seven reservoirs one below the other, and the remains of ancient chains which once carried a water conduit across the Shahrud valley. 'There should be a garden somewhere,' said I, 'for it is written that Hassan-i-Sabah kept a garden hidden in the fortresses here.' 'Oh, that must be up in such and such a place,' says this wonderful man. And he explained that in coming over a pass right at the back – exactly in the position one would expect, too – and about 11,000 feet up, he had been surprised to see fruit trees growing on a space of ground about three to six acres as far as I could make out and far above the level of any cultivation now. The place is yet deep under snow and will not be clear for another two months – but it is a thrilling thought isn't it? I got so excited I felt my fingers *trembling*. Ever since I went up to the castle and indeed came into the valley I have felt there must be a good deal in the old legend (as there usually is). People told me that there is no sign of the garden by the castle now, but the very meaning of the legend points to the fact that the garden was somewhere else, far out of the ordinary way: and this barren valley which looks like a desert until you come on some patch of incredible greenness and fertility is exactly the place where such a little paradise could be made.

The Government and two little daughters came back with us across the wobbly bridge (three poles filled in with mud) with the torrent yellow below, and the stars coming out over the valley, and a damp smell of cultivated ground where the little channels are made to run through; and I walked along talking to my friend about natural history and tried to tell him the story of the cuckoo in Persian (not so easy); but he said that it is not really such a useless bird since its right eye is an excellent medicine for sick human eyes. And he says that all these things are written in a book called *The Peculiarities of Animals* which you can buy in the bazaar. I find I get much more information if I take these things seriously and they think me quite sensible to be ready to believe it all.

This morning we left Iatish, at seven, after taking a family group: rather painful with films running low. When I got to this village about twelve, very glad to sit under the trees in the grass, a woman seized me and made me walk about half an hour, and I had the sick of all the village round me and knew very little of what to do: my quinine and castor oil are all exhausted (except for a little quinine for myself these five days) and I hope not to have done any harm. The people were very nice and it seems tragic there should be no arrangement at all in this malarial country.

Today was a pleasant journey. The valley made a sharp turn and became green – village touching village with dark green fields of corn, and little terraced lakes where the baby rice is growing. The peasants in their round caps and tight waistcoats look just like some of those early Italian fresco figures. The whole place is purely medieval. Sitting out on the veranda this morning, while the laird saw the two or three persons who had brought their business to him and arranged his little court, I thought how unchanged it all is. It has been a wonderful time altogether, and I can now *see* how the story of the Assassins really was; can see their life here in the valley and the devotion of their people, and the remoteness from all the world: and the comparative wellbeing which there still is, though it has to be practically independent from all outside.

Dear love,

FREYA

Darling B.,

This village is 7,500 feet, and I have just been up and down again to 10,250 – and seen the whole valley below from end to end, a green winding streak between its red hills, to where the western castle of Badasht must be above the cliffs that close the other outlet. One must go up to this old castle of Nevisar Shah (who fled from it in the shape of a dog as I told you and was killed by Ali at Kafir Kuh down the valley) to realise the marvellous strength of this valley which is really a pre-fortified camp. The Bolshies found it so, for they got down into it and were 'broken' over the two passes as the Persians say.

I have had a proper bit of Alpine climbing up real rock, holding on with my hands and looking sheer down, and without the moral support of a rope, and my native givas not yet familiar and apt to slip on their heels from under me. Having now again lost the trail of my only Englishwoman – and in fact of any English at all, for only one European is remembered to have climbed up to Nevisar, and that before this generation, – I have been setting the standard and the next lady will have to be some climber. We went off on the mules till we came to a little green col with the immense stony mass of the castle rising like a battlement 1,500 feet above. Here was their little grave-yard and four or five shallow rifled graves from which the people here got a few rings and things – and, alas, sold them 'in the town'. We left the mules at the col and began to climb, and got wonderful cliff views – one rugged cliff and gulley after the other. Then we finally distinguished the heaps of masonry crowning all the top of the rock – it must have been a little village below the fort and top tower, with a wall all round, like a wasps' nest sticking to the cliff: a bit of battlement outer and inner wall left, and two loopholes at the very top – and all the circle from Elburz to Taht-i-Suleiman gleaming with their snows.

You can see that the place is absolutely closed. I sat up there for an hour, finding the points of the compass, getting the names of the hills sorted, and trying in vain to disentangle the absolute wrongness of my map, which has actually got the Elburz *range* in the wrong valley. However, I have got about half a dozen new mountains and two really important villages in the pass that figures as uninhabited in the maps.

Here I am staying at 'Aziz's house. Such a pretty wife, and knows it too, and gave him a terrific rating for staying away so long. It is so pleasant to be welcomed by the whole village: all the relatives and friends coming in –

and three ladies sitting round me while I washed which I could have done without but it gave them so much more pleasure than my own discomfort that it didn't seem kind to interfere with it. The muleteer Isma'il has become really clever at setting up my bed and mosquito net. He is very rough but always willing and good tempered and I believe it is he who sees that each mule has a blue bead tied into its tail by one hair.

There was a bit of old worship when we left the castle: 'Aziz told me one must salaam to Elburz, whenever one leaves the sight of him.

Later

I have just been seeing how the women do their head-kerchiefs: they make themselves look just like the heads of queens on playing cards. I am getting to like the quaint dress of the women – their trousers and shirts just like a man's, and a man-like waistcoat and then the very feminine frilled ballet-skirt coming out from under all this. Then they tie themselves round with a big cotton plaid with the point down behind them to the knees or lower, and tied tight round the waist, and into that the babies are tucked when they want to carry them, so that they look like snails walking round with their houses. The men look just like the medieval pictures except that they have trousers instead of tights.

Your own

FREYA

FLORA STARK

Salambar
21 May 1930

Darling B.,

I have crossed the watershed and am now on the Caspian side, still very high up (the pass just above is 11,290 feet) and surrounded by mountains and snow. *Such* a pass, six hours from Garmrud and nearly all the time the magnificent massif of Elburz in full view across the valley. There are two villages above Garmrud, then nothing but rock and snow and water, a really wonderful wilderness of hills. Mr. Watelin, who appears to be the only one across here, told me it was the finest thing he remembered after a life spent in Asia. We started at six. Such an affectionate farewell from the family. I wasn't able to pay for anything, but left a shawl and the half sack of sugar I was so uselessly burdened with.

Last night our guide and a few village people dropped in, the guide bringing the precious antiquity which his father had handed down and which he evidently thought might be worth great wealth – and what do you think it was? A glass marble, one of those with a curly pattern inside: how it came to the Elburz mountains is a mystery for ever – as much as my yellow silk powder sachet will be to the next people who find it in Nevisar's castle. We went through the eastern *serra* – one cliff a sheer precipice, the other nearly so and just room for river and path to tumble through together. Then up and up and up, and a chaos of river beds and narrow glacier courses to look down on, the barren red of the Assassins' rocks looking small now compared to the more awful fastnesses of the mountains. Half way up we stopped: the two men to consume an enormous armful of wild rhubarb which they gathered, while I tried to draw the lovely peaks of Elburz across the valley.

It was cold on the pass, and when we finally got there and had tea in a little hovel of a *chaikhana* with three young boys in white felt jackets over their blue cotton clothes, we were glad to hurry down out of the wind. The whole pass felt like the very high hills: three sorts of lovely little yellow flowers, one a tiny campanula, the other like a wee primrose, the third like buttercups with as many petals as a marguerite – and coming down on this side, big pale yellow iris were out in bloom, and yellow tulips. ('Aziz is just stirring my tea with the big packing needle used to goad the donkey. It is so pleasant to sit beside a samovar in the grass.)

Your

FREYA

FLORA STARK   The Caspian 'Jungle'; below Yuj
                               22 May 1930

Darling B.,

It seems very strange to be here, in a narrow valley wooded with tall and beautiful trees, and no one near for miles and miles except the muleteers who have their packs stacked round and their sleeping figures laid beside them, while the mules with their saddles on are grazing about on the steep hillside. The air is filled with the noise of the stream rolling its boulders and the wind turning the shiny side of the leaves as it blows up the narrow gorge from the sea. We have been coming for hours down the long shaft of the valley – with hardly a side valley off it and no human dwellings except about four villages and here and there a little wooden *chaikhana* where the traffic of the road can have a rest. I have got a new pass for the map, and the name of two lonely valleys, and a little village that no one has ever I believe heard of before, where the people of Khurramabad send their flocks in summer. It is all green here, kept so by the mists and dews. At 8.10 this morning, as we rode along, the bushes of hawthorn and sweet briar threw heavy showers on to me as I passed. I feel like one of this gipsy fellowship now: a moving sort of confraternity which lives on the roads, with its friends and gossips at the resting places: the same sort of bronze faces, with black thick hair coming out from the felt caps, the sash tied round the waists over the coat and a long thong wound round over with a leather satchel behind for knives, and two blue beads on the tassels to make it lucky: the same laden mules and jingling bells come up to meet us or wait for us to pass in the narrow places, or pass us as we are resting or greet us passing as they sit with the samovar by the wayside: and 'Aziz will say 'They come from Garmrud, or Rudbar, or away over the hills of Talaghan,' and greet them with every variation from cordiality to mere politeness.

We had a ghastly number of biting things last night – the first time I have really felt unhappy over them, and I have mislaid the Keatings. I have got an influenza cold from 'Aziz (one never knows whose cup one is drinking out of and must be grateful for catching only colds), and felt rather tired altogether, but now I have been sleeping in the sun with my head under my umbrella and am all right again.

Last night we sat round the fire waiting for the pilau and discussed religion, 'Aziz having with a little self-consciousness got through his sunset prayer which took up all the available room in the centre of our small village group. I am quite an expert in Shi'a theology, however, and was able to explain how Muhammad and Jesus and Moses are to meet and co-operate on the Day of Judgement. 'Aziz told me that Noah is buried in the right eye of 'Ali at Nejf. 'Aziz walked from here to the holy places, taking a month over it.

Later at Gavar

– where there is a decent wooden house built by the Emir Sipahsalar and where he used to stay. I took one of the upper rooms, on a nice wooden balcony where my bed is being put up, but the glory is rather dimmed by having the two men and all their fleay possessions up too. The owner of the *chaikhana* came too to give tea which was not from a samovar but warming on an earthenware brazier. Then our host of yesterday turned up, and a strange old man who saw a tea-party and joined, as anyone may do, and so here we are in a circle again, and the caravans arriving one by one, depositing their packs in the various *grangie* and rubbing down their animals. A pleasant feeling of leisure and the end of the day's work about it all.

This valley might be Switzerland now, or rather Pyrenees: the lonely woods and streams, and the few houses built of wooden trunks, with stones to hold the slates on the roofs, which slant. Very familiar it all looks and

286

European: and the men are not foreign, but just medieval. They are much impressed because this morning I disagreed about a mountain, and this evening we hear that I was right and they wrong as to the position. It is a difficult business to get accurate information and needs great patience: the hills and streams rarely have names of their own but take them from the nearest place, and the streams vary according to each place you pass.

Your own

FREYA

FLORA STARK

Nr. Khurramabad
23 May 1930

Dearest B.,

It is a most extraordinary sight to come out on to the Caspian after all the forest — all yesterday afternoon and six hours today riding through it, lovely in the lower parts like some lonely bit of Pyrenees with its rushing streams and enormously tall trees. One leaves the big river, the two Hizars they are, which have joined their waters and rush down foaming together: one crosses a small col which the Emir Sipahsalar paved with boulders before he was asked by the government to commit suicide: then one crosses the Valmirud — a broad slow stream in a big bed: up another steep, short col — and there is the Caspian, and between you and it a landscape that has walked out of a lacquered tray: a flat landscape shining like a dull mirror with endless little sub-divisions of rice plots divided by tiny mud barriers: islands of green trees, oranges and pomegranates in flower, rise all among these water plots, and every island has a few houses under enormous beehive roofs of rice thatching. Little observatories on four pillars, under a dome of thatching, stand about in the water, and beyond it all is a pale streak of sea without shadows that also might come out of a Japanese print. Blue dragonflies, with the outer half of their wings velvety black, dart about doing their little best with the mosquitoes: but, of course, this is a perfect trap for malaria and even the poorest house has a veranda which you climb to by a ladder and are supposed to be out of their way. I am sitting on one now, after lunch, and the centre of an interested row of onlookers who look very much more Russian than Persian, with darker eyes, and pretty oval faces, and a generally softer expression. Their language is quite incomprehensible — and especially today because my cold is so bad that I could scarcely understand English if there were any to be heard within fifty miles.

My coming has evidently been heralded by the muleteers who went ahead, for I was greeted with looks of expectant surprise by all we met. It is quite a shock when you are jogging along amiably absent-minded to see people meeting you suddenly petrified with surprise.

I had quite a good night having rediscovered the Keatings; and a nice airy balcony: and in the early light could see the caravans getting under way, the mules being groomed down and the packs fixed on, all in the cold wet light with mist overhead and everything drenched in dew. The men wore woollen stockings and a bit of leather or fur gathered round their feet by way of shoes. I believe these people used to be very wild and a man who is now political officer in Fars was kept a year or so as a prisoner tied to a tree: at least that is what Captain Holt told me, and said I should get to know him as he is as mad as me. Anyway they seem friendly enough now.

24 May 1930

I am waiting to know whether or no a motor is going to take me to Resht or not this evening. I had been hearing so long of Tunakabun as the centre of all things here, and was thinking of it as a kind of metropolis where civilisation, films and chairs were flourishing. What it is, is a peaceful little village with a market twice a week where people from Resht spread awnings and all sorts of bright cottons, buttons, beads, elastic, and such European oddments for the rice growers round to buy. It would be a charming spot with its green gardens and the row of wooded slopes rising to snow behind, if it were not a perfect death-trap for malaria; I dose myself with quinine which may explain why I feel so peculiar – but I shall be glad to get away to a drier country.

I felt rather depressed: having come to the end of my objective, and also having left the hills. The hill people are all gentlefolk in their way; one likes to be with them; on the plains, if you go into the same sort of house, you find just peasants, and it isn't good enough.

Resht

26 May 1930

I had just got so far when a motor car finally turned up. Two in fact; one which had been ordered from Shahzavar came along, but with the intention of taking me only half-way and then stopping: so we took the other one, which had a charming chauffeur like a Mujik with an enormous beard. The first car wanted to be paid for coming so far, but even the easy benevolence of the Doctor came to the conclusion that a car which comes to take you to a place where you haven't asked to go, needn't be paid. To make all sure we appealed to a village Elder with a red hennaed beard: and the verdict being in favour, started off without more ado. Most affectionate farewells. I felt I was leaving quite a familiar place: having sat under the orange trees, drinking tea in the Emir's garden: and spent the morning with a little procession of Bahai notables behind me, visiting the bazaar (and buying a silk bedcover which I regret, for the sum would have just prevented me from being impecunious now): and having visited the school, which is a lonely old dilapidation in a garden with a tank and big trees where the little boys read out short moral stories in high sing-song voices. It was good to make for the coast and see the Caspian, grey in the grey evening, stretching away shallow and flat. The mountains were hidden, and it was drizzling now and then, but it is a magnificent coast. We got to a place called Ab-i-Garm, where some pools of steaming water spring up by the roadside and you can see the skinny Persians bathing while a little circle of *chaikhanas* and cars and crowd make it into a sort of fair: there was even a conjurer with his wares spread on the floor making the same jokes in Persian which his colleagues make in their European languages. I lost my people, who disappeared to drink tea, and when at last they reappeared it was with a fat blond chauffeur and a really nice car.

It was now about seven o'clock, and I had discovered that it would be another four hours at least to Resht, and was not too pleased when it turned out that the fat chauffeur was taking me alone through the Caspian jungle. It did seem very lonely: the forest here reaches almost to the water's edge; the sea lay very quiet and dull with a last light in it; and this road drifted along through sand or gravel, with not a soul on it. Luckily the chauffeur was a really good man and not fond of talking: his only remark was as we came to a particularly shadowy bit under the trees, that there used to be a lot of robbers here. We met a woodcutter or two trudging home: a horseman now and then: and about one car an hour coming the opposite way. Here and there were clearings for rice fields. We punctured conveniently in one of these clearings – and the chauffeur turned out really capable and put it right quickly. After that I saw no more of the country; we went through like a dream, and it was extraordinarily like England – the green hedges, and trees, and thatched roofs. Only the little towns with their bazaars still busy looked foreign enough – shoemakers and tailors stitching away at ten o'clock at night round a big lantern, and the tea-shops handing round their little glasses. About 10.30 we waded up to the footboards through the first branch of the Safid Rud which I had crossed a week before near Chala; when we got across, a man in a little hut sounded a gong, and by the time we reached the second branch the ferry was waiting and a posse of men ready to get us across. It was so like a dream. I could not help wondering all the time how I came to be there on the edge of the Caspian in the middle of the night. A little after eleven, I got to Resht and asked for the Grand Hotel – having been told this name by the A's: it was a mistake, however, of theirs, for the Savoy is the one to go to, and the Grand is an awful little place with nothing clean except its notice board. I was too exhausted to care much however.

Next day I decided to go and call on the Consul – whether I knew him or not. We went and looked at maps: he had done some exploring himself – farther east – and, by the time I was going, he asked me to stay to dinner and rang up Mr. Ward the bank manager. Dinner with candles and silver: and the two men so friendly. They discussed Valerian and the Persian wars, very agreeably remote – and by the time Mr. Ward took me back to my disgusting hotel and asked me next time to stay at his house, I was feeling much refreshed.

Later, Kazvin
27 May 1930

After refusing to go from Resht at 5 p.m. I thought I was fairly safe to travel by daylight, leaving at nine-thirty. The motor turned out to be one of these lorries with a wire grill like a menagerie behind where the passengers sit on whatever the freight may be: rice done up in straw bales it was. I sat in front, rather dubiously – but there was nothing for it – and I was only paying about 8/- for 110 miles, so I couldn't be particular. It was only after a couple of hours, noticing what a very small impression we seemed to make on the map, that I began to ask if it was really only a six-hour drive and if I would be in Kazvin by four. 'Oh, no, not four: possibly by eight *inshallah*.' Then the wheel broke down: they said nothing was the matter with it, but went on tinkering for a long time. The seat had no springs and an abyss behind just in the small of one's back where the jolts come: I wondered how I could bear it, as eight o'clock was an endless way off. The road runs along the Safid Rud valley, clothed in jungle, but dusty and small after our lovely solitary jungle: then into hills with bare patches. One comes to a wide open desolate country full of small disordered hills like a moon landscape where the two rivers from west and east meet and become the Safid Rud: the eastern river, far above this, was the Shahrud I crossed below Chala; and its northern branch was the Alamut, so that this was still the water that runs below Salambar. The wind was blowing huge curtains of dust all up the wide valley: the tumbled hills stretched away beyond eyesight, and our poor old ramshackle lorry, puffing and smelling horribly, crawled along the little dips and rises in the most exasperating way.

My temper was long ago ruined inwardly, but I was hoping I could keep it in outward control: the one thing that never pays in the East is to lose one's temper: it doesn't anywhere but especially here. When seven o'clock came and they said cheerfully that if God willed we might arrive in another three hours, I did lose it however. I had had no lunch, not having any money and not wanting to borrow off the chauffeur. It really did seem the last straw after all the fatigues of my real trip, and then when it was eight o'clock, and already dark, and the wind like ice over the pass, we all had to wait for half an hour shivering while one of the passengers in the menagerie cage behind got out to smoke a pipe of opium. These people were putting up quite cheerfully with all the discomforts, and the chauffeur even suggested not wearing his greatcoat because it was being used to support my back: so I recovered as best I could, and finally at 11 p.m., after thirteen and a half hours in that unspeakable lorry, arrived in Kazvin.

Everyone here so nice: the doctor is a dear. They have all been following my journey with great interest and the head of the *Municipio*, with three gold lacings on his cuff, came rushing up to salute me. I shall take three days in Hamadan before going on to Baghdad.

Dear love to you. FREYA

FLORA STARK Lunchtime at Kangavar
1 June 1930

Dearest B.,

I am now on my way [to Baghdad]. Everyone [in Hamadan] was so kind – except the Bank which told me that 'quite distinguished-looking people, generals and such', come and pay un-cashable cheques: I was not particularly pleased at being put in this category, and very glad when my money finally came.

It is very hot driving over these greeny-yellow plateaux. Baghdad will be awful. Hamadan now is a city of poppies; everywhere a field of great white flowers, with a few mauve ones among them, stands out in the foreground, with the mountains and their last patches of snow behind. The Persians gather their wild flowers in tight little bunches round a stick, so that they carry coloured staffs, very pretty: they will stick a rose anywhere – on their leban-bowls or in their mouths – but they could not understand that I just loved to look at them and not to pick them.

[continued] Tinkering at a groggy wheel, Karind
2 June 1930

I got in to Kermanshah late, at four yesterday, and thought I would make an effort and reach Taq-i-Bustan (seven kilometres out) and see the sculpture: a fine new road with the finishing touches being put on, to a dilapidated village, dilapidated even for Persia, and a shell of what was once a good house where the water, a deep green stream, bursts out of the sheer mass of rock of the mountain side. They are sculptured figures on horseback, with chain mail and helmet and plume, and the horse panoplied with tassels all over him: on the two sides were hunting scenes in relief, and much smaller: elephants, deer, wild boar, with the king and queen in boats shooting arrows, and boatloads of musicians playing harps. What strikes one is how extraordinarily medieval it looks, so that the big figures might come off some early Gothic cathedral.

Everyone has really been charming in Persia. This morning I suggested leaving at six, and so thought it would be eight or so, and was astonished to hear the thing hooting under the window at five. So I kept them all waiting while I dressed, breakfasted and came down three-quarters of an hour later to find four gentleman in the car, and no sign of impatience.

Later

Have now got to the frontier. Found at the last Persian town that I had no visa: luckily the young Iraqi man took me round and we woke the head of customs and the secretary of police from their sleep in their homes: they were so amiable about it, and bribes out of the question: we sat in a cool room over hot tea, on the floor, with the Secretary's wife sleeping under a mosquito net nearby, and wrote out the visa on a slip of paper as there is no room in my passport.

The only man I could bribe was the head of police's servant, to make him wake his master up, and that wasn't dear. When I got up to go I found I could wring the water from my underwear. The wind is just like the warm fan at a hairdresser's: it feels like a hot hand on your eyelids. And all this bit of land is a waste moon-land of treeless red ridges: the heat beating on it is fierce beyond words.

It is nice to come among a more capable people: the Persian 'has mistaken a promiscuous amiability for the whole conduct of life', as I once read in Santayana.

Love

FREYA

FLORA STARK

Baghdad
4 June 1930

Darling B.,

I got here yesterday morning and found there was to be a big party for *everyone* for the King's birthday in the Residency garden after dinner. I found evening things (which I haven't used all the time I was away) – and we sat at tables on the big lawn with coloured lights and a band. Hilton Young was there, a fine looking man with an eyeglass and eighteenth century artistic sort of head so that one quite sees how Lady Scott married him and why the official people think him peculiar. He is supposed to set right the Iraq finance, so Hercules isn't in it.

Your

FREYA

ROBERT STARK

On board SS *Carnaro*
18 June 1930

Dearest Pips,

Just before leaving I got your letter and the most surprising and altogether too overpowering news of your present. I don't even know how one says thank you for such large sums. I am just £66 overdrawn, so my bank says, and suggested in a tactful way that one might sell securities: so you see it will be such a nice moral satisfaction to tell him 'nothing of the kind'. Thanks most awfully dear Pips. Only *can* you really afford it? It is a most lovely present, and lets me get home without that awful feeling of having to economise so strenuously to make up for Persian dissipations.

I had a very good trip across the desert, in a respectable manner in the huge six-wheeler Nairn car with all the British. There were no other women travelling so I had all the attention to myself. Left 7 a.m.; got very hot by the time we were out in the open desert through the afternoon though it was all greener than when I came over in October. We had sandwich lunch at Ramadi and then tea out of kettles, very neatly done: the whole kettle is smothered in wood, and a little paraffin poured over, and it boils in no time – and tastes so good. We reached Rutba about 9 p.m. – barbed wire, and the fortress walls, and great gate and sentry of the Arab desert police, looking very grim under stars. I got a bath of sorts, and had my arm dressed (septic mosquito, now all right). Then dinner, and back into the car the whole night: rather weary. I found my head resting on somebody's knee who didn't seem as pleased with it as he should. People with longer legs were worse off than me however. We had breakfast inside the Syrian border, in the desert among thousands of camels. Sausages cooked in their tins while a man of the Persian Oil told me how he came through this place some years ago when it was strewn with 10,000 dead Druses.

Then ages at the Damascus quarantine where a doddering old man looked slowly through our certificates and murmured 'Pas de précipitation'. So that I had very little time in Damascus and had to *rush* out to the bazaar and buy an *'abba* which I had promised to Mrs. Granville, and then just time for bath and lunch and off in another car with a young Air Force man who was also starting for Haifa. We had a lovely drive: looking towards my Druse country far on the east and going down across the head waters of Jordan where it comes in a peaceful little stream out of the marshes and a shallow lake in to the blue lake of Tiberias. All lovely uplands round, green and brown. The neat building strikes one, and altogether all so much more European as you come from Baghdad. The young man suppressed my proposal for a bath in Tiberias but suggested one at Nazareth, which is quite a fine white town on a hill with cypress and figs and olives and rich convents and a clean hotel: all marvellously *clean* after Iraq. Result was we got to Haifa quite late and I went straight to bed and only discovered various Baghdad friends this morning.

It seems quite strange to be talking Italian again. We sail at one from Jaffa – where we are at present – and our first land is Brindisi. I feel quite sad at leaving Iraq. It was a good time in spite of all its difficulties.

Your

FREYA

Notes and Index

Notes

1. Flora Stark was living at Dronero, together with F.S.'s sister, Vera, and her husband, Count Mario di Roascio. The association with Dronero had begun when F.S. was ten, soon after Mario had acquired the carpet factory there from the local priests. Flora Stark took a house outside the town, became interested in the venture, and finally started working herself. For the next fifteen years the factory's affairs totally absorbed her. Family friends despaired of her reluctance (or inability) to extricate herself from Mario's influence, but F.S.'s relationship with her mother seems to have been exceptionally strong. If outside criticism did have an effect, it was perhaps that F.S. gradually saw her mother as someone not merely to be adored but also to be protected.

2. F.S. liked and admired the sculptor Leonardo Bistolfi, who lived in Turin. He was a great friend of Toscanini, whom F.S. met at his house.

3. F.S. had gone in 1914 to learn nursing at the Clinic of St. Ursula in Bologna. While there she met Guido Ruata, a bacteriologist, and in 1915 became engaged to him. The marriage was first deferred because of F.S.'s serious illness with typhoid; then, in 1916, Ruata wrote breaking off the engagement without explanation. Flora Stark's subsequent behaviour towards Ruata (who had always disliked her) caused a serious rift between herself and F.S.

4. Viva Jeyes was a family friend of long standing. In the autumn of 1911 F.S. had stayed at her house in St. John's Wood while working for matriculation at Bedford College.

5. F.S. had met W.P. Ker at Viva Jeyes' house when she was fifteen. He taught her English literature at Bedford College, became her adopted godfather and remained a profound influence in her life.

6. F.S. had also met the writer Margaret Jourdain with Viva Jeyes before the outbreak of war. She became devoted to her 'with her quiet biting sparkle of wit'.

7. Edwin Bale had married Viva Jeyes' mother as her second husband. Before marriage he had made his way as a painter, but afterwards took to business, becoming a director of Cassell's. He regarded F.S. as a second daughter.

8. With Flora Stark's preoccupation with the Dronero factory, the marriage,

which had always been difficult, gradually faded away. Robert Stark spent longer and longer periods in England, then went to Canada. At the outbreak of war, although he was then aged fifty-nine, he had returned to England to try (unsuccessfully) to enlist.

9. The Varwell family had come to live at Thornworthy, the neighbouring estate on Dartmoor to the Starks' Ford Park. After Ford Park was sold in 1912 F.S. stayed from time to time at Thornworthy with the Varwells. Dorothy, the elder daughter, married Maurice Waller.

10. The De Bottini family came closely into F.S.'s life. There was an old mother called Honorine, two brothers in the army, and an elder sister, Clotilde. They were 'a real old Piedmontese family untouched by any outside influence at all, something belonging to an age before 1789; they talked French not Italian.' Clot, plump and eccentric, 'conceived an affection for me, embarrassingly demonstrative, but so genuine that I soon came to be very fond of her.' (*Traveller's Prelude*)

11. Joan Carr was a friend F.S. met in England about this time.

12. Vera di Roascio, F.S.'s younger sister, had been married in 1913 at the age of eighteen. She loathed Dronero and took no interest in the house. In 1916 (much to F.S.'s pleasure, as she was convalescing there) she had a flat in Turin, where Mario was doing work for the government.

13. Aunt Mary was Mary Androutzos, daughter of Alfred Fripp, the watercolour painter. She had been a neighbour on Dartmoor, 'had married a Greek and been sorry when he left her', and was now living in Italy. She had always been particularly encouraging to Vera, who looked on her as a dearest friend. As children, F.S. and Vera stayed with her in a series of villas rented in Mussa in Tuscany. No villa lasted very long as the tenancy nearly always ended in a lawsuit.

14. Professor Allen was professor of history at Bedford College. F.S. was much impressed by him.

15. Leonard Whibley, a writer, had been with his wife to L'Arma on the introduction of W.P. Ker.

16. Herbert Olivier, the painter, was an old friend of F.S.'s parents. He was so enchanted by L'Arma that he bought the next property above.

17. Olivia Horner (later the wife of Sir Ernest Barker) was a goddaughter of W.P. Ker. At the end of December she went to Scotland with F.S. and the Professor.

18. Poldores MacCunn, a doctor, was also a goddaughter of W.P. Ker. She had met F.S. at Tarbet, where her parents lived.

19. Venetia Buddicom had become a friend that year. Her parents had a villa in Bordighera.

20. The Biancheri family, neighbours of F.S.'s at L'Arma, were close friends. The Colonello had left the army to look after his mother and his property. His father had been President of the Council of Ministers in Florence, and his brother was a diplomat in Rome.

21. Herbert Young, the painter, had been a student friend of Robert Stark's in Paris. It was he who introduced the family to Asolo and bought the house there which later became F.S.'s home.

22. Minnie Granville was a new neighbour at L'Arma in 1923, 'county and clergy, who had never met anything artistic in her life.' But she settled happily into the casual life and proved a sensible and charitable friend.

23. Lionel Smith had been a friend of W.P. Ker. Although they had this background in common, he and F.S. had not met.

Index

301

Batworthy Mire, 65, 190
Beach, Mrs., 92, 186
Bébé, see Roascio, Angela di
Beecham, Sir Thomas, 36
Beerbohm, (Sir) Max, 57
Beirut, 114, 131, 133, 136, 141, 165, 168, 204
Belever, 190
Bell, Gertrude, 212, 229, 238, 254, 258; her *Syria,* 187
Bellegarde, 178
Belle Isle, Straits of, 179
Belluno, 63
Belshazzar, great hall of, 250
Belston, 110
Belvedere, 195
Ben Cruach, 107
Benetti, Signor, 124, 125
Ben Lomond, 67
Bennington, Miss, 144, 145
Bentwichs, The, 172
Bernini, 90
Bevera, 80
Bhopal, Begum of, 97
Biancheri, Agostino, 81, 82, 98, 101, 111
Biancheri, Colonello, 80, 82, 88, 89, 97
Biri, see Stark, Mrs. Flora
Biron, Mr., 44
Birs Nimrud (once Borsippa), 250
Bistolfi, Leonardo and wife, 1, 7, 38
Black Mountains, 171
Black Prince, 76
Black Sea, 232
Boccaccio, 41
Boethius, 227
Bologna, 1, 3, 9, 19, 27
Bordighera, 56, 81, 82, 134
Boris Godunov, 36
Borrow, George, 54
Bottini de Ste. Agnès, Achille de, 50
Bottini de Ste. Agnès, Clotilde de, 6, 41, 50, 68, 89, 94, 105
Bottini de Ste. Agnès, Gabriel de, 6, 43, 51, 93, 94
Bramley, Mrs., 101-2
Brenta, 174
Brindisi, 46, 121, 122, 294
British Museum, 16-17, 35, 36, 189, 191
Brock, Dr., 51
Brooke-Popham, Lady, 245
Browne, Professor, 83
Browning, Robert (poems of), 163
Brumana, 114, 118, 119, 128, (letters from) 130-51, 154, (letters from) 163-8, 174, 198, (letters from) 199-203
Buddicom, Venetia, 76-9, 95, 108, 110-12, 118-19, 134, 140, 141, 144, 147, 155, 168-72, 269; letters to, 118-19, 128, 131, 132-3, 137, 139-40, 141, 146, 154, 156, 166-7, 174, 200,

208-9, 215-16, 222-3, 232-3, 246, 250-1, 266-7, 271-2, 274-5
Bullecourt, 35
Busbecq, 178
Byblos (Jubail), 140, 148

Cadore, 92
Caetani, 99
Cairo, 172-3
'Canada and the *Odyssey',* 190
Canalone, 84
Cantlie, Mrs., 35
Capanna Margherita, 84-5
Caparn, Mrs., 219, 237, 240
Cap Martin, 54
Caporetto, 51
Carcassone, 76
Carlton Grill, 11, 60
Carnaro, S.S., 198-9, 293-4
Carr, Joan, 14, 15, 25, 26, 29, 35
Carr, Mrs., 24-5
Carr, Ursula, 14
Casale, Mme (embroidery school, Asolo), 92
Caspian Sea, 271, 284, 287, 289
Castel d'Appio, 61
Castelfranco, 192
Cenotaph, 58
Cette, 77
Chagford, 57, 64
Chala, 276-8, 289, 290
Chaldeans, 238
Chaucer, 154
Chauve-Souris, 60
Chester, 111
Chiappera, 63
Chopin, 51
Christie's, 113
Churchill, Lady Randolph, 36
Churchill, (Sir) Winston, 59
Cleobolus, 124
Clyde, 178
Cogne, 24, 91
Col des Géants, 52
Col Maurin, 62, 63
Col Traversières, 63
Consolation of Philosophy, 227
Constantinople, 178, 239
Cooke, Mr., 229, 230, 247-50, 257
Cooke, Mrs., 229, 230, 251
Corfu, 122, 173
Cornford, Mr. (Cope), 101
Cornhill, The, 175, 190
Corriere, 39
Cortina, 174
Courmayeur, 52
Creston, B.C., 61, 180-8
Criterion, 11
Csarevitch, 231

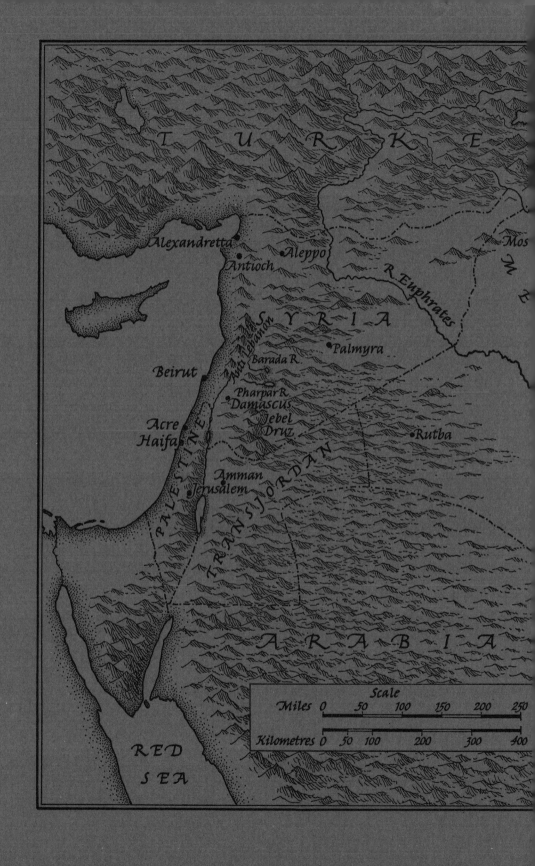